I LAUNCH AT PARADISE

A Consideration of John Donne, Poet and Preacher

by

FREDERICK A. ROWE

LONDON: THE EPWORTH PRESS

FIRST PUBLISHED IN 1964

© THE EPWORTH PRESS 1964

Book Steward
FRANK H. CUMBERS

SET IN MONOTYPE BASKERVILLE AND PRINTED IN
GREAT BRITAIN BY THE CAMELOT PRESS LTD
LONDON AND SOUTHAMPTON

In Memory of my Parents

They who one another keepe
Alive, ne'r parted bee

CONTENTS

PREFACE

THE invitation to me to deliver the Fernley-Hartley Lecture at the Methodist Conference of 1964 is an honour which I wish to acknowledge. It has given me an opportunity to explore farther a subject on which I addressed a gathering of fellow-Methodist Ministers in the Birmingham District. The interest in John Donne then evoked confirmed my judgement that the republication of his sermons in ten notable volumes is an important event for the preacher today. His fertilizing thought, expressed with distinction, stimulates the mind and helps it to become articulate. His early verse has had a similar effect upon our age; the republication of his sermons (and other writings) has been dictated by the revival of his poetic fame, and through this means a bridge has been built between the pulpit and the contemporary scene; over this, as preacher, he will pass, penetrating a society which, though agitated by his realism and embodiment of meaning to seek new forms of artistic expression, is by no means reconciled to orthodox Christianity which he expounded with grace and power.

I believe that the sermons cannot be adequately appreciated and used apart from an understanding of the author and his works, his place in the tradition of Christian preaching, and his influence as a poet upon our age. My purpose has been to consider these matters as well as the sermons themselves, and to indicate the range of reading which the subject offers. I hope that some service has been done to my brethren in the ordained Ministry and that younger men especially will find here some suggestions for reading which will be of value; but the ever-increasing significance of the preaching ministry of laymen and laywomen in the universal Church has been constantly in mind, and the study which is here presented is addressed also to them.

The Reverend W. Russell Shearer, a former President of the Methodist Conference, when Chairman of the Birmingham District, invited me to address the gathering to which I have referred. I have been much encouraged by his constant interest as I have sought to present what I then said in this expanded and altered form. I wish to thank the Reverend Richard S. Monkman of

New York for his help in the preparation of Chapter 6. I acknowledge the kindness of many friends in the Scotland Synod, and recall how, at a time of indecision, the late Reverend Frank W. R. Salisbury, then its Secretary, urged me to regard the Lecture as a duty not to be avoided. I am especially indebted to Mr Henry Hargreaves, Lecturer in English in the University of Aberdeen, who offered to read the manuscript and who generously put his professional knowledge and experience at my service, saving me from certain inconsistencies and making many suggestions to improve the presentation, which I have followed, though I am alone responsible for my views and their expression. I wish also to record my appreciation of special reading facilities at the libraries of Glasgow University and Trinity College, Glasgow.

I acknowledge, with thanks, the permission, readily given, by the University of California Press, to quote extensively from the text of the sermons as given in *The Sermons of John Donne*, in ten volumes, edited by the late George R. Potter, and Evelyn M. Simpson; by the author and publishers, Chatto & Windus Ltd, to quote, on p. 13, from *The School of Donne* by A. Alvarez; by the author and publishers, Dobson Books Ltd, to quote, on p. 67, from *The Well Wrought Urn*, by Cleanth Brooks.

F. A. R.

SUMMARY OF CONTENTS

ONE

MY STORY, IN THY ETERNALL BOOKE

('Metempsychosis, The Progresse of the Soule', stanza IV)

BY the year 1601, when John Donne wrote these words, he had lived half his life. The critical event of that year, his marriage, divides his story into two equal parts, each of thirty years: 1571-1601; 1601-1631.

He was born, lived, and died in the city of London, destined to live through the greatest days of the reign of Elizabeth, to see the arrival on the London scene of James VI of Scotland, and to experience the opening years of his son's tragic reign. He was born into a Roman Catholic home, where, from his first moments, religion was made to matter supremely. For the sixty years of his life it never ceased to matter. He became an Anglican; in 1615 he was ordained to the Christian Ministry; in 1621 he became Dean of St Paul's, and in his remaining years he was the most illustrious preacher of his day.

His father, John Donne, who died in 1575, was descended from a family of Welsh extraction, and had been sent to London to be apprenticed to a merchant named Harvey who became an Alderman of the city; the father prospered in business and became Warden of the Ironmongers' Company shortly before his death. His mother, Elizabeth Heywood, outlived her son and remained a Roman Catholic to the end. She was the third child of Elizabeth Rastall, whose father's mother was a sister of Sir Thomas More, Lord Chancellor of England, a famous martyr for the Roman faith, executed in 1536. In this family religion meant martyrdom. John Rastall, married to the sister of Sir Thomas, strongly opposed Henry VIII's Reformation, and died in prison in 1536; Margaret Griggs, the Lord Chancellor's adopted daughter, who married in 1530, died in exile for her faith at Malines in 1570, two years before her husband, Dr John Clement, who also died in a foreign land; their daughter Winifred had died at Louvain in 1553—she married William Rastall (son of Sir Thomas More's sister) who died at Louvain in 1565 and was buried beside his wife. Their daughter Elizabeth married John Heywood the epigrammatist, whose sympathies with Catholicism were well known, and who, on the accession of Elizabeth, went into exile, to Malines, where he died in 1580. Of this marriage there were three children: Ellis, who became a Jesuit, Secretary to Cardinal Pole, dying at Louvain in 1578; Jasper, who became leader of the English Jesuits and was banished, dying at Naples in 1598; and Elizabeth, the mother of John Donne.

He was the third child; only one daughter grew to maturity; his brother Henry, a year younger, was arrested at the age of nineteen for harbouring a seminary priest in his chambers at Thavies Inn (an Inn of Chancery), and died of jail fever soon afterwards. In Donne's inheritance, in his own experience, death was part of life. It was also part of religion. When it meant the loss of his father submissive acceptance of a mystery was right; but when it meant the loss of an only brother and was preventable by the detachment of religion from martyrdom an entirely different issue was raised. It is not possible to discover when John Donne first began to rebel against his circumstances; perhaps the references to the martyrs were too frequent; or the simple fact that 'during four generations, at least five blood relations of Donne had suffered cruelty in their persons or their estates for what they believed to be the true faith of a Christian'[1] brought him to a determination not to be a martyr; or certain Jesuits, confident of their power over the youthful mind, overreached themselves, not considering that their influence might achieve, as it did in this case, a lifelong hostility to their Order.

Two references which he made in prose writings to his early years reveal the influence of his Catholic upbringing upon him. In the Preface to *Biathanatos*, a work on suicide, he wrote:

I had my first breeding and conversation with men of a suppressed and afflicted religion, accustomed to the despise of death, and hungry of an imagined martyrdom . . . [2]

In 1610 he published *Pseudo-Martyr, Wherein out of certaine propositions and gradations, this conclusion is evicted, That those which are*

---

[1] Augustus Jessopp, *John Donne, Sometime Dean of St Paul's*, p. 5; see Appendix A, p. 223, 'Pedigree showing the descent of Dr Donne from Elizabeth, sister of Sir Thomas More, the Lord Chancellor, executed in 1536'. In future notes this book is referred to as 'Jessopp'.

[2] Edmund Gosse, *The Life and Letters of John Donne, Dean of St Paul's*, I. 260. In future notes this book is referred to as 'Gosse'.

of the Romane Religion in this Kingdome, may and ought to take the Oath of Allegeance. A little before his birth, Pope Pius V had issued a Bull proclaiming the excommunication of Queen Elizabeth; and in answer it was made a penal offence for a Roman priest to absolve or exercise other priestly functions upon any of Her Majesty's subjects. In 1581 the death penalty was imposed on Jesuits and seminary priests in the Queen's dominions. The Catholics who acknowledged Queen Elizabeth and outwardly conformed to her settlement of religion were unmolested; an irreconcilable minority, under Jesuit leadership, who repudiated her authority and regarded her as excommunicated by the Pope, were in danger of banishment or death, and it was this rebellious Catholicism to which Donne's family was committed. The oath of allegiance was the testing-point, and in the Preface to his discussion of this subject he said,

I have been ever kept awake in a meditation of Martyrdom, by being derived from such a stock and race, as, I believe, no family, (which is not of far greater extent, and greater branches), hath endured and suffered more in their persons and fortunes, for obeying the teachers of Roman doctrine, than it hath done. . . . I had a longer work to do than many other men; for I was first to blot out, certain impressions of the Roman religion, and to wrestle both against the examples and against the reasons, by which some hold was taken; and some anticipations early laid upon my conscience, both by persons who by nature had a power and superiority over my will, and others who by their learning and good life, seemed to me justly to claim an interest for the guiding and rectifying of mine understanding in these matters.[3]

For forty years his family had made great sacrifices for the Roman faith, and each generation supplied a martyr; perhaps his brother's death set him free, in his own mind, from any farther obligation, and he determined to rebel against the coercion of his origins. This he did very thoroughly. The term 'pseudo-martyr' expressed moral disapproval as well as disagreement. He gave Ignatius Loyola particular attention in his prose work, *Ignatius his Conclave*, a satirical treatment of the Jesuits; and concentrated his views on martyrdom as they interpreted it in the lines in 'A Litanie', written about the same time (the same period as *Biathanatos*),

---

[3] See Gosse, I. 3, 25f, 250; E. M. Simpson, *A Study of the Prose Works of John Donne*, pp. 183f, 188.

B

             . . . to some
Not to be Martyrs, is a martyrdome.[4]

His sermons make frequent allusion to false martyrdom (the
theme of *Pseudo-Martyr*) and the need to take this present life
seriously and positively—for example, in the first sermon, speaking of the persecutions of the early Christians, he says:

though the Christians did then with a holy cheerfulness suffer those
persecutions, when they could not avoid them, without prevaricating,
and betraying the hour of Christ Jesus, yet they did not wilfully thrust
themselves into those dangers, they did not provoke the Magistrate.[5]

He is not at ease with the word 'martyr', and stresses the dangers
of an over-emphasis on dying for the faith—

The shedding of our blood for God is not a greater service then the
winning of souls to God.[6]
Since I am bound to take up my crosse, there must be a crosse that is
mine to take up. . . . I must not go out of my way to seeke a crosse.[7]
God shall thanke no man, for dying for him, and his glory, that con-
tributed nothing to his glory, in the actions of his life. . . . The love
of this life, which is *naturall* to us, and imprinted by God in us, is not
sinfull. . . . It is ill, in many cases, *not to love this life*. . . .[8]

His uncles Ellis and Jasper had both been Fellows at Oxford,
and John entered Hart Hall in 1584. He left three years later
without taking a degree, because he would not take the oath of
allegiance—but one wonders if this marks the beginning of his
rebellion against his situation. It is supposed that, on leaving
Oxford, he spent three years at Cambridge, but confirmation of
this is lacking; then he followed in the steps of members of his
family and entered Thavies Inn in 1591, and Lincoln's Inn in
1592. Although he did not adopt the legal profession, his training
was invaluable for the controversial writings of later years, and
his sermons, apart from many allusions to and illustrations from
legal matters, are enriched by his clear, orderly arrangement and
precise definition and statement.

[4] Herbert J. C. Grierson, *The Poems of John Donne*, I. 341; title as in Miss Helen
Gardner, *The Divine Poems*, p. 16. In future notes these books are referred to as 'Grierson' and 'Gardner' respectively. Throughout, titles of poems are as given in Grierson's
text unless otherwise stated. The reader who prefers to use the one-volume edition of
Donne's poems (*Oxford Standard Authors, 1933*), which is, essentially, Grierson's first
volume, will find references to this edition in the Appendix, p. 247, *infra*.
[5] George R. Potter and Evelyn M. Simpson, *The Sermons of John Donne*, I. 151f.
In future notes this edition of the *Sermons*, in ten volumes, is referred to as 'PS' followed
by the number of the volume, or by the volume number alone.
[6] I. 189f.   [7] II. 301.   [8] III. 201f.

Not only did he not take up the profession of Law, it also seems certain that, as a student, he did not give these legal studies close attention. As H. C. Beeching said, Donne was 'trained for the law but far more interested in theology.'[9] He was athirst for knowledge and experience of every kind, and the various studies which he seriously undertook laid the foundation of that interest in total knowledge which so much enriched all he wrote and spoke. At the same time he sought and enjoyed human society. In a sermon preached at The Hague in 1619 he said:

it were not hard to assigne many examples of men that have stolne a great measure of learning, and yet lived open and conversable lives, and never beene observed, (except by them, that knew their Lucu-brations, and night-watchings) to have spent many houres in study.[10]

In his writings allusions to Greek and Latin literature are significantly few; he was eager to learn living languages and to speak them, and enjoyed a reputation as a traveller abroad; through human contacts, the interaction of personalities, as much as through the private study of books, he perceived Truth and sought the enrichment of his understanding. His *Songs and Sonets* were part of a sustained correspondence and contact with friends, and their subject-matter must have been influenced by many a conversation; however independent in spirit, their origin was social. Much later, in his preaching, he paid close attention to his relationship with his audience, striving to create an atmosphere of sympathy and understanding. His appreciation of others was deep and sincere, and theirs of him equally so; the portraits that we have of him introduce us to an attractive man, with the gifts and graces which give ready access to society.

In the summer of 1596 a large, well-equipped expedition under Lord Howard of Effingham and the Earl of Essex set sail against Cadiz. Donne was swept along by an outburst of popular enthusiasm into service with the land forces under Essex, and two of his friends on this expedition were Thomas Egerton and Francis Wooley. The first was the eldest son of Sir Thomas Egerton, afterwards Lord Ellesmere, who had been made Lord

---

[9] 'Izaak Walton's *Life of Donne*: An Apology', *The Cornhill Magazine*, n.s. VIII. (1900) 264.
[10] II. 275; see Izaak Walton, *The Life of Dr John Donne* (The World's Classics), p. 67. In future notes this book is referred to as 'Walton'.

Keeper of the Great Seal and Lord High Chancellor a month before the fleet set sail. There were few more influential persons in the realm. Francis Wooley was Sir Thomas's stepson, a few years younger than Donne, and his father had been private secretary to the Queen. After this adventure, and the expedition to the Azores in the following year, Donne returned home to become secretary to Sir Thomas Egerton, through the influence of his son Thomas. This was extreme good fortune such as some never find; a few receive it, though it is too rare to be trusted; yet, in its coming, it can create a recklessness in the recipient which leads him to his ruin.

Sir Thomas had married again in 1596 and his wife Elizabeth, mother of Francis Wooley, had a sister, married to Sir George More, Lieutenant of the Tower, about ten years younger than Egerton, who was in his late fifties. He had an unmarried daughter, Anne, born in 1584. When Lady Egerton removed to the Lord Keeper's home at York House, her niece accompanied her as companion. With this young girl the secretary fell in love. He was many years her senior; there is nothing to suggest that his action was unpremeditated in proposing marriage, and events proved the wisdom of his choice, for they were bound to each other by abiding affection. His action was reckless in that he seemed to regard it as a matter for Anne and himself alone; he did not sufficiently consider others who were involved. Anne was a minor, entrusted to the care of his employer, the daughter of a man in a much higher social position than himself.

Suddenly events moved toward a crisis. In January 1600, Lady Egerton died, and Anne became the lady of the house until October, when the Lord Keeper married once more. Anne could not remain at York House; 'forwardnesse is the best argument of love, and dilatory interruptions by the way, argue no great desire to the end',[11] they were pledged to each other before she left, and the marriage took place secretly in December 1601, with the assistance of two old friends, Christopher Brooke, who gave the bride away, and his younger brother Samuel, who performed the ceremony. The act was done, as he said in a letter to Anne's father, knowing 'that to have given any intimation of it had been to impossibilitate the whole matter'.[12]

[11] From a sermon preached in 1624, VI. 155.   [12] Gosse, I. 101.

Anne's father was a tempestuous man, and when he received the news of the marriage he determined to break this man who had aimed too high and to impoverish his daughter twice over by depriving her husband of employment and herself of her dowry. He demanded that Sir Thomas, his brother-in-law, should dismiss Donne immediately.

Egerton was a contrast to the angry father; a careful, deliberate man. He was well aware that the marriage had taken place through a secret association under his own roof; that it was an offence against Canon Law and Common Law, for Anne, a minor, to be married without her father's consent. He was reluctant nevertheless to dismiss so good a secretary, and, less involved personally than Sir George, saw more wisdom in what had happened. The father was adamant; he was determined to humiliate Donne, and made escape for Sir Thomas impossible by publicly challenging the legality of the marriage; once there was general discussion of the action of his secretary, the Lord Keeper had no alternative to the action forced upon him, and Donne was dismissed. His end achieved, the father cooled down, and perhaps he began to make a more favourable estimation of Donne, who behaved throughout with a disarming dignity and candour, presenting himself to Sir George as 'a sorrowful and honest man'.[13]

In a short time he became reconciled and asked Sir Thomas to restore the secretary to his appointment. Sir George, hot-tempered, was now pacified. Sir Thomas was slow to act, but what he had done he would not undo. He replied, saying that he had 'parted with a friend and such a secretary as was fitter to serve a king than a subject, yet that, though he was unfeignedly sorry for what he had done, it was inconsistent with his place and credit to discharge and readmit servants at the request of passionate petitioners'.[14] One in his position had great responsibilities, and must be above the influence exerted upon him by a 'passionate petitioner', and Sir George had certainly been that. He could not restore Donne to the secretaryship.

In 'A Sermon of Valediction at my going into Germany' preached at Lincoln's Inn just before going to the Continent in 1619, Donne spoke words the meaning of which had been written into his own experience—

[13] Gosse, I. 113.   [14] Jessopp, pp. 25f.

remember that he can make thy sun to set at noon, he can blow out thy taper of prosperity when it burns brightest,[15]

and in another sermon he said:

do not arm thy self with that vulgar, and triviall saying. . . . It suffices me, that mine own conscience is cleare, and I care not what all the world sayes; thou must care what the world sayes, and thinks.[16]

He could not at first believe that the disaster had happened, for want of 'That which love worst endures, *discretion*'.[17]

Following upon his dismissal came ample leisure in which to repent, not his marriage to Anne, but the manner of it. We find him, several years later, writing to his friend Lord Hay, who had been trying to promote his fortunes:

I have been told, that when your Lordship did me that extreme favour of presenting my name, his Majesty remembered me by the worst part of my history, which was my disorderly proceedings, seven years since, in my nonage . . . that intemperate and hasty act of mine.[18]

When one recalls his intention, later, to publish his poems just before his ordination,[19] itself an imprudent disregard of public opinion, one recognizes in his character an element of impulsiveness, made dangerous for him by an incapacity to calculate the consequences of proposed conduct; one suspects that the circumstances of his marriage did not present to his contemporaries in high office an offence to be noted and at length forgiven, but evidence of an inclination to rashness not to be trusted; sometimes in this world a single crime of almost monstrous proportions is more easily forgiven than an imprudent act is forgotten. As he himself said in a letter:

sometimes I think it easier to discharge myself of vice than of vanity, as one may sooner carry the fire out of a room than the smoke.

In a poem written a little later he said:

> For good, and well, must in our actions meete;
> Wicked is not much worse than indiscreet.[20]

---

[15] II. 242—Titles of sermons are as given in PS.   [16] X. 82.
[17] 'Loves diet', Grierson, I. 55.   [18] Gosse, I. 201f.
[19] See Gosse, II. 68-70.   [20] Gosse, I. 185; Grierson, I. 241.

In a letter to Sir Henry Wotton, 1612, he said, 'I died ten years ago';[21] and the years from his dismissal to his ordination in 1615 brought to him an intense, protracted experience of unfulfilled ambition, poverty, and sickness. His life was an experience of nihilism from the age of thirty to nearly forty-four, in some ways the best years of a man's life; many children were born to enrich a happy union, but family life was far from sufficient to exercise the extraordinary scholastic and human qualities which were rebelliously unsatisfied in days when most of his friends, less talented but with more wisdom, made steady progress in the world.

But his friends did not forsake him. The Donnes' first home was at Pyrford, the country residence of Francis Wooley, his wife's cousin, but, to be nearer London, they moved to Mitcham, where the dreariest and most melancholy years were spent. This period was not uncreative, and the subjective verdict in depression will not be that of posterity. Apart from a considerable amount of poetry, he helped Thomas Morton, later Bishop of Durham, in controversy with Roman Catholics, whose strength and influence were reviving; he developed, by the employment of his legal training, powers of argument which enabled him to write the very effective *Pseudo-Martyr*, a work which brought him to the notice of the King, who now had good reason to visualize for him a career of distinction in the Church. 'A book that pleased the King was an easy road to advancement.'[22]

His position in life was one of dependence and insecurity, and any criticism of his attitude toward patrons must be linked to the poverty which had little relief until his father-in-law paid his wife's dowry; even so, as he approached the fourth decade of his life he was economically dependent on two men, Sir George More and Sir Robert Drury. He had studied law but was not professionally established in it, and it is clear that these studies never commanded his full attention; he was 'betroth'd to no 'one Art'.[23] Walton, who says 'he was earnest and unwearied in the search of knowledge', speaks of him as a student 'often changing his studies . . . which had been occasionally diffused'.[24]

In a sermon preached at Lincoln's Inn, he said:

---

[21] Gosse, I. 291.   [22] D. H. Willson: *King James VI and I*, p. 212.
[23] 'To Mr *Rowland Woodward*', Grierson, I. 185.
[24] See Walton, pp. 84, 24, 48.

the study of our conversion to God, is in this like the study of your
profession, it requires a whole man for it. It is for the most part losse of
time in you to divert upon other studies. . . .[25]

He seemed almost excessively aware of the diffuse, allusive,
varied nature of his learning, and began his own epitaph, at the
end of his life, with the words, 'John Donne, Doctor of Divinity,
after various studies, pursued by him from his earliest years
with assiduity and not without success'[26]—but this attractive,
accomplished man was for many years handicapped by his quest
for knowledge, undisciplined by a particular calling, and when
this is added to the touch of recklessness associated with him
through his marriage, the reason for his failure to secure advancement is not hard to find. In the Preface to *Pseudo-Martyr* he wrote:

My natural impatience not to dig painfully in deep and stony and
sullen learnings; my indulgence to my freedom and liberty, as in all
indifferent things, so in my studies also, not to betroth or enthral
myself to any one science, which should possess or denominate me. . . .[27]

As late as 1612 he wrote to his friend George Gerrard:

For my purpose of proceeding in the profession of the law so far as to
a title, you may be pleased to correct that imagination wheresoever
you find it. I ever thought the study of it my best entertainment and
pastime, but I have no ambition nor design upon the style.[28]

A student of human nature could readily infer, from these quotations, a want of purpose, of intention to achieve, as characteristic
of him from his early days; the student of his life, confronted by
the view that is sometimes expressed that he never underwent
conversion, and that his motives for entering the Ministry were
at best mixed and scarcely creditable, must account somehow for
the fact that, from his ordination onward, indecision, uncertainty,
and want of purpose left him, never to return.

It is essential, to understand the message of Donne the preacher,
to experience, as far as possible, the terrible catharsis which he

[25] II. 156.
[26] Gosse, II. 282: the epitaph was in Latin and Gosse gives this, together with a
translation by Francis Wrangham.
[27] Gosse, I. 249—Gosse suggests 'dominate' for 'denominate', but Donne meant,
'link me with a particular profession'; presumably Walton recalled this passage when
he wrote: 'About the nineteenth year of his age, he . . . did . . . lay aside all study
of the Law: and, of all other Sciences that might give him a denomination. . . .'
(Walton, p. 25).
[28] Gosse, I. 303.

underwent. This is narrated by Gosse, who gives us Donne's own words on the protracted melancholy and dejection which descended upon him when he was poor, often unwell, thwarted and near to despair. These were the days when he wrote *Biathanatos*, a mitigation, to some degree, of suicide; this work was kept from the eyes of the public, and in the Preface he confessed that he felt sometimes the temptation to suicide—

whensoever any affliction assails me, methinks I have the keys of my prison in mine own hand, and no remedy presents itself so soon to my heart as mine own sword;[29]

but this casuistical exercise was itself a positive creation sufficient to check his self-despair, and the means whereby, stating a position, he disentangled himself from it, 'when my fortune was very low, as God knows it was'.[30]

Some of his finest prose letters belong to this period, and they served a similar purpose; by writing of his dejection, he saved himself from it. He wrote to Sir Henry Goodyear:

Because I am in a place and season where I see everything bud forth, I must do so too, and vent some of my meditations to you; the rather because all other buds being yet without taste or virtue, my letters may be like them. The pleasantness of the season displeases me. Everything refreshes, and I wither, and I grow older and not better, my strength diminishes, and my load grows. . . .[31]

Again:

I write from the fireside in my parlour, and in the noise of three gamesome children; and by the side of her, whom because I have transplanted into a wretched fortune, I must labour to disguise that from her by all such honest devices, as giving her my company and discourse.[32]

Again:

There is no one person but myself well of my family; I have already lost half a child, and with that mischance of hers, my wife is fallen into such a discomposure as would afflict her too extremely, but that the sickness of all her other children stupefies her; of one of which, in good faith, I have not much hope; and these meet with a fortune so ill provided for physic and such relief, that if God should ease us with

[29] Gosse, I. 260.   [30] Walton, p. 76.   [31] Gosse, I. 185f, Walton, p. 37.
[32] Gosse, I. 214f.

burials, I know not how to perform even that: but I flatter myself
with this hope that I am dying too; for I cannot waste faster than by
such griefs. . . .

From my Hospital at Mitcham. . . .[33]

Although one of the most quoted of his letters, the following,
to Sir Henry Goodyear, must be included as one of the great
letters of our literature:

Sir,—Every Tuesday I make account that I turn a great hour-glass,
and consider that a week's life is run out since I writ. But if I ask
myself what I have done in the last watch, or would do in the next,
I can say nothing; if I say that I have passed it without hurting any,
so may the spider in my window. The primitive monks were excusable
in their retirings and enclosures of themselves; for even of them every
one cultivated his own garden and orchard, that is, his soul and
body, by meditation and manufactures; and they ought the world no
more since they consumed none of her sweetness, nor begot others to
burden her. But for me, if I were able to husband all my time so
thriftily, as not only not to wound my soul in any minute by actual sin,
but not to rob and cozen her by giving any part to pleasure or business,
but bestow it all upon her in meditation, yet even in that I should
wound her more and contract another guiltiness. As the eagle were
very unnatural if because she is able to do it, she should perch a whole
day upon a tree, staring in contemplation of the majesty and glory of
the sun, and let her young eaglets starve in the nest.

Two of the most precious things which God hath afforded us here,
for the agony and exercise of our sense and spirit, which are a thirst
and inhiation after the next life, and a frequency of prayer and meditation in this, are often envenomed and putrified, and stray into a corrupt
disease; for as God doth thus occasion, and positively concur to evil,
that when a man is purposed to do a great sin, God infuses some good
thoughts which make him choose a less sin, or leave out some circum-
stance which aggravated that; so the devil doth not only suffer but
provoke us to some things naturally good, upon condition that we
shall omit some other more necessary and more obligatory. And this
is his greatest subtlety, because herein we have the deceitful comfort
of having done well, and can very hardly spy our error because it is
but an insensible omission and no accusing act. With the first of these
I have often suspected myself to be overtaken, which is with a desire
of the next life; which though I know it is not merely out of a weariness
of this, because I had the same desires when I went with the tide, and

[33] Gosse, I. 189; he reproduces this in II. 36 as part of a later letter probably to Sir
Robert Drury, without explanation; see also Walton, p. 36.

enjoyed fairer hopes than now; yet I doubt worldly encumbrances have increased it. I would not that death should take me asleep. I would not have him merely seize me, and only declare me to be dead, but win me and overcome me.

When I must shipwreck, I would do it in a sea where mine impotency might have some excuse; not in a sullen weedy lake, where I could not have so much as exercise for my swimming. Therefore I would fain do something, but that I cannot tell what is no wonder. For to choose is to do; but to be no part of any body is to be nothing. At most, the greatest persons are but great wens and excrescences; men of wit and delightful conversation but as moles for ornament, except they be so incorporated into the body of the world that they contribute something to the sustentation of the whole.

This I made account that I begun early, when I understood the study of our laws; but was diverted by the worst voluptuousness, which is an hydroptic, immoderate desire of human learning and languages—beautiful ornaments to great fortunes; but mine needed an occupation, and a course which I thought I entered well into when I submitted myself to such a service, as I thought might (have) employed those poor advantages which I had.

And there I stumbled too, yet I would try again; for to this hour I am nothing, or so little, that I am scarce subject and argument good enough for one of mine own letters; yet I fear, that doth not ever proceed from a good root, that I am so well content to be less, that is dead. You, sir, are far enough from these descents, your virtue keeps you secure, and your natural disposition to mirth will preserve you; but lose none of these holds, a slip is often as dangerous as a bruise, and though you cannot fall to my lowness, yet in a much less distraction you may meet my sadness; for he is no safer which falls from an high tower into the leads, than he which falls from thence to the ground; make therefore to yourself some mark, and go towards it alegrement. Though I be in such a planetary and erratic fortune that I can do nothing constantly, yet you may find some constancy in my constant advising you to it.

Your hearty true friend,

J. Donne.[34]

[34] Gosse, I. 190-192; Walton, pp. 37f. A. Alvarez speaks of it as 'a magnificent letter', and observes: 'This was written during the period of his disgrace, when he was unemployed, child-ridden and in danger of being patronized merely as a poet. The letter makes wonderfully clear that vibration behind all his verse: his desire for fulfilment within the body of society as an active, intelligent, professionally trained man. This is why he objected so strongly to being known as a poet: from this masculine point of view a poet was somehow parasitic, a mere entertainer who did not fulfil any serious function' (The School of Donne, p. 125). George R. Potter, in his lecture 'John Donne: Poet to Priest', quotes from this letter and stresses that the declaration 'to be no part of any body is to be nothing' is the key to understanding his dejection of spirit;

Yet in another letter written in bed, when ill, he tells us that during his illness he has written his poem 'A Litanie', a poem of rich complexity with profound spiritual insight:

Since my imprisonment in my bed, I have made a meditation in verse, which I call a Litany . . . for lesser chapels, which are my friends. . . .[35]

Sickness was a period of spiritual quickening, and his later *Devotions upon Emergent Occasions*,[36] his last sermon, and many of his sermons as we have them, all testify to this. We know that at times of deep emotion he wrote in verse as well as prose; he wrote 'A Hymne to Christ, at the Authors last going into Germany', at about the time of his 'Sermon of Valediction at my going into Germany', 'A Hymne to God the Father' at the time that he wrote his *Devotions*, and very probably the 'Hymne to God my God, in my sicknesse' was written almost at the end of his life. 'A Litanie' belongs to his years of melancholy, but does not express it. For this we must go to the great soliloquy, 'A nocturnall upon S. Lucies day, Being the shortest day'. The occasion is religious, for it is St Lucy's Day and the word 'nocturnal' carries the sense of 'an evening service in a Church'. But as it is a private meditation there is also the meaning, familiar in the musical term 'nocturne' of 'a composition of a pensive, melancholy character'. The saint commemorated is St Lucy (Lucia), Virgin and Martyr, said to have been put to death at Syracuse in the year 303; the name itself is associated with light, and, in various forms, became very popular in the Stuart period; and St Lucy became the patron saint of those afflicted in the eyes; suitably, her Day is 13th December, so fixed in the Julian calendar for the shortest day of the year, which might be regarded as the martyrdom of light;[37] this conjunction of the night season and the longest night provided just that concentration of significance in a moment of time which could excite and agitate his poetic nature;

he was happy when, as a priest, he 'belonged'; see *Five Gayley Lectures, 1947-1954,* p. 105. J. B. Leishman quotes the letter and underlines the nothingness of which Donne speaks, his isolation and unrelatedness; see *The Metaphysical Poets: Donne, Herbert, Vaughan, Traherne,* p. 55.

[35] Gosse, I. 195f.

[36] In future notes, as in the text, this is referred to as *Devotions*.

[37] In a sermon Donne refers to this Day, 'The eye of the Lord upon mee, makes midnight noone, and *S. Lucies* day *S. Barnabies*' (i.e. 11th June), PS, IX. 367; see Grierson, I. 254.

meaning became focused, held, expressed. The poem seems to refer to a beloved lady, recently dead. The objections to her identification with his wife, as is sometimes suggested, are that the poem expresses an altogether different reaction to the subject of the poem, 'Nothing', from what we find when he became a preacher; and that his wife died two years after his ordination. The preacher's message stressed his deliverance from nothing and the impossibility of returning to nothing. The poem is an experience of nothing, and of surrender to it.

Nevertheless, the reference may be to his wife, whose death, at a time of illness during these years of struggle and depression, was a real possibility to be reckoned with; in a mood of deep dejection, fearing such a loss, contemplating the consequences, he would realize what was only a fear of the mind. This is in harmony with what we know of his foreboding on going to Germany in 1619, and of his proleptic approach to his own death when he reconstructed its external form by means of a portrait, and enacted it before his own eyes. This theory must gain support, one supposes, from reflecting upon the influence of the darkness and the gloom of fear upon an extremely active imagination in solitude; and it could be urged that this dramatic projection of the mind to apprehend and realize a thought is the secret of the intensely realistic achievement of his verse. The XIIIth 'Holy Sonnet' begins: 'What if this present were the worlds last night?' His powers of imaginative realization were very great. When he charged his beloved, probably his wife, on parting from her, not to worry—

> Let not thy divining heart
> Forethinke me any ill,
> Destiny may take thy part,
> And may thy feares fulfil[38]

he had as much need to give this counsel to himself.

It is not necessary, however, to identify the lady of the poem, who may be the saint herself, whose death is now commemorated and who embodies his idea of Woman, without whom life has no positive meaning. The mood of the poem is that of the Mitcham days.

The poem is controlled by this experience of darkness in its

[38] Grierson, I. 328, 19.

intensest form, at double strength, the darkest part of the day
for the longest possible time; the structure is much simpler
than many of his poems, the argument does not move forward
and backward or suffer distraction from complicating side-issues;
instead, a very unusual thing in him, the last line reiterates the
first, the argument is static and the purpose of the poem is to
apply this double darkness to his own annihilation and show that
it also is the intensest possible. The darkness is not ordinary
darkness, but, to use a musical term for this nocturne, darkness
fortissimo; likewise, his deprivation through bereavement is not
ordinary nothing, it is the very essence of nothing, that Nothing
which preceded the creation of the world.

Stanza 1

> 'Tis the yeares midnight, and it is the dayes,
> *Lucies*, who scarce seaven houres herself unmaskes,
> The Sunne is spent, and now his flasks
> Send forth light squibs, no constant rayes;
> The worlds whole sap is sunke:
> The generall balme th'hydroptique earth hath drunk,
> Whither, as to the beds-feet, life is shrunke,
> Dead and enterr'd; yet all these seeme to laugh,
> Compar'd with mee, who am their Epitaph.

> *Line* 1—the year and the day stand in the relation of
> 'correspondence' like the macrocosm and the micro-
> cosm.
> 3—*flasks*: may refer to the stars.
> 6—*hydroptique*: a word often used by Donne; the reference
> to dropsy suggests disease; the dying earth has
> drawn into itself the life-spirit of the world.
> 9—notice the religious allusion, and the statement that
> he is, not that he writes, the epitaph. Is he lying on
> a bed, like a marble effigy lying on a tomb?[39]

'It is the darkest, and the longest, night of winter, and nature
sinks away on her deathbed; yet it can laugh, knowing that life
will be renewed; but I am really dead.'

---

[39] Donne was a skilled epigraphist, and he wrote his own epitaph; the subject is
discussed by John Sparrow, 'Two Epitaphs by John Donne', *The Times Literary
Supplement* (26th March 1949), p. 208.

Stanza 2

10   Study me then, you who shall lovers bee
     At the next world, that is, at the next Spring:
     For I am every dead thing,
     In whom love wrought new Alchimie.
     For his art did expresse
     A quintessence even from nothingnesse,
     From dull privations, and leane emptinesse:
     He ruin'd mee, and I am re-begot
     Of absence, darknesse, death; things which are not.

    Line 13—*Alchimie*: alchemy, chemistry as practised in ancient
          and medieval times.
      14—*expresse*: press out, extract.
      15—*quintessence*: this word, together with the words
         'elixir' (line 29), 'element', and 'philosophers'
         stone', are part of the vocabulary of alchemy.

It was believed from ancient times that, in addition to the four
elements of earth, air, fire, and water, dwelling in them all and
so unifying them in itself, was a fifth element, purer than any
of the four, the fifth element or quintessence. It was held that,
extracted from the four elements, it could be used (1) to endow
mankind with perpetual health, and in this sense was known as
the 'elixir'; (2) to endow base metals with perpetual health, i.e.
purge them of imperfection and turn them into gold; in this
sense it was known as 'philosophers' stone'—as in the well-known
lines of George Herbert,

     This is the famous stone
     That turneth all to gold.

   This unremitting quest of the alchemists had for its objectives
two great benefits for mankind, and for its method an involved
chemical process (to which the word 'sublimation', e.g., belongs),
with the alembic (line 21—'limbecke') or retort, for distillation.[40]
   Whatever one believed about alchemy, the quest was useful
illustrative material, with its search for what is held to be good,
promoted by the purification of what is impure; Donne did not
necessarily approve of this quest because he used it as a picture

---

[40] These words are discussed by M. A. Rugoff, *Donne's Imagery*, pp. 58f; see also
E. C. Brewer, *A Dictionary of Phrase and Fable*, 'elements', 'elixir of life', 'philosophers'
stone', 'quintessence'.

to represent meaning; here his purpose is to create a surprise, and to show that, though usually the alchemist sought to extract what was good, indeed perfect (line 19), in this case the alchemist Love has extracted from nothing an even more intense and perfect form of Nothing. He is not an example of creation out of nothing, but of the quintessence of Nothing, which he is, extracted from it.

'Come, next season's lovers, read me, an epitaph on all dead things. For you there is the prospect of renewal, but not for me —I have died through love, which has taken all human deprivation and made it me, and then proceeded to extract from it the very essence of Nothing; yes, I have a resurrection, I am remade, more Nothing than before, through my bereavement. What I have suffered through Love I thought was nothing; but it has assumed a more intense form even than that—the worst is yet to be.'

Stanza 3

> 19   All others, from all things, draw all that's good,
>   Life, soule, forme, spirit, whence they beeing have;
>   I, by loves limbecke, am the grave
>   Of all, that's nothing. Oft a flood
>   Have wee two wept, and so
>   Drownd the whole world, us two; oft did we grow
>   To be two Chaosses, when we did show
>   Care to ought else; and often absences
>   Withdrew our soules, and made us carcasses.

'The alchemist's quest for the quintessence is to achieve a greater good, but Love has made my nothing even more intense. In our Love for each other we became aware of Nothing—if the strains of life brought us to tears it was like the Flood over again, drowning the world; if anything drew us away from each other we went back farther, to the first Chaos, each of us a world in chaos; and if we were parted, it was as though life itself had ceased.'

Stanza 4

> 28   But I am by her death, (which word wrongs her)
>   Of the first nothing, the Elixer grown;
>   Were I a man, that I were one,
>   I needs must know; I should preferre,

If I were any beast,
Some ends, some means; Yea plants, yea stones detest,
And love; All, all some properties invest;
If I an ordinary nothing were,
As shadow, a light, and body must be here.

'I have been taken back—back to the Flood; back beyond the
Flood to Chaos; back beyond Chaos to Death; back beyond
Death to Nothing before Creation, for I am the very stuff of the
first Nothing. I am not an ordinary nothing—a man, beasts,
plants—mention what you will—have some positive qualities of
soul, and even stones attract and repel; nothing suggests
something, a shadow suggests a substance, and light. There is
something to be said, even about nothing!'

Stanza 5

37   But I am None; nor will my Sunne renew.
     You lovers, for whose sake, the lesser Sunne
     At this time to the Goat is runne
     To fetch new lust, and give it you,
     Enjoy your summer all;
     Since shee enjoyes her long nights festivall,
     Let mee prepare towards her, and let mee call
     This houre her Vigill, and her Eve, since this
     Both the yeares, and the dayes deep midnight is.

   Line 39—*the Goat*: Capricorn.
       41—*all*: this word reduces the love of others to ordinari-
            ness, and is meant to be as undistinguished as
            saying 'a good time was had by all'—it is just the
            fulfilment of lustful appetite, to serve which the
            lesser sun (i.e. the sun) has moved on.
       43—*prepare*: a religious act; Donne had a due sense of
            the place of preparation in religion—see, e.g. the
            first stanza of 'Hymne to God my God, in my
            sicknesse' (Grierson, I. 368), and his religious
            meditation on himself in his shroud, before his
            death.

'A shadow requires light, but I am before Light was created,
and the real Sun of my life has gone for ever, and I cannot be
even a shadow. You who read this Epitaph, Me, run along and

c

enjoy yourselves, the sun is your accomplice. Now leave me, for I make ready to keep vigil, and spend this night in prayer.'

The repetition of 'enjoy' in lines 41f is deliberate. He achieves enjoyment through her. The poem ends with a reaffirmation of its beginning, but it is more than a repetition, for through this meditation one who could not laugh (9) now rejoices as a Festival approaches. This is a deeply religious poem. Particularly, one notes his spirit of meditation; his submission to and acceptance of the unalterable; he does not demand a miraculous alteration of life (or, rather, death), and he does not question and rebel; he is not far from saying,

> . . . I resigne
> My selfe to thee, O God,[41]

and the poem ends with a paradox: it becomes a religious celebration of Nothing, and is itself something, one of our great poems, created at a time of dereliction.[42]

Before his dejection came upon him Morton had urged him to enter the Ministry. Then and for years afterwards Donne still hoped that a suitable secular appointment would be offered to him; he was not indifferent to money, and to the social prestige which the Ministry lacked. Not without reason Dr Morton said to him, when seeking to persuade him to enter the Ministry, 'No mans Education or Parts make him too good for this employment. . . .'[43] Leslie Stephen rightly says: 'His whole career was forced upon him, not carved out by his own taste';[44] James I, when requested even by a favourite, refused to give Donne secular employment, believing that his career should be in the Church as a preacher—he predicted that he would become 'a powerful Preacher'[45]—and it was through his inflexibility and his persistence that Donne, half-hoping even to the end for employment in law or diplomacy, at length capitulated. All other doors were shut and locked.

Donne was always ready to acknowledge his debt to his monarch, and he had his own particular affection for the words

[41] Grierson, I. 322.
[42] For the poem itself see Grierson, I. 44f; and for discussions of it, II. xxii f, xlv, 37-39; and the Bibliography, pp. 230f infra.
[43] Walton, p. 33.
[44] Leslie Stephen, Studies of a Biographer, Second Series, III. 59.
[45] Walton, p. 45.

in Proverbs xxii.11, 'the king shall be his friend', part of the text of his first sermon at St Paul's Cross. In a letter to Sir Robert Ker he said:

For, as when I sit still and reckon all my old master's royal favours to me, I return evermore to that, that he first inclined me to be a minister.[46]

In another letter he wrote of

his Majesty, from whom I have not only (as other men have) received my livelihood, but my priesthood.[47]

He dedicated his *Devotions* written after his grave illness in 1623, to the Prince of Wales, later Charles I, and in the dedicatory epistle he said:

I have had three births; one, natural, when I came into the world; one, supernatural, when I entered into the ministry; and now, a preternatural birth, in returning to life, from this sickness. In my second birth, your Highness' royal father vouchsafed me his hand, not only to sustain me in it, but to lead me to it.[48]

James was not always a good judge of men, but for once he did not make a mistake.

In the year of his ordination Donne became Chaplain to the King, and the Court, so much bound up with his secular hopes and seemingly ever beyond his attainment, received him as a preacher. Fortunately for Donne, at the beginning of his ministry a vacancy occurred in the appointment of Reader in Divinity at Lincoln's Inn, and this important post became his in 1616; in this place, where he had studied law to little purpose, he was received with affection as a preacher, and, to add to his good fortune, he held office during the years when the new Chapel was being erected. Thus, after a short 'probation', he occupied one of the important London appointments, a sphere of influence and note. Fortune seemed disposed to favour him the moment he surrendered to the sacred calling.

It is generally supposed that John Donne as a young man was of loose moral character, and that his acceptance of ordination was a penitent repudiation of his former way of life. According to

---

[46] Gosse, II. 190.   [47] Gosse, II. 214.
[48] See also *Devotions*, 8, Expostulation and Prayer; and his own epitaph, Gosse, II. 282, Walton, p. 79.

Walton, 'some irregularities of my life' were a reason given by
Donne for not taking Holy Orders earlier than he did; he records
him saying, 'I cannot plead innocency of life, especially of my
youth', and Walton himself says: 'He was by nature highly
passionate. . . .'[49] The student of his life and works must make
up his own mind on this matter. The prodigal returning home to
Lincoln's Inn as preacher is an exciting spiritual drama, but one
must pause to consider how likely it would be for a responsible
governing body to appoint him, so early in his ministry, if his
character was notorious; Sir Richard Baker's comment on him,
often quoted, deliberately denies the charge—

Mr John Dunne, who leaving Oxford, liv'd at the Inns of Court, not
dissolute but very neat: a great Visiter of Ladies, a great Frequenter
of Plays, a great Writer of conceited Verses.[50]

In a letter to Sir George More soon after the wedding Donne
denied 'that fault which was laid to me of having deceived some
gentlewomen before' and declared it to be 'vanished and smoked
away'.[51] The names of any parties to illicit intrigue, if they ever
existed, have been lost, leaving no more trace, to use a favourite
analogy of Donne, than the fish or the human hand leaves trace
in water.[52]

Gosse did his best to put this right by threading a number of
the poems together on the theory of an intrigue with a married
woman; this is so convincing to himself, and he writes with such
ardour upon it, that one forgets it is only conjecture, even when
he alludes to 'his great criminal liaison' as a fact.[53] He is not
alone in interpreting the poems by the principle that 'there is
hardly a piece of his genuine verse which, cryptic though it may
seem, cannot be prevailed upon to deliver up some secret of his
life and character'.[54]

The fact is that Gosse's discussion makes dramatic 'realization'
of something in the imagination so convincing that he destroys
his own argument. If he was able to recreate this woman, Donne
was no less able to realize the imaginary. Sensuous, some would
say salacious, passages in his verse can as easily be explained in

[49] Walton, pp. 34, 76, 84.   [50] Grierson, II. 172.
[51] Gosse, I 106.
[52] Grierson, I. 125, lines 41f; p. 182, line 56; PS, IV. 149; V. 318; see Evelyn Hardy,
John Donne: a spirit in conflict, pp. 72f.
[53] Gosse, I. 75; see the whole chapter.   [54] Gosse, I. 62.

this way as supposed to be narratives of actual experiences, an essentially untypical poetic style. Long after his ordination he wrote of his verse: 'I did best when I had least truth for my subjects.'[55] The charge of immorality must be held not proven if it rests solely on the interpretation of his poems. As for the poems themselves being immoral at times, apart from divergent views on impropriety, there is always the tricky point Donne himself made, that

Martial found no way fitter to draw the Roman matrons to read one of his books, which he thinks most moral and cleanly, than to counsel them by the first epigram to skip the book, because it was obscene.[56]

And there is much in the poems that points the other way—

> I never stoop'd so low, as they
> Which on an eye, cheeke, lip, can prey,[57]

and his character in relation to his 'secular' poetry suffers serious damage only if it can be held, by its teaching or influence considered as a whole, to promote immoral conduct. The argument of 'The triple Foole' is that his verse had a moral purpose toward himself—

> Then as th'earths inward narrow crooked lanes
> Do purge sea waters fretfull salt away,
> I thought, if I could draw my paines,
> Through Rimes vexation, I should them allay,
> Griefe brought to numbers cannot be so fierce,
> For, he tames it, that fetters it in verse.[58]

Gosse himself wrote that 'The early writings of Donne are not those of a depraved or even of an immoral man, but they are reckless in language, sensuous in imagery, full of the pagan riot of the senses, and far indeed from any trace of the pietist or the precisian'.[59]

Donne referred frequently to the sins of his earlier life, 'the sinfull history of mine own *youth*',[60] 'the wantonnesse of my

[55] Grierson, I. 288.
[56] Gosse, I. 123; there is weight in the observation that the poems on Elizabeth Drury, which are discussed in Chapter 5 of this book, 'may be a warning that we must not infer genuine autobiography from his utterances, for, if the truth had been unknown, injudicious critics might have constituted a romance out of lines intended simply to attract a patron'. (Leslie Stephen, *Studies of a Biographer*, Second Series, III. 56f.)
[57] Grierson, I. 66.   [58] Grierson, I. 16.   [59] I. 27.   [60] PS, II. 53.

youth',[61] but he began to preach with more of a past than an expectation of a future; these, and other references, as in his poetry to the days of his 'idolatry' and his 'profane mistresses'[62] are too vague to establish the specific charge of sexual licence. A fact which bears both upon his imaginativeness and his perception is his repeated reference in sermons to the sinfulness, for different reasons, of confessing sins never committed—e.g.

I would bely my self, and say I had done that, which I never did, lest I should be under-valued for not having done it.[63]

Donne's ministry began in 1615 and continued until his death in 1631; it was interrupted by illness, but also enriched by it, and his whole life became dominated by the desire to preach the Gospel. Jessopp entitled the third chapter of his book on Donne, in a series on 'Leaders of Religion', 'Steps to the Altar'. A pulpit also has steps. Donne refers to himself occasionally as a Priest, but more often as a Minister, and his references to preaching are frequent and emphatic. It was as a preacher that he found fulfilment.

During these years he became Vicar of Keyston in Huntingdonshire (1615; resigned 1622), Rector of Sevenoaks (1615), Rector of Blunham in Bedfordshire (1622), and Vicar of St Dunstan's-in-the-West in 1624, and on these appointments Jessopp comments:

In those days the holder of a benefice was considered to have done his duty to the parish from which he derived his income, if he took due care that the ordinary ministrations of divine service in the sanctuary were adequately provided for, and the parsonage occupied by a curate who ministered to the necessities and spiritual wants of the people. There was no feeling against a man of learning and eminence holding two or more livings in plurality. It was thought better that a clergyman of great gifts should be supported out of the surplus income of a rich benefice, and allowed to exercise his talents in a sphere which needed his personal presence and influence, rather than that he should be buried in a country village where he would be likely to live and die forgotten and unknown.[64]

[61] PS, X. 56.
[62] Grierson, I. 323 (III, line 5); p. 328 (XIII, lines 9f); see *Devotions*, 10, Prayer.
[63] II. 107f; see p. 295, III. 128; and *Devotions*, 10, Expostulation.
[64] Jessopp, pp. 112f.

The inscription on the paten presented with a chalice to Blunham, by Donne, and still in use, 'From Dr Donne Deane of Pauls, for Blunham Church',[65] realizes an advantage of the arrangement, whereby a remote country living was linked with an illustrious name. It is possible that Izaak Walton, a parishioner of St Dunstan's, would not have known Donne and written his Life, on which we greatly depend, had Donne not been appointed his Vicar.

Anne, Donne's wife, shared his improving fortunes for only two years, and died in 1617, after giving birth to a still-born child. When Donne wrote to her father after the marriage, he promised, 'as my love is directed unchangeably upon her, so all my labours shall concur to her contentment',[66] and he wrote to him again in 1614, 'So much company, therefore, as I am, she shall not want; and we had not one another at so cheap a rate, as that we should ever be weary of one another'.[67] They were faithful to each other, as Donne might have said, '*et in finem*', and she partakes of his enduring fame.

Fortune again favoured Donne in that there was a vacancy in the Deanery at St Paul's in 1621, and James was his friend once more in appointing him; to this responsibility he brought his ripened powers as a preacher, and here his massive contribution was made; the sermons that he preached in the Cathedral are his sufficient memorial. But not the only one. In the south choir aisle of St Paul's may be seen his effigy and epitaph, erected in old St Paul's, and the only monument of the former building still surviving in the new. The strange story is told by Walton, who thus narrates the preparations for the monument to be erected after his death, and the Dean's meditations shortly before his end:

A Monument being resolved upon, Dr *Donne* sent for a Carver to make for him in wood the figure of an *Vrn*, giving him directions for the compass and height of it; and to bring with it a board of the just height of his body. 'These being got: then without delay a choice Painter was got to be in a readiness to draw his Picture, which was taken as followeth.—Several Charcole-fires being first made in his large Study, he brought with him into that place his winding-sheet in his hand, and, having put off all his cloaths, had this sheet put on him, and so tyed

---

[65] PS, V, Appendix, 'Donne's Tenure of the Rectory of Blunham', pp. 425-30.
[66] Gosse, I. 102.   [67] Gosse, II. 48.

with knots at his head and feet, and his hands so placed, as dead bodies are usually fitted to be shrowded and put into their Coffin, or grave. Upon this *Vrn* he thus stood with his eyes shut, and with so much of the sheet turned aside as might shew his lean, pale, and death-like face, which was purposely turned toward the East, from whence he expected the second coming of his and our Saviour Jesus'. In this posture he was drawn at his just height; and when the Picture was fully finished, he caused it to be set by his bed-side, where it continued, and became his hourly object till his death: and, was then given to his dearest friend and Executor Doctor *Henry King*, then chief Residentiary of St *Pauls*, who caused him to be thus carved in one entire piece of white Marble, as it now stands in that Church.[68]

This imperious author of his own epitaph and designer of his own effigy stands, at his own command, proclaiming a triumphant faith by standing, not lying, upon his tomb. This monument is endowed with indelibility; its survival after three centuries is a significant emblem of one whose influence upon our age is as potent and disturbing as upon his own.

[68] Walton, p. 78.

TWO

A WHOLE UNWASTED MAN

('Metempsychosis, The Progresse of the Soule', stanza V)

A LADY was introduced to Sabine Baring-Gould, priest of the Church of England; preacher and hymn-writer; novelist and antiquarian. She asked, 'Are you the good Mr Baring-Gould who writes such beautiful sermons, or the other Mr Baring-Gould who writes novels?' John Donne, priest of the Church of England, was also a poet; and some would wish to meet the one, but not the other; the good Dr John Donne who, instead of writing poems, preached wonderful sermons; but not the bad Jack Donne, whose poems, it was supposed, were evidence of an immoral past. For them his life is in two contrasting parts, his verse belonging principally to his earlier life and to English Literature, his prose to his later life and to Divinity. His first biographer, Izaak Walton, presented his story in the contrasting terms of youth and age, of secular frustration and fulfilment in his sacred calling. Donne himself must bear some responsibility for this dichotomy. At the close of his 'Obsequies to the Lord Harrington', a tribute in verse to the memory of a young nobleman who died in February 1614, he announced his intention to write no more poetry—'. . . in thy grave I doe interre my Muse'.[1] He did not keep absolutely to this undertaking, but the fact that he made it a few months at most from his ordination suggests a contrast in his mind. His sacred calling greatly altered his way of life, but not as decisively as he seems, by this evidence, to have expected; the non-fulfilment of this declaration established the very continuity of his life which he appeared to deny.

About two years after becoming Dean of St Paul's, Donne wrote to the Marquis of Buckingham, who was in Spain with the Prince of Wales in connection with the proposed marriage of the Prince with the Infanta:

MOST HONOURED LORD,—I can thus far make myself believe that I am where your Lordship is, in Spain, that, in my poor library, where

---

[1] Grierson, I. 279.

indeed I am, I can turn mine eye towards no shelf, in any profession from the mistress of my youth, Poetry, to the wife of mine age, Divinity, but that I meet more authors of that nation than of any other. Their authors in Divinity, though they do not show us the best way to heaven, yet they think they do.[2]

This emphatic contrast, significantly linked with morality, and much to the advantage of Divinity, is made, nevertheless, when the Dean surveys his bookshelves and reflects upon books of Spanish poetry associated there with works on Divinity.[3]

About seven years, probably, before his ordination, he wrote a prose work entitled *Biathanatos, A Declaration of that Paradoxe, or Thesis, that* Selfe-Homicide *is not so Naturally Sinne, that it may never be otherwise.* This conclusion, which he knew would be widely opposed, deterred him from seeking to publish it. In 1619, four years after he had entered the Ministry, preparing to accompany Viscount Doncaster on his mission to Germany on the eve of the Thirty Years War, and depressed by the foreboding that he might die abroad, he gave a manuscript copy of this work to Sir Robert Ker, a Scotsman who had come south with King James in 1603 and who was and remained a close friend. In presenting him with the book, he wrote the following letter:

. . . besides the poems, of which you took a promise, I send you another book to which there belongs this history. It was written by me many years since, and because it is upon a misinterpretable subject, I have always gone so near suppressing it, as that it is only not burnt; no hand hath passed upon it to copy it, nor many eyes to read it; only to some particular friends in both universities, then when I writ it, I did communicate it. And I remember I had this answer, that certainly there was a false thread in it, but not easily found. Keep it, I pray, with the same jealousy; let any that your discretion admits to the sight of it know the date of it, and that it is a book written by Jack Donne, and not by Dr Donne. Reserve it for me if I live, and if I die I only forbid it the press and the fire; publish it not, but yet burn it not, and between those do what you will with it.[4]

He found it hard to destroy anything that he had created, and though he speaks of his former self as 'Jack Donne', it is when he sends to a lifelong friend copies of poems, and a controversial

[2] Gosse, II. 176.
[3] This letter and his reading of Spanish writers are considered by E. M. Simpson, 'Donne's Spanish Authors', *Modern Language Review*, XLIII (1948) pp. 182-185.
[4] Gosse, I. 258, II. 124.

prose work, to be kept. As he said in his Will, he bequeathed
to this same 'honourable and faithful friend ... that picture of mine
which is taken in shadows and was made very many years before
I was of this profession'.[5] This portrait has been found and is
reproduced as a frontispiece to the latest edition of J. B. Leishman's *The Monarch of Wit*.[6] In *The Times*, 13th October 1959,
John Bryson, writing on the 'Lost Portrait of Donne', tells the
interesting story of the identification of this picture, and draws
attention to the words in Latin around the head, 'ILLUMINA
TENEB. NOSTRAS DOMINA' ('Lighten our darkness, Mistress'),
which, he suggests, are a deliberate alteration of the third Collect
for Evening Prayer, '*Illumina quaesumus Domine Deus tenebras
nostras*' ('Lighten our darkness, we beseech thee, O Lord'). The
irreverent substitution of '*Domina*' for '*Domine Deus*', whatever
one thinks of the taste, is characteristic both of the poet and the
preacher, who, as the former, can transubstantiate manna to
gall,[7] and as the latter, declares, with reference to St Andrew and
recalling St Matthew vii.7, that those who find, seek.[8] This
picture was 'taken in shadows'—a reference, first to the dark
background, then to the mood of melancholy resting upon a
young lover, which the picture represents, but, at the deepest
level, a reference to human darkness and the Light of the world,
which was to be the theme of his first sermon as Dean of St Paul's,
on St John i.8, on Christmas Day, 1621; the preservation of the
picture by the Dean was a symbolic act whereby he represented
to himself the unity that belongs to personality; and the bequest
was his last endeavour to ensure that the memory of him as a
youth would be preserved, after his death.

In the year 1616 he was appointed Reader in Divinity at
Lincoln's Inn. He could not escape from his earlier life if he
would, for here he had studied Law as a young man, and many
to whom he preached had known him then. Five useful and happy
years of preaching were set in the context of his early days. On
becoming Dean of St Paul's, and terminating his appointment,
he presented to the Benchers a handsome recent edition of the
Vulgate, printed at Douai in 1617, in six volumes, and containing
the Postills of Nicholas of Lyra and the *Glossa Ordinaria* then
attributed to Walafrid Strabo. He wrote in his own hand on the

---

[5] Gosse, II. 363.   [6] 5th edition, 1962.   [7] Grierson, I. 28.
[8] See pp. 203-206, *infra*.

flyleaf of the first volume a Latin inscription,[9] in which he says
that he went to Lincoln's Inn to study Law, and that he turned
aside from this to other studies and matters, including foreign
travel; but although, by his own confession, his study of Law was
neglected, he states emphatically that throughout this time he
never neglected theological studies.[10] Though he began his
ministry later than most, we have here almost a sworn statement
written by his own hand into the Book, that he had been a student
of Divinity all his days. This was his principal, life-long interest.
He experienced the call to the service of God long before he was
aware of it, and looking back, saw it set at the heart of all his
restlessness.

For him, as for his age, Truth was realized in Emblems. The
library, the manuscripts, the portrait, the parting gift: these are
four emblems of the truth that, to consider him aright, one must
study him altogether, in the whole course of his life and in the
entire range of his writings.

The verdict of history has been decisive. The interest of his
contemporaries was his own interest, himself, and, never more so
than at the present time, students have insisted on learning all
that can be known about him. Soon after his death, in 1633,
his poems were collected and published; only a few, and none of
early date, had been printed during his life, and the rest, in various
manuscripts and in private ownership, were now made accessible
to all. He had himself prepared his sermons for the Press; these
were published, successively, in three collections, and 160 have
come down to us. It seems certain that he did not desire that
Biathanatos should be published, yet his own son caused it to be
printed in 1644; seven years later, he gave to the world his father's
Essayes in Divinity, which the author had not prepared for the
Press. About the same time, a number of prose letters, greatly
prized and so preserved, were published. Interest in him would
be satisfied with nothing less than the publication of all that he
had written which was still procurable. In the latter half of the
seventeenth century this interest waned, and practically ceased
in the century following, but in the middle of the nineteenth
century a few enthusiasts turned to him again, notably two who,

[9] Given in full in Gosse, II. 114; PS, II. 3 note 5.
[10] Qui huc, in prima juventute, ad perdiscendas leges, missus,
Ad alia, tam studia, quam negotia, et peregrinationes deflectens,
Inter quæ tamen nunquam studia Theologica intermiserat. . . .

like him, were Ministers of Religion, Augustus Jessopp, an Anglican, who concentrated on the prose, reprinting the *Essayes in
Divinity* in 1855—'I have never been able to feel much enthusiasm
for Donne as a poet', he confessed;[11] and Alexander Grosart, a
Minister of the United Presbyterian Church,[12] who edited his
poems in 1872, about the time, according to Bishop Lightfoot,
that Donne's effigy was rescued from neglect and removed from
the crypt to its present position.[13] Their labours were permanently
established by the *Life* written by Sir Edmund Gosse and the
edition of the *Poems* by Sir Herbert Grierson, who wrestled with
the problems of canon and text created by the private circulation
of the poems. The impact of all this, and the powerful influence
of Mr T. S. Eliot, have led to the publication of a great number
of books and essays in literary journals on every aspect of the
subject, and many of these writings are of great merit and
significance.

Most of his major works have now been reissued, and it is
reasonable to suppose that, before many years, everything that
he wrote that is extant will be accessible in a pleasing, convenient
form, his life rewritten and his letters edited anew in the light of
fresh knowledge. Miss Helen Gardner's edition of *The Divine
Poems* is a work of major importance for students of Divinity no
less than for students of English Literature. Mrs E. M. Simpson's
edition of the *Essayes in Divinity*[14] gives to them a significance not
conceded before. The years 1953-1962 have seen the publication,
in ten volumes, edited by the late George R. Potter and Mrs
E. M. Simpson, of all the sermons; this is a noble edition, presenting them, as far as can be determined, chronologically, with
critical apparatus and textual notes, and with essays on the
literary value of the sermons, the preacher's life in relation to
them, and the various authorities which he used—a worthy,
impressive monument to a preacher of renown.

The unity of Donne's life may be presented in the word 'entire-
ness', which is used notably by him in a poem and in a sermon,
both of which reveal his understanding of the importance of
wholeness to true personality. He wrote a number of love poems

[11] Jessopp, p. viii.
[12] See Robert Small, *History of the Congregations of the United Presbyterian Church*, I. 388f.
[13] J. B. Lightfoot, 'Donne the Poet-Preacher', *Historical Essays*, p. 222.
[14] All references to the *Essayes in Divinity* are to this edition with the abbreviation 'Essayes'.

of parting; one of these is called 'A Valediction: of my name, in
the window'—it reminds one of the famous latticed window in
Shakespeare's birthroom, bearing the names of distinguished
visitors. He has engraved his name with a diamond on his
mistress's window, and nothing can remove it, though he must
depart; his handwriting, his signature, suggests to him, for the
parting will surely kill him, his skeleton which she, contemplating
it, will restore to a human form—'this ragged bony name'[15] will
not be a skeleton to her—the reader finds himself thinking of the
reanimation of the dry bones of the valley in Ezekiel xxxvii.1-10,
and of passages in the sermons.[16]

His name will remain in the window, whole and indelible—

> As no one point, nor dash,
> Which are but accessaries to this name,
> The showers and tempests can outwash,
> So shall all times finde mee the same;
> You this intirenesse better may fulfill,
> Who have the patterne with you still.[17]

The first line recalls 'one jot or one tittle' (St Matthew v.18);
the last two lines, in which he says that his name, in expressing
his devotion, will help her to give herself even more entirely to
him, link themselves spontaneously with a sermon which he
preached at a christening, on 1 John v.7f, in which he uses one of
his most powerful original Latin expressions, 'Integritas Iesu'. He
gives to the first part of the sermon the title 'Integritas Christi',
and translates 'integritas' by 'intirenesse', the word used in the
poem for the same idea of a personality that remains indelible,
indivisible. He does not state the source, if any, of the expression,
but it is clearly inspired by St John xix.24, 36, and his mind
dwells upon the garment which remained whole, upon the bone
that was not broken, as he says:

That spirit which receives not Jesus intirely, which *dissolves* Jesus and
breakes him in peeces, that spirit is not of God . . . that Jesus, whose
bones God provided for, that they should not be broken, whose flesh
God provided for, that it should not see Corruption, and whose gar-
ments God provided, that they should not bee divided . . . here is

---

[15] Grierson, I. 26.   [16] See Grierson, II. 24f.   [17] Grierson, I. 26.

Integritas Iesu, quæ non solvenda, the intirenesse of Christ Jesus, which must not be broken. ... [18]

In stanza cxiv of his poem, 'The Two Poets of Croisic', Browning quotes from one of John Donne's poems:

> *He's greatest now and to de-struc-ti-on*
> *Nearest.* Attend the solemn word I quote,
> O Paul! *There's no pause at per-fec-ti-on.*
> Thus knolls thy knell the Doctor's bronzed throat!
> *Greatness a period hath, no sta-ti-on!*
> Better and truer verse none ever wrote
> (Despite the antique outstretched *a-i-on*)
> Than thou, revered and magisterial Donne!

The words quoted, in italics, refer to a whale, about to be destroyed by a thresher and a sword-fish, two smaller fishes. Browning addresses the poet Paul Desforges Maillard, and Donne may have come to his mind through his reference in stanza lxx to Paul at thirty years of age; this and the three stanzas following describe a situation and undertaking closely comparable to that of Donne in the circumstances of the poem from which Browning quoted. The work is 'Metempsychosis, The Progresse of the Soule',[19] the first poem in the collected edition published after his death. His earliest poems had been satires, and this was to be a satire of epic proportions, introduced with (1) an impressive dedication; (2) the date; (3) the title; (4) the words '*Poêma Satyricon*'; (5) an Epistle; (6) another title; and when he is ready to begin, we have (7) the words 'First Song', to encourage the expectation of an elaborate poem in many parts; but although the whole title-piece thus has seven different elements before we begin to read, the first is the only song; it opens in true epic style, but he tires of the subject for the sufficient reason that the poem, despite the title, does not progress very much, and he

---

[18] V. 134, 137; and see pp. 133-138.
[19] This is referred to by Grierson and others as 'The Progresse of the Soule', but Donne, who was prepared to alter and parody a prayer to make a title for his portrait, used his own work in the same way, and later adopted this title, in the form 'Of the Progresse of the Soule', for a poem which, unlike the earlier, was published. The two poems are easily confused, and to avoid misunderstanding the word 'Metempsychosis', which is the true title, and by which the poem was known to Ben Jonson, is always included in the title of the earlier poem.

terminates it abruptly, perhaps deliberately, the essence of the
satire being embodied in the flatness of the close and the uncompleted treatment of the theme. In the course of the poem he
indulges in a favourite pastime of ridiculing what is merely large,
and the whole poem, in being what it is, a fragment, satirizes the
epic.[20]

The poem bears the date, not at the end, but as part of the
title—16th August 1601. So much of his verse is undated that
attempts to relate it to his life depend on very dubious internal
evidence, but here we have a comparatively long poem of over
500 lines with a precise date. Although we have no information
on the date of composition of very many poems, they establish
that he was not unconcerned about time; particular occasions
affected him deeply; he wrote a poem 'Upon the Annunciation
and Passion falling upon one day. 1608';[21] a 'Hymne to Christ'
on going to Germany in 1619; a poem on his journey westward on
Good Friday, 1613; and a Verse Letter to the Countess of Bedford
on New Year's Day, beginning,

> This twilight of two yeares, not past nor next,
> Some embleme is of mee . . .

He wrote nothing finer than 'The Anniversarie' and 'A nocturnall upon S Lucies day, Being the shortest day', which depend
upon a sense of time and occasion.[22] By placing a date as part of
the title he anchored the poem to his personal history. The date
of his birth is not known, and the study of relevant documents,
which is of great interest, is indecisive, though the year given by
Izaak Walton, 1573, is agreed to be too late, and should be 1572
or even the year before. H. W. Garrod suggested that 16th
August was Donne's birthday and 1571 the year of his birth;
and although this has not been generally accepted it remains a
possibility; we know that he was nearly thirty when he wrote the

[20] There is an unfinished character about much of Donne's work. He intended to
continue the sequence of poems on Elizabeth Drury annually, but wrote, in all, two
poems. The last two chapters of *Pseudo-Martyr* appear in the Table of Contents, but
not in the work (see Gosse, I. 247f). He intended to consider the opening verses of
the books of the Bible, beginning with Genesis, in his *Essayes in Divinity*, but travelled
no farther than Exodus. It may be that the *Holy Sonnets* were not completed. A
Verse Letter to the Countess of Bedford and a poem entitled 'Resurrection, imperfect', conclude with the words '*Desunt cætera*' (Grierson, I. 221, 334).

[21] Grierson, I. 334-336; title as in Gardner, p. 29.

[22] Grierson, I. 352f, 336f, 198, 24f, 44f.

poem, for he makes the statement at the beginning of the fifth stanza.[23]

There is uncertainty on many of the titles of the poems, but it is not questioned that the words '*Infinitati Sacrum*' were written by Donne at the head of this one, as a dedication. The opening words of the Epistle which followed suggest that he intended to include a portrait of himself, and the possibility that this was to be the one 'in shadows' suggests a comparison of its Latin inscription with this one; this mock-epic, introduced with serious, religious words, will seem to many readers unworthy of this dedication, which, nevertheless, with the precise date, reveals an underlying seriousness not usually associated with it. Three lines from the VIIIth stanza, easily separable from the poem, reappear later in the second of the sequence of sonnets entitled '*La Corona*', as a striking symbol of his essentially religious nature, his 'crown of prayer and praise' incorporating words from an earlier and very different poem,

> That All, which alwayes was all, every where;
> Which could not sinne, and yet all sinnes did beare;
> Which could not die, yet could not chuse but die.[24]

The introductory Epistle refers to the Pythagorean doctrine of metempsychosis, or the transmigration of souls, which gives to the poem its title—

the Pithagorian doctrine doth not onely carry one soule from man to man, nor man to beast, but indifferently to plants also . . . [and, in harmony, he will narrate the story of the soul] . . . when shee was that apple which Eve eate, to this time when shee is hee, whose life you shall finde in the end of this booke.[25]

When Ben Jonson conversed with Drummond of Hawthornden in 1619, he said of this poem: 'The conceit of Donne's Transformation, or Μετεμψύχωσις was, that he sought the soul of that apple which Eve pulled, and thereafter made it the soul of a bitch, then of a she-wolf, and so of a woman: his general purpose was to have brought in all the bodies of the Heretics from the

---

[23] On the discussions of the date of Donne's birth see Bibliography, pp. 228f, *infra*.
[24] Grierson, I. 298, 319; compare p. 298, lines 77f with 'Hymne to God my God, in my sicknesse', lines 21f, p. 368.
[25] Grierson, I. 294; for a derogatory reference to this doctrine by Donne in a sermon, see PS, I. 316.

soul of Cain, and at last left it in the body of Calvin. Of this he
never wrote but one sheet, and now, since he was made Doctor,
repenteth highly, and seeketh to destroy all his poems.'[26]

The poem itself suggests that the end of the soul's journey
would be Queen Elizabeth, not Calvin, and a change in the
course of the poem, despite the introductory Epistle, is much
more characteristic than the alliterative theme, 'Cain to
Calvin'.

The poem narrates the progress of the soul of heresy—a religious theme—from the apple in the Garden of Eden, in which
the soul dwelt. The soul, in a series of metamorphoses, proceeds
from the apple to a succession of various creatures—a mandrake,
a sparrow, a fish's roe, a swan, another fish, an oyster-catcher
(sea-pie), a whale, a mouse, a she-wolf, a bitch (half-dog, half-
wolf), an ape, and, finally, to Siphatecia, daughter of Adam and
wife of Cain; at this stage the poem ends, and it is only introductory to the declared purpose; it is the first song preparing the
way for Cain.

This poem, praised by Lamb and De Quincey,[27] and signally
honoured by Browning, has been widely disregarded, though
Gosse, his biographer, devoted his fifth chapter to it, and gave it
more attention than any other poem. More recently Miss M. M.
Mahood in her *Poetry and Humanism* has given it fresh significance,
and Professor W. A. Murray has asked, and answered, the
question, 'What was the Soul of the Apple?'[28]

He argues that the key to the poem is not the supposed study of
heretics, and not the supposed reaction against Queen Elizabeth
who was at this time most unpopular through the execution of
Essex, but the circumstances of the poet himself. He emphasizes
the critical decision upon his marriage which he had to make, and
quotes the words, 'for to choose is to do', from a later prose letter[29]
as a heading and summary of the essay. The poem, he contends,
presents the soul of the apple in a series of dilemmas involving
choice; because man is fallen, every act of choice is a quest for
self-preservation and progress; the wrong decision is made, and
the penalty of error has to be paid; there is no real progress, and
the same process and result—error followed by the doom of

[26] Gosse, I. 132f.
[27] See H. W. Garrod, *John Donne: Poetry and Prose*, pp. 122, lii.
[28] *Review of English Studies*, n.s. X(1959) 141-155.
[29] See p. 13, *supra*.

death—form the plot of the successive episodes. This theory, applied to the poem in detail, raises it to the level of a highly serious discussion of man's responsibilities, truly epic in the purpose, though not the result.

Further, he demonstrates the poem's affinity with the thought of Philo, the Jew of Alexandria and contemporary of our Lord, in whose writings are to be found (a) the idea of the soul, or reason, in plants; (b) the Pythagorean philosophy; (c) an emphasis upon the importance and place of choice, and destiny, in life. Study of Donne's 'secular' poems suggests the probability of 'religious' sources for some of them, making them less original than has been supposed, and the separation of 'secular' from 'religious' poems untenable. Philo allegorized the Genesis account of the creation of the world, and could be the source of the names of Adam's children given by Donne toward the end of the poem, and found in Philo. As an allegorist he stressed every significant detail, as Donne does in these passages—

(1)   Thee, eye of heaven, this great Soule envies not,
      By thy male force, is all wee have, begot . . .
      Yet hast thou not more nations seene then shee,
      That before thee, one day beganne to bee. . . . [30]

—a reference to the creation of the sun on the fourth day, as told in Genesis i.14-19.

(2)   Prince of the orchard, faire as dawning morne,
      Fenc'd with the law, and ripe as soone as borne. . . . [31]

These two references introduce us to ideas which are found in his sermons.

Professor Murray quotes from Philo's *De Plantatione*, xi, 'Noah's Work as a Planter', a passage in which we may recognize this reflection upon the detail of the scriptural account of Creation; and also the possible source of the poem:

It is with deliberate care that the law-giver says not of the man made after God's image, but of the man fashioned out of earth, that he was introduced into the garden. . . . The earthly man has a disposition of versatile subtlety, fashioned and concocted of elements of all sorts. It

[30] Grierson, I. 295.
[31] Grierson, I. 298; and see p. 302, lines 187-189, 191f for this idea, and p. 308, line 320, for a reference to Genesis i. 7.

was to be expected, then, that God should plant and set in the garden, or the whole universe, the middle or neutral mind, played upon by forces drawing it in opposite directions and given the high calling to decide between them, that it might be moved to choose and to shun, to win fame and immortality should it welcome the better, and incur a dishonourable death should it choose the worse.[32]

Murray makes a highly interesting analysis of the various incidents of the soul's progress, contrasting man's repeated failure to choose aright, indeed his lack of freedom to do so, with 'the infinity of right choice',[33] as he terms it, exercised by Jesus Christ, alluding, doubtless, to the words '*Infinitati Sacrum*' which, in the light of this impressive discussion, have an altogether more serious and devout purpose than to satirize the idea of the religious epic. If the poem is dedicated to the one right choice of history, it is a religious poem, and has at its heart an aspiration that, since Jesus Christ has thus ended the entail of sin's wrong choices, he may do what is right in the hour of decision.

The date, the portrait, the theme of choice shortly before his marriage, the references to himself, show this to be a poem of a personal character; to the autobiographical allusions we turn, in conclusion. He fails, almost at the start, to separate himself from the soul whose adventures he is narrating. The IVth, Vth, and VIth stanzas of the poem, lines 31-60, are as follows:[34]

IV

31   Great Destiny the Commissary of God,
       That hast mark'd out a path and period
       For every thing; who, where wee of-spring tooke,
       Our wayes and ends seest at one instant; Thou
       Knot of all causes, thou whose changelesse brow
       Ne'er smiles nor frownes, O vouch thou safe to looke
       And shew my story, in thy eternall booke:
       That (if my prayer be fit) I may 'understand
       So much my selfe, as to know with what hand,
       How scant, or liberall this my lifes race is spand.

[32] op. cit., p. 145.   [33] ib., p. 154.
[34] These stanzas, together with stanza VII, appear as no. 68 in the *Oxford Book of Christian Verse*.

V

41   To my six lustres almost now outwore,
    Except thy booke owe mee so many more,
    Except my legend be free from the letts
    Of steepe ambition, sleepie povertie,
    Spirit-quenching sicknesse, dull captivitie,
    Distracting businesse, and from beauties nets,
    And all that calls from this, and to others whets,
    O let me not launch out, but let mee save
    Th'expense of braine and spirit; that my grave
    His right and due, a whole unwasted man may have.

VI

51   But if my dayes be long, and good enough,
    In vaine this sea shall enlarge, or enrough
    It selfe; for I will through the wave, and fome,
    And shall, in sad lone wayes a lively spright,
    Make my darke heavy Poëm light, and light.
    For though through many streights, and lands I roame,
    I launch at paradise, and I saile towards home;
    The course I there began, shall here be staid,
    Sailes hoised there, stroke here, and anchors laid
    In Thames, which were at Tigrys, and Euphrates waide.[35]

Line 31—The poem begins:

    I sing the progresse of a deathlesse soule,
    Whom Fate, which God made, but doth not controule, . . .[36]

Fate, Destiny, is permitted by God as His deputy to appoint to each man the unalterable circumstances, including the duration, of his life; and thus to determine the dramatic setting for his exercise of choice.

Line 35—'Knot' is used sometimes by Donne for 'a knotty problem'—'O knottie riddle . . .'[37] and may carry this sense in 'the knottie Trinitie',[38] but it is also used in the positive sense of a knot which joins and holds together—

    . . . to knit
    That subtile knot, which makes us man.[39]

---

[35] Grierson, I. 296f.
[36] Grierson, I. 295; see the important note, II, pp. 150f.
[37] Grierson, I. 181; cf. p. 328, *Holy Sonnets*, XIV, line 11.
[38] Grierson, I. 329, and Gardner, p. 73.
[39] Grierson, I. 53; and see p. 303, line 207.

In the sermons the word is used frequently, and much more often in a positive sense for that which draws or holds together. Of Jesus Christ he declared in another christening sermon, similar in thought to the one referred to earlier:[40] 'the Holy Ghost hath presented him unite, and knit together.'[41] A characteristic use of the word is in passages like the following—

at last, as the knot of all, created man . . . this text is the knot, . . . of all the second part . . . the knot of his life . . . command your *souls* to have their conversation in heaven by meditation of this Scripture, and you shall meet company, which no stranger shall interrupt, for they are all of a knot, and such a knot as nothing shall unty, as inseparably united to one another, as that God, with whom they are made one Spirit, is inseparable in himself. . . .[42]

In a passage to be noticed for its intrinsic importance, both senses are found—

A net is *Res nodosa*, a knotty thing; and so is the Scripture, full of knots, of scruple, and perplexity, and anxiety, and vexation, if thou wilt goe about to entangle thy selfe in those things, which appertaine not to thy salvation; but knots of a fast union, and inseparable alliance of thy soule to God, and to the fellowship of his Saints, if thou take the Scriptures, as they were intended for thee, that is, if thou beest content to rest in those places, which are cleare, and evident in things necessary. A net is a large thing, past thy fadoming, if thou cast it from thee, but if thou draw it to thee, it will lie upon thine arme.[43]

The knot is for Donne an image of personality, both divine and human, complex, but held together in wholeness.

Line 41—*lustres*: lustre or lustrum: a period of 5 years.

  55—*light, and light*: in two different senses, referring to the preceding words 'dark' and 'heavy'.[44]

[40] See pp. 32f, *supra*.   [41] PS, V. 123.
[42] See II. 342, III. 116, IV. 294, V. 97 (another christening sermon), respectively; cf. *Essayes in Divinity*, p. 30.
[43] II. 308.
[44] In the third line of 'The Curse' (Grierson, I. 41) 'only' is used similarly in two different senses: (1) 'his "one and only" purse', (2) 'nothing but his purse'; one recalls the prayer in a Lenten sermon: 'Forgive me my . . . sinnes against *Thee* and *Thee*, against thy Power O Almighty Father, against thy Wisdome, O glorious Sonne, against thy Goodnesse, O blessed Spirit of God; and sinnes against *Him* and *Him*, against Superiours and Equals, and Inferiours; and sinnes against *Me* and *Me*, against mine own soul, and against my body, which I have loved better then my soul. . . .' (VII. p. 361f).

56—See 'Hymne to God my God, in my sicknesse', where he writes of the 'streights' through which alone the traveller may reach home.[45]

59—cf. the opening words of the second sermon on Genesis i.26, preached before Charles I in 1629:—'By fair occasion from these words, we proposed to you the whole Compasse of mans voyage, from his lanching forth in this world, to his Anchoring in the next; from his hoysing sayle here, to his striking sayle there'.[46]

60—this last line brings to mind the last line of Francis Thompson's 'The Kingdom of God'.

Donne could penetrate a little farther than most beyond the veil.[47] Izaak Walton narrates an extraordinary vision of his wife which Donne had when parted from her.[48] He was very sensitive to the foreboding that came upon him at times of parting. He had in fact come half-way in his life, and exactly thirty more years, 'so many more', would be given him. He prayed, if his life were to continue, to be free from the very things which in fact he suffered, yet, though he was not prevented from launching out, he remained, despite 'th' expense of braine and spirit', 'a whole unwasted man'. And the spirit of prophecy, which, through his catalogue of those things he would most avoid, wrote the story that was his destiny, dictated to him the source of the message that he would deliver to the world as a preacher of the Gospel. He launched at Paradise.

He began where the Scriptures began. God's greatest work was the Creation, seen in its splendour contrasted with Nothing which preceded it. Even God's work of regeneration is not a creation from nothing, but a recreation, a redirecting, of that which had been made. Once the creative act has taken place, life is essentially continuous, and grace works upon, not apart from, nature. In a sermon preached before Queen Anne in 1617, on Proverbs viii.17, on the theme of Love, he makes the interesting reflection, at the beginning, that within the Scriptures we can trace the

[45] Grierson, I. 368.   [46] IX. 68.
[47] Hugh I' A. Fausset regards the words quoted on p. 67, *infra* from 'Satyre III' as a prophecy of Donne's attempt to take life by direct assault, his struggle and eventual victory—see *John Donne: A Study in Discord*, p. 54.
[48] Walton, pp. 39-42.

effect on authors of their former occupations: the courtier, the town-dweller, the shepherd, the fisherman, may be found in their writings, 'ever inserting into their writings some phrases, some metaphors, some allusions, taken from that profession which they had exercised before'. So also the converted person brings to his religious experience his own particular temperament, which is not eradicated, but redirected upon God. There is a place in religion for covetousness, voluptuousness, anger, and passion; Solomon, 'whose disposition was amorous, and excessive in the love of women, when he turn'd to God, he departed not utterly from his old phrase and language . . . as we see . . . in this text . . .'. Donne illustrates this idea in other sermons. The penitent thief stole his salvation at the Cross; Paul, who asked for Letters of Commission of the State to persecute Christians, became the great letter-writer of the Church; Rahab let down the spies out of her house with the same cord with which she drew up her adulterous lovers into it; the fishers of men were first fishermen. This truth to which Donne gave frequent expression was his personal experience. The same amorous nature is revealed in the *Songs and Sonets* and the *Divine Poems*, as the XVIIth Holy Sonnet and the third stanza of his 'Hymne to Christ' clearly show. He tells us that his personal preference for the Psalms of David and the Letters of Paul is based upon his activity first as a poet and then as a letter-writer. Suitably, Donne returned as preacher to Lincoln's Inn, where he studied Law, and in the prayer before the sermon preached by him at the dedication of the new Chapel on Ascension Day 1623 he prayed:

And in these walles, to them that love *Profit* and *Gaine*, manifest thou thy selfe as a *Treasure*, and fill them so; To them that love *Pleasure*, manifest thy selfe, as *Marrow* and *Fatnesse*, and fill them so; And to them that love *Preferment*, manifest thy selfe, as a *Kingdome*, and fill them so; that so thou mayest bee all unto all. . . .

As John Chudleigh stated in his Elegy:

> He kept his loves, but not his objects; wit
> Hee did not banish, but transplanted it,
> Taught it his place and use, and brought it home
> To Pietie, which it doth best become. . . .

Mortification, he would say, is not to kill nature, but sin; be ambitious for a place in the Kingdom of Heaven; let anger become zeal; love above all others the face of Jesus.[49]

The influence of this thought on Donne, together with his Jesuit upbringing, accounts for a principal defect in his presentation of the Gospel; of martyrdom, which he saw at close quarters as a reckless negation of life's essential worth, he has not much to say, and of renunciation, or self-mutilation to enter into life, even less; his early training turned him rebelliously against self-denial, pain, death, in the cause of religion. His words in *Pseudo-Martyr* state his position well: 'We are not sent into this world *to suffer* but *to do*, and to perform the offices of society required by our several callings.'[50] It is not easy to present the Gospel both as life-affirming and life-denying. Donne, repelled by a rigorism which seemed to dishonour God's created work, gave all his powers to affirm that God created the world and saw that it was good. In his preaching he declared the value for religion of a man's temperament and nature, and reinforced his message by its exposition in his life. Great Destiny had appointed to him the task, by the discipline of experiencing self-negation, of communicating the worth of the created order, and of himself as part of it. His acceptance, late in life, of the call to the pulpit charged with purpose the years that remained, but the light that fell upon them shone also on the way that he had come.

[49] See PS, I. 236f, 156, 286; II. 287, 304f; Grierson, I. 330, 353; PS, II. 49; IV. 363; Grierson, I. 394; Walton, p. 49f., PS, IV. 228; and cf. V. 177; IX. 354f; X. 110.
[50] Gosse, I. 253.

THREE

OF THAT SHORT ROLL OF FRIENDS WRIT IN MY HEART

('To Mr I. L.')

AMONG the human influences upon his message as a preacher none was more constant or enriching than his many friendships. There is a blaze of glory igniting his prose as he speaks of the sociableness of God; his nature is excited as he urges his hearers to an answering eagerness to associate with one another; and this distinctive emphasis was sustained by his experience of human friendship. He was never a solitary recluse; he depended on the stimulus of human company, and even in 'A Hymne to Christ, at the Authors last going into Germany', in which the relationship between himself and his Lord is the controlling thought, he struggles to give Christ His sovereign place, vividly aware of those he is leaving behind him—

> I sacrifice this Iland unto thee,
> And all whom I lov'd there, and who lov'd mee. . . .
>
> Nor thou nor thy religion dost controule,
> The amorousnesse of an harmonious Soule,
> But thou would'st have that love thy selfe . . . '[1]

and his dedication is to Christ as Lover who fulfils, not denies, all human friendship. Many of his closest friends travelled life's road with him, and when the passing years took some away, others replaced them, and he who gave so much to others was given imperishably to the world by the loving tribute of his latest friend, Izaak Walton. Jessopp fittingly entitled his second chapter, '*Noscitur a sociis*'. In a prose letter Donne declared, 'there is a Religion in friendship'.[2] Writing to the Countess of Bedford he said (though it would have helped us much had his letters all been dated):

though in inheritances and worldly possessions we consider the dates of evidences, yet in letters, by which we deliver over our affections and

---

[1] Grierson, I. 353.   [2] Gosse, I. 290.

assurances of friendship, and the best faculties of our souls, times and days cannot have interest nor be considerable, because that which passes by them is eternal, and out of the measure of time.[3]

To George Gerrard he wrote:

(for our letters are ourselves, and in them absent friends meet) . . . If we write to a friend, we must not call it a lost letter, though it never find him to whom it was addressed, for we owe ourselves that office to be mindful of our friends,[4]

and in a sermon, speaking of the value of letters, he said:

by this meanes wee overcome distances, we deceive absences, and wee are together even then when wee are asunder.[5]

Donne was a notable letter-writer; his poem, 'A Valediction: of the booke' imagines the love-letters between himself and his 'deare Love' made into a book, and in contemplation of it he declares:

> Here Loves Divines, (since all Divinity
> Is love or wonder) may finde all they seeke.[6]

We have no such book, but we possess poems, letters in verse and prose, *Biathanatos*, *Paradoxes and Problemes*, and sermons, because of his correspondence, and the value put upon it, and the writings issuing from it or entrusted to friends by it. John Donne the younger published in 1651 'the first collection of private letters ever published in England',[7] consisting of prose letters written over many years by his father to those whom the son described as 'persons of honour', and preserved by their recipients, who felt as their writer did, that they were not business communications to be read, noted, and finally destroyed, but emblems of friendship, enriching the affection which they expressed, to be re-read and preserved. Warmth of feeling and serious discussion of important religious matters were combined to invest human relationships with a sense of the eternal. We have noticed already the memorable letter written to Sir Henry Goodyear.[8] He wrote to him weekly, and his relationship stimulated him to write some of his best letters, in one of which he makes the declaration:

[3] Gosse, II. 43.
[4] Gosse, II. 266f; see I. 181 for a letter of the Mitcham period on friendship, with its declaration: 'There is some of the honour and some of the degrees of a Creation to make a friendship of nothing.'
[5] I. 285.   [6] Grierson, I. 30.   [7] Jessopp, p. 92.   [8] See pp. 12f, *supra*.

You know I never fettered nor imprisoned the word Religion, not straightening it friarly, *ad Religiones factitias* (as the Romans call well their orders of Religion), nor immuring it in a Rome, or a Wittemberg, or a Geneva; they are all virtual beams of one Sun, and wheresoever they find clay hearts, they harden them and moulder them into dust; and they entender and mollify waxen. They are not so contrary as the North and South Poles, and that they are co-natural pieces of one circle. Religion is Christianity, which being too spiritual to be seen by us, doth therefore take an apparent body of good life and works, so salvation requires an honest Christian.[9]

He began his Easter sermon, 1625, with the same analogy of the sun's diverse working[10] and long before he began to preach he expressed many of his religious views in his private letters.

Jessopp says of Sir Henry, that he 'was a gentleman of many accomplishments, with cultivated tastes, and of a poetic temperament; he had a large and apparently well-chosen library; but his almost romantic devotion to his friend has won for him an immortality which he could not otherwise have achieved',[11] but he deserves his place in the biography of his friend for evoking such memorable phrases as 'my second religion, friendship', 'the coarse but durable garment of my love'.[12] He was the same age as Donne, and died four years before him, and he was a constant friend, who helped him to bear the lean years by exercising the high art of so conducting correspondence that it did not cease.

Among many other friends were the Earl of Northumberland, scientist and mathematician, who was imprisoned in the Tower for fifteen years for supposed complicity in the Gunpowder Plot; James Hay, some years junior, a Scotsman who came south with King James in 1603, prospered at Court, and became Viscount Doncaster and later Earl of Carlisle, one of his most faithful friends, affectionate and generous; Robert Ker, another Scotsman who accompanied the King to England, and who became Earl of Ancrum in 1633;[13] Sir Thomas Roe, Sir Thomas Lucy, Henry King, Sir Julius Caesar; and, linking him with the following years, George Herbert and Izaak Walton.[14]

Donne owed much to his friends—his appointment as secretary to Sir Thomas Egerton, his ordination, the first preaching in

[9] Gosse, I. 226.   [10] PS, VI. 262.   [11] Jessopp, p. 49.
[12] Gosse, I. 170; II. 7.   [13] See p. 28f, *supra.*
[14] See A. Alvarez, *The School of Donne*, p. 36f, and Appendix I, 'Donne's Circle', pp. 187-195.

villages outside London, accompanied by a friend,[15] the return
to Lincoln's Inn (with Christopher Brooke behind the scenes),
the promotion to St Paul's, his biography by Izaak Walton, a
parishioner.

For a full understanding of the matter we must turn, not only
to his prose letters, but also to the verse letters, *Letters to Severall
Personages*, thirty-five in number,[16] a considerable and varied
correspondence over many years, from the later years of Elizabeth's reign almost to his ordination, preserved by recipients who
were honoured by them. We know nothing of Mr I. L., save
that he lived somewhere in the north country, beyond the river
Trent, and was married, but he had a distinction of primacy
which many might have envied—

> Of that short Roll of friends writ in my heart
> Which with thy name begins. . . .[17]

and Donne says that of all his friends who have gone far away
'there's none that sometimes greets us not' except the friend to
whom he writes, who is failing in his 'duties of Societies' if he has
time only for his wife and his interests in country life. Two
friends from early days were the brothers Christopher and Samuel
Brooke, to whom letters were addressed; four were sent to Sir
Henry Wotton, Ambassador to Venice, later Provost of Eton,
in one of which he says;

> I aske not labored letters which should weare
> Long papers out. . . .
> Nor such as from the brayne come, but the hart.[18]

Mr Rowland Woodward was the recipient of five of these letters;
Donne gave to him a copy of his poems, a sure proof of his
affection; and wrote letters also to his brother, Thomas Woodward. The collection includes letters addressed to certain ladies;
these are much more formal, using the plural form of address,
and also much more involved and scholastic, intellectual exercises
in wit and compliment. Donne was stimulated by the society
of cultivated people, and Mrs Magdalen Herbert, the mother of
Sir Edward and George Herbert, influenced him considerably;
probably he sent to her his sequence of sonnets, '*La Corona*'; and,

---

[15] See Walton, p. 48. [16] Following Grierson, *The Poems of John Donne*, 1933.
[17] Grierson, I. 212. [18] Grierson I. 189; see Walton, p. 20.

later, in 1625, when the plague drove him from the heart of
London, he found refuge in her home, and opportunity to prepare
some of his sermons for publication. Lucy, Countess of Bedford,
his patroness in the seven or eight years before his ordination,
was a great lady, of Court and aristocratic connections, who
stimulated him when the spirit of poetry might have died away;
seven of these letters are addressed to her, and the declaration at
the beginning of one of them, 'You have refin'd mee . . .',[19] was
probably a simple statement of fact; she was the patroness of
scholars and poets, and was noted for her love of gardens, and
paintings. The last letter but one of this collection of verse
epistles, to the Countess of Salisbury, is dated August 1614, and
brings us very near to his ordination. In lines 11-21 we have an
analysis of the human situation resulting from the disintegration
of the medieval world; mankind is seen as in a condition of decline,
sinking into the state of Nothing preceding Creation—

> All the worlds frame being crumbled into sand,
> Where every man thinks by himselfe to stand,
> Integritie, friendship, and confidence,
> (Ciments of greatnes) being vapor'd hence,
> And narrow man being fill'd with little shares,
> Court, Citie, Church, are all shops of small-wares,
> All having blowne to sparkes their noble fire,
> And drawne their sound gold-ingot into wyre;
> All trying by a love of littlenesse
> To make abridgments, and to draw to lesse,
> Even that nothing, which at first we were. . . .

In lines 39-50 we have an example of his meditation upon the
story of Creation, which, with the passage just quoted, shows how
important this was to him as the great change in his life drew
near—

> For had God made man first, and man had seene
> The third daies fruits, and flowers, and various greene,
> He might have said the best that he could say
> Of those faire creatures, which were made that day;
> And when next day he had admir'd the birth
> Of Sun, Moone, Stars, fairer then late-prais'd earth,
> Hee might have said the best that he could say,
> And not be chid for praising yesterday;

[19] Grierson, I. 191.

> So though some things are not together true,
> As, that another is worthiest, and, that you:
> Yet, to say so, doth not condemne a man,
> If, when he spoke them, they were both true than.[20]

Donne expressed intense emotion at times of parting. Poems
called valedictions, and some others of similar character, come
straight from, and go straight to, the heart; 'Sweetest love, I do
not goe' and 'A Valediction: forbidding mourning', whatever
opinions are held on other poems, will keep his name as a poet
secure. 'Elegie XII. His parting from her' contains the defiant
lines addressed to 'Fortune':

> Do thy great worst, my friend and I have armes,
> Though not against thy strokes, against thy harmes.
> Rend us in sunder, thou canst not divide
> Our bodies so, but that our souls are ty'd,
> And we can love by letters still and gifts,
> And thoughts and dreams; Love never wanteth shifts.
> I will not look upon the quickning Sun,
> But straight her beauty to my sense shall run;
> The ayre shall note her soft, the fire most pure;
> Water suggest her clear, and the earth sure.
> Time shall not lose our passages; the Spring
> How fresh our love was in the beginning;
> The Summer how it ripened in the eare;
> And Autumn, what our golden harvests were.[21]

We recognize the same man in the words of the preacher, as he
says farewell for a season to the Lincoln's Inn where he was well
content to be:

And so as your eyes that stay here, and mine that must be far of, for
all that distance shall meet every morning, in looking upon that same
Sun, and meet every night, in looking upon that same Moon; so our
hearts may meet morning and evening in that God, which sees and
hears every where; that you may come thither to him with your
prayers, that I, (if I may be of use for his glory, and your edification
in this place) may be restored to you again. . . .[22]

The emotion had to be concentrated and made tangible, in a
name scratched on a window, in a book of love-letters, in the

---

[20] Grierson, I. 224f.   [21] Grierson, I. 18f, 49-51, 102f.
[22] PS, II. 248. One of his sermons in connection with the Feast of the Conversion
of St Paul was based on Acts xx.25: see VIII, sermon 6.

'Hymne to Christ' written when going to Germany, in a farewell gift of books to Lincoln's Inn. Izaak Walton tells us

that not long before his death he caused to be drawn a figure of the Body of Christ extended upon an Anchor, like those which Painters draw when they would present us with the picture of Christ crucified on the Cross: his varying no otherwise then to affix him not to a Cross but to an Anchor (the Emblem of hope), this he caused to be drawn in little, and then many of those figures thus drawn to be ingraven very small in *Helitropian* Stones, and set in gold, and of these he sent to many of his dearest friends to be used as *Seals*, or *Rings*, and kept as memorials of him, and of his affection to them.[23]

The Mayor of Casterbridge might ask 'that no man remember me', but Donne the Christian is near to his Lord when, like Him, he asks his friends to remember him.

They did, and his legacy to us is immeasurably enriched by the writings which would not have been preserved otherwise. Lady Drury kept twenty-five of Donne's letters sewn together in a bundle;[24] these, most unfortunately, have not survived; but, lost though they are, the fact that they were kept at all is an emblem of the special value put upon them and their author. Gosse said of him, 'he was a priest in the temple of friendship', and Izaak Walton said, with simple adequacy, that he was 'a lover of his friends'.[25]

[23] Walton, p. 63; this adaptation of the cross into an anchor is an example of the characteristic noted on p. 29, *supra*.
[24] R. C. Bald, *Donne and the Drurys*, pp. 4, 158.
[25] Gosse, II. 289; Walton, p. 68.

FOUR

DEIGNE AT MY HANDS THIS CROWN OF
PRAYER AND PRAISE

('La Corona', first and last lines)

IN July 1607, probably, John Donne wrote a religious poem called 'La Corona'. It was, he says, 'Weav'd in my low devout melancholie'.[1] If this refers to the depression which had then settled upon him, the poem shows a vigorous resistance, for it is a noble, positive offering of devotion to Christ. Seven sonnets are linked together, taking successively the subjects of the Annunciation, our Lord's Nativity, His presence in the Temple 'in his ages morning',[2] His Crucifixion, Resurrection, and Ascension. There are many memorable lines,[3] and the poem is a significant expression of Donne's personal religious life, based upon the prayers and praises of the Church on which he drew to create his own offering of worship. The last line of the first sonnet is the first line of the second, and so on, the last line of the seventh being the same as the first line of the poem; thus, so far as this can be achieved on a flat page of print, the poem is a crown. It is not of many of his poems that his own words can be used—

'And makes me end, where I begunne',[4]

but they apply to this work, in which the subject affects the form, the expression realizes the idea. The purpose of this chapter is to note other examples of this embodiment of meaning in some of his writings, both verse and prose; and to consider its significance. To do this we must, first, discuss some of the characteristics of his verse.

The introductory Epistle to 'Metempsychosis, The Progresse of the Soule' expresses the self-awareness and self-concern found throughout his writings, in prose and verse—

Others at the Porches and entries of their Buildings set their Armes; I, my picture; if any colours can deliver a minde so plaine, and flat,

---

[1] Grierson, I. 318.   [2] Grierson, I. 320.   [3] See, e.g., p. 208 *infra*.
[4] Grierson, I. 51 (referring to a circle drawn with compasses).

E

and through light as mine. . . . Now when I beginne this booke, I have
no purpose to come into any mans debt.[5]

The poem begins with the announcement that he will sing the
progress of a deathless soul (not himself); but he is soon writing
about himself, his lifelong interest. His love poems are not
conventional expressions of praise of the beloved; he is not
concerned with her portrait; it is his which should be set also at
the beginning of the *Songs and Sonets* which begin suitably in
Grierson's edition with, 'I wonder . . .'. Even his name he takes
seriously (in the form of 'Don' or 'Dunne' it is still in use, but in his
day his name was pronounced 'done', to rhyme with 'sun'),
and, as others also did, he makes puns upon it. He ends a verse
letter to Sir Henry Wotton with his signature incorporated into
the poem—

> . . . But if my selfe, I'have wonne
> To know my rules, I have, and you have
> DONNE.[6]

Izaak Walton tells us that immediately after his dismissal from
Egerton's service, 'he sent a sad Letter to his Wife, to acquaint
her with it: and, after the subscription of his name, writ:

> *John Donne, Anne Donne, Vn-done,*

and God knows it proved too true'.[7]

At the end of his life he wrote the line which he intended should
appear beneath the picture of himself in his shroud: '*Corporis
haec Animae sit Syndon, Syndon Jesu. Amen.*' *Sindon* or *Syndon* is the
word for a fine thin linen fabric, a kind of cambric or muslin,
and was a familiar religious word, used in the Rheims[8] translation
into English of Matthew xxvii.59: 'Joseph taking the body,
wrapt it in cleane sindon', or Mark xiv.51: 'a certaine yong
man followed him clothed with sindon'; and for a shroud, and
especially that of our Lord, 'the holy syndon, wherein they say
our Saviour's body was bound up and buried':[9] it is a translitera-
tion of the Greek word σινδών in the Gospels,[10] first into Latin

---

[5] Grierson, I. 293.   [6] Grierson, I. 182.   [7] Walton, p. 29.

[8] The Rheims version (1582), the New Testament part of the Douai Bible (Roman
Catholic) was strongly Latin in character; Tyndale and Coverdale both used 'linen'
instead of 'sindon'.

[9] Quoted in *New English Dictionary*.

[10] Matthew xxvii.59; Mark xiv.51f, xv.46; Luke xxiii.53—the only verses in which
the word occurs.

(the Vulgate translates by *sindon*) and then into English. This scriptural use of the word, confined to the Passion narratives, with reference to the shroud of Christ and the garment worn by Mark, was exactly appropriate to the dying Donne, contemplating himself in his shroud, an emblem of his meditation on the Christian hope of the resurrection of the body, in which he believed passionately—the emblem with motto was a familiar form of religious devotion. This motto, prefixed to the published last sermon, *Deaths Duell, or, a Consolation to the Soule, against the dying Life, and living Death of the Body,* concentrates attention on the subject of the sermon, body and soul, and the inscription may be taken to mean: 'May this shroud of the body also signify the shroud of the soul, namely the shroud of Jesus.'

Yet into this traditional religious expression and scriptural allusion he inserts a reference to himself, and in 'sindon' we have his last pun on his own name, alluding to the death of sin. It is a mistake to regard these puns as trivialities; Donne would not have been capable of such irreverence in the preparation that he made for death. Deliberately he obtruded his name because he was concerned for himself—as he had been when near to death in 1623, when he wrote his 'Hymne to God the Father', which he caused to be sung frequently in St Paul's 'to a most grave and solemn Tune';[11] this is a poem of three stanzas on the words 'sin' and 'done', which occur eight and seven times respectively, and is the probable origin of the later *sindon*, and it is throughout a pun, but a very serious one, on his own name. One cannot understand him, as poet or preacher, unless one recognizes that he took himself seriously.[12]

The 'Elegies upon the Author', printed by Grierson after the Poems, contain important statements about Donne; and the 'Elegie' by Thomas Carew stressed the originality of the poet—

> The Muses garden with Pedantique weedes
> O'rspred, was purg'd by thee; The lazie seeds
> Of servile imitation throwne away;

[11] Walton, p. 62, following the poem, which is also in Grierson, I. 369.

[12] For a discussion of the epigraph, see Gardner, pp. 53, 112f, and Sir Geoffrey Keynes, *Bibliography of Dr John Donne,* (3rd edition, 1958), p. 42f, and John Sparrow, *The Times Literary Supplement,* (13th March 1953), p. 169, F. Kermode, *John Donne,* p. 41. Walton (pp. 79f) contrasts the portrait made just before his death with the portrait of 1591 with the Spanish motto *Antes muerto que mudado* (reproduced in Grierson, I. 7). For further references to puns on the name see PS, II. 2 note 4; Gosse, I. 277, II. 50.

And fresh invention planted, . . .
           . . . open'd Us a Mine
Of rich and pregnant phansie, drawne a line
Of masculine expression. . . .[13]

He was a rebel against the Petrarchan tradition in love poetry,
with its lovers in flower gardens; smooth lawns and gently mur-
muring streams; its goddesses of mythological and pastoral
imagery; and conventions of chivalry. Now, instead, we have a
violent assertion of sexual realism; he is neither platonic nor
ascetic, but frankly, yet honestly, sensuous. His interest is in his
experience of love, and his endeavour is to understand it, not to
deny or suppress it, and still less to present it untruthfully. The
presentation is anything but romantic—

I sing not, Siren like, to tempt; for I
Am harsh. . . .[14]

Ben Jonson said that Donne's 'verses of the Lost Chaine he
hath by Heart', a reference to 'Elegie XI. The Bracelet. Vpon
the losse of his Mistresses Chaine, for which he made satisfaction'
—he has lost her bracelet; and what he says about this is not that
it was the colour of her hair, not that it was precious because it
had been touched by her, not that the links symbolized their
relationship; but, frankly, that to replace it would cost money—

Not that in colour it was like thy haire,
For Armelets of that thou maist let me weare:
Not that thy hand it oft embrac'd and kist,
For so it had that good, which oft I mist:
Nor for that silly old moralitie,
That as these linkes were knit, our love should bee:
Mourne I that I thy seavenfold chaine have lost;
Nor for the luck sake; but the bitter cost.[15]

In a variety of ways his early poems communicated the realism
of familiar, conventional, contemporary life. His language is
colloquial and many of his love-poems are, simply, talk; they
are essentially contemporary, in the present tense; and the reader
finds himself at once *in media res*.

[13] Grierson, I. 378f.
[14] Grierson, I. 211; see PS, IV. 164, 'things of sweetnesse, and of delight grow not
in my ground'.
[15] Grierson, I. p. 96. His realism was not confined to amatory verse; see 'Elegie
VIII', with its reference to war, and the ugly, repellent realities of life.

The first of the *Songs and Sonets* begins with natural, probable human speech:

> I wonder by my troth, what thou, and I
> Did, till we lov'd? were we not wean'd till then?
> But suck'd on countrey pleasures, childishly?[16]

describing an experience of awakening, and astonishment at it, which is both real and familiar; but stating it by making it part of what it describes, like a love-letter. One is made aware at once of dealing with real people in true, dramatic situations. Who can fail to relive opening words like these?

> For the first twenty yeares, since yesterday,
> I scarce beleev'd, thou could'st be gone away. . . .[17]

An analysis of one's reaction will disclose, however, an awareness that his hand closes round the situation to hold it and examine it, to get at its meaning; quickly the poem will move on to consider implications and objections, and one finds oneself in an argument. The speech is not only colloquial, but also argumentative and sometimes contentious, and realism is achieved by the poem itself presenting the familiar human situation of an argument exposed in its falsity, or carried too far and made to retreat. The poem itself comes alive, and, through the developing, changing argument—he is essentially a poet who thinks aloud—the position at the end may be different from that at the beginning—indeed this is commonly so, as in 'Song. Goe, and catche a falling starre', 'The Sunne Rising', 'The triple Foole', 'A Valediction: of my name, in the window',[18] 'Twicknam garden', 'The Message', 'The Extasie', 'The Primrose', 'A Ieat Ring sent', 'The Prohibition'; 'The Undertaking' stands apart, with 'A nocturnall . . .' as a poem of reiteration.[19] With the repeated use of words like 'yet', 'but', these poems have astonishing agility. This is assisted by the great variety of stanza forms in the *Songs and Sonets*, well over forty in number and rarely repeated; and this diversity is in close relation with the changing mood and attitude of the

---

[16] Grierson, I. 7; Saintsbury commented on this opening, 'The enshrining once for all in the simplest words of a universal thought' (*Prefaces and Essays*, p. 287).

[17] Grierson, I. 69; see pp. 9, 48, for examples of dramatic opening lines, provocative in character to gain attention; there are many others, projecting the reader immediately into a living situation needing no further description.

[18] On this Valediction see D. Louthan, *The Poetry of John Donne*, pp. 128-131.

[19] Grierson, I. 8f, 11f, 16, 25-28, 28f, 43, 51-53, 61f, 65f, 67f, 10, 44f.

poet toward the theme of love, over many years, the varied
experiences requiring varied stanzaic forms to embody them.
Sometimes, as in 'Loves Vsury', 'Loves Alchymie', 'The Dampe',
the theme is, to quote the first of these poems, ' . . . let my body
raigne . . .'[20] Or he presents woman as fickle, changeable, and
himself as expounding the variety which is opposed to the errors
of the 'poore heretiques in love', who 'thinke to stablish dangerous
constancie'.[21] Sometimes he is bitter, almost savage; but much
more often he is positive and affirmative. These poems study the
subject from every possible angle, but they are not about love,
they are communications from one experiencing an aspect of it.

The argument alters its course, the stanza forms vary from
poem to poem, because he changes too; now he is impudent,
reckless, irresponsible; now his mind, instead of his emotions,
dominates the subject, and in a moment of scintillation he throws
out ideas and suggestions which ask to be explored. As a result
the poems are rich in pregnant thought, and once our minds
are stirred we share his sense of vitality; for him a thought was a
deep, enriching experience; he was at home with paradox and
seeming contradiction because such true thoughts are our nearest
approach to God, who is a Mystery; Donne's obscurity and
difficulty are not meant to irritate, they are a valid communication of the essential nature of truth.

The poems are natural in being colloquial and argumentative
and diverse. The same realism is achieved through the innumerable allusions to the familiar, contemporary scene—everyday
home life, a window, a dream, maps and voyages, the human
body and its health, law, astronomy, war, time, love, death,
business. There are, it is true, allusions in his verse which appear
recondite to us, but which had a familiar meaning in his day;
Leslie Stephen's words may well be remembered when reading
his poems: 'What strike us as unaccountable conceits are simply
applications of the current philosophy'.[22] In his sermons, as in his
poems, he refers to the 'Schools', and has in mind the vast range
of medieval philosophical, and theological teaching which
comprehended human knowledge synthetically, expressed
supremely in the *Summa Theologica* of Aquinas. Words which are

[20] Grierson, I. 13, 39, 63.
[21] Grierson, I. 13, 'The Indifferent'; see Elegies III, XVII.
[22] *Studies of a Biographer*, III. 50; and see R. Tuve, *Elizabethan and Metaphysical
Imagery*, p. 221, note 28.

still part of our vocabulary—wit, conceit, essence, quintessence, elixir, correspondence, balm, humour, concoction, element, intelligence, simple, sphere, neutrality, spirit (e.g. animal spirits), —carried suggestions of ideas long since forgotten by most people, and we have to understand their meaning in his day to appreciate his use of them (their meaning was much more precise, making possible a plural use—e.g. intelligences, correspondences, humours, conceits, accidents). The rival claims for Ptolemy and Copernicus, for Paracelsus, provide a background for the poems, and modern scholarship has been devoted to an exposition of these many allusions. In view of the dangerous but understandable separation of the 'secular' from the 'divine' poems, it is the more necessary to indicate that the former carry many references to religious matters, and, just as it is necessary to perceive allusions to medicine, law, and astronomy, so it is essential to acknowledge the religious interest of many of the *Songs and Sonets*, with their references to body and soul, faith and works, death and burial, the oath, the anathema, heresy, canonization, profanity, the clergy, religious orders, sacrilege, relics, martyrs, epitaphs: 'A Valediction: of the booke' is an extended reference to religious matters—a book compiled from love-letters becomes a missal or breviary for Love's Divines.

Some of the characteristics of his poetry are well expressed in the following poem, which is chosen, somewhat arbitrarily, to set them forth—

Lovers infinitenesse

1   If yet I have not all thy love,
　　Deare, I shall never have it all,
　　I cannot breath one other sigh, to move,
　　Nor can intreat one other teare to fall,
　　And all my treasure, which should purchase thee,
　　Sighs, teares, and oathes, and letters I have spent.
　　Yet no more can be due to mee,
　　Then at the bargaine made was ment,
　　If then thy gift of love were partiall,
　　That some to mee, some should to others fall,
　　Deare, I shall never have Thee All.

12   Or if then thou gavest mee all,
　　All was but All, which thou hadst then;
　　But if in thy heart, since, there be or shall,

New love created bee, by other men,
Which have their stocks intire, and can in teares,
In sighs, in oathes, and letters outbid mee,
This new love may beget new feares,
For, this love was not vowed by thee.
And yet it was, thy gift being generall,
The ground, thy heart is mine, what ever shall
Grow there, deare, I should have it all.

23   Yet I would not have all yet,
Hee that hath all can have no more,
And since my love doth every day admit
New growth, thou shouldst have new rewards in store;
Thou canst not every day give me thy heart,
If thou canst give it, then thou never gavest it:
Loves riddles are, that though thy heart depart,
It stayes at home, and thou with losing savest it:
But wee will have a way more liberall,
Then changing hearts, to joyne them, so wee shall
Be one, and one anothers All.[23]

There is not an obscure word in this poem, which cross-examines an expression all too easily made, because conventional—'with all my love'. Possibly she has said or written it, without appearing to mean it very much. What does it mean, when you come to think about it?

Stanza 1: If I have not won all your love, I cannot hope to now, I can do no more to win it; you certainly have all *my* love! I realize my only claim is on the love you meant to give me—you may not have intended it all for me.

Stanza 2: But, supposing you did, 'all' was only what you were capable of giving then. Love, once it is roused and exercised, increases; and—torturing thought—through my love for you, other men may seek you and, with their unexhausted charms, fare better. I admit you are under no obligation to give this new love to me— but wait a moment, I am wrong—I have a claim to it, for you would not be able to love at all apart from me; so I do claim all your love!

Stanza 3: But no, I do not want it all—I shall exhaust it! though

[23] Grierson, I. 17f, II. 17f; see Bibliography, p. 231, *infra*.

we can both grow in love and so exchange more. But surely it is not a matter of 'exchange'. What a paradox, what a riddle, it all is, but I am sure we must stop thinking of giving, which is a finite idea, and so, exhaustible; we do not give all, we become all, and, joined together, our love will be infinite.

The poem is an argument, controlled by 'if', 'or', 'yet', or 'but'. It is much more than a clever game with bargains and contracts, although it can be that for those who will not look for more; the poet penetrates to the little explored deeper levels of personality, and, especially in lines 13, 27f, lights up its potentialities. More aware at the beginning of her possibilities than of his own, he astutely demonstrates in the third stanza the falsity inherent in ever saying one has done all one can, by confessing that he also can grow in love; lines 25f contradict 3-6.

Later, as a preacher, Donne would sometimes take a simple idea and work upon it in this way. His insight into the human heart, by which he held a mirror before his hearers, is illustrated by the convincing detection in the argument of the potentialities of a person, and the exposure of his supposed thoroughness of self-giving. It is among these poems that we must search for the sources of his preaching. In the case of this particular poem, the central idea recurs later. In the *Essayes in Divinity* he writes: 'For if thou couldest express all which thou seest of God, there would be somthing presently beyond that.' And in a Christmas sermon at St Paul's, probably in 1629, on John x.10, he says: 'in the Christian Church, he hath given us meanes to be better to day then yesterday, and to morrow then to day. That grace which God offers us in the Church, does not onely fill that capacity, which we have, but give us a greater capacity then we had: And it is an abuse of God's grace, not to emprove it, or not to procure such farther grace, as that present grace makes us capable of.[24] Certainly 'Lovers infinitenesse' is not by or for a sensual person, for whom line 23 would have no appeal. Its theme is the growth of love, and after looking at 'all' from every angle, the poet discovers that it has itself grown in meaning during the argument, to mean much more, in the last line, than the first. It is one example among many of an emotional idea invested with thought

[24] *Essayes in Divinity*, p. 23; PS, IX. 150.

which makes it attractive with new meaning. This application
of thought to feeling enabled him as preacher to hold the attention
as he considered the great themes of religion, so that he was never
just sentimental or intellectual but, in the fusion of thought and
feeling, truly passionate.

His freedom from 'servile imitation', his realism and his
spontaneity are revealed repeatedly in the creation of surprises.
The sense of astonishment, the expectation of truth confounding
conventional attitudes, irrupting violently to shatter assumptions,
may be discovered in a number of these poems. Reality's first
impact is to shock, to surprise, to astonish. This was his own
experience: the shock of Protestantism breaking into his Catholic
training, the shock of his dismissal from Egerton's service, the
surprise of his appointment to Lincoln's Inn at the beginning of his
ministry but in middle life. Donne's contribution to the study of
Christian experience has much to do with this sense of surprise,
which he never lost.[25]

The pleasant dream, an escape from harsh reality, becomes, in
'The Dreame' the prelude to reality.[26] Though 'Elegie X. The
Dreame', urges caution with any generalization, dreams and
sleep, which is a kind of death, are given no high honour; 'The
good-morrow', in the second stanza, contrasts the snoring and
dreaming of the opening lines with the declaration:

> And now good morrow to our waking soules . . .[27]

The truth about a matter will be astonishing, not commonplace.
Donne lived in days when 'the Copernican revolution' of a helio-
centric instead of a geocentric universe was displacing the Ptolemaic astronomy; the impact of this new truth was disturbing
to many people, and it seemed to imply that man himself was less
significant than had been supposed. But to Donne these changed
opinions made man, their author, more, not less, significant; in
Ignatius His Conclave he refers to Galileo, 'who of late hath sum-
moned the other worlds, the Stars to come neerer to him, and give
him an account of themselves'.[28]

---

[25] On this use of the 'surprise', see G. Williamson, *The Proper Wit of Poetry*, pp. 32,
35.

[26] Grierson, i. 37f; see Mario Praz, 'Donne's Relation to the Poetry of His Time',
A Garland for John Donne, pp. 53ff.

[27] Grierson, I. 7.

[28] J. Hayward, *John Donne Dean of St Paul's: Complete Poetry and Selected Prose*, p. 359.

Instead of saying that man was centred on the sun, he made a habit of depreciating the sun. 'Busie old foole, unruly Sunne', is mockingly addressed in 'The Sunne Rising', and discharged from his normal task because 'Thine age askes ease'[29]—'you're getting old, ease up a bit, concentrate on us'. In the sermons references to the sun and the Son, a deliberate pun, are numerous, but the true glory is the Son—'his begotten Son exceeds his created Sun'.[30] The lovers' world in 'The good-morrow' is better than the natural world—

Without sharpe North, without declining West . . .[31]

Twice in the sermons he alludes to the drowning man—

Quid mihi, sayes that man, who looked upon the Rainbow when he was ready to drown; though God have promised not to drown the world, what's that to me, if I must drown?[32]

In a world where people usually attach importance to what is physically large, the surprising truth is that physical size does not determine importance. In 'Metempsychosis, The Progresse of the Soule', the great whale is at the mercy of the thresher and the sword-fish, and the next incident repeats the lesson; Donne exalts the traditional enemy of the elephant, the mouse, by whom the great creature is destroyed—

Natures great master-peece, an Elephant,
The onely harmlesse great thing; the giant
Of beasts . . .
His sinewy Proboscis did remisly lie:
In which as in a gallery this mouse
Walk'd, and surveid the roomes of this vast house,
And to the braine, the soules bedchamber, went,
And gnaw'd the life cords there; Like a whole towne
Cleane undermin'd, the slaine beast tumbled downe. . . .[33]

The same allusion is made in sermons and the *Devotions*—

some very little creatures, contemptible in themselves, are yet called enemies to great creatures, as the Mouse is to the Elephant.[34]

It was fitting that in an intended epic the great beast was brought

[29] Grierson, I. 11f; see p. 46, line 6; p. 47, lines 13-16; p. 295, stanza II.
[30] PS, VI. 173.   [31] Grierson, I. 7.   [32] PS, I. 263f, III. 82.
[33] Grierson, I. 310f.
[34] PS, X. 134; *Devotions*, 12, Meditation.

low—bringing the epic with him: whether in verse or prose, the excellence of Donne is in the sudden flash of insight, the inspired phrase, the qualities that qualify for anthologies.

While accepting conventional terms like macrocosm and microcosm, and sometimes saying simply that man is a little world—

> If men be worlds, there is in every one
> Some thing to answere in some proportion
> All the worlds riches. . . .[35]

he did not approve of man being described as anything in little—

It is too little to call *Man* a *little World*; Except *God*, Man is a *diminutive* to nothing. Man consistes of more pieces, more parts, then the world; then the world doeth, nay then the world is.[36]

The importance of little things, especially in moral action, is a familiar theme of preaching, and it is found repeatedly in Donne, whose favourite verse of Scripture on this is The Song of Solomon, ii.15, 'Take us the foxes, the little foxes, that spoil the vines'.

It is not a little request to you, to beware of little sins . . . as little as those Foxes are, they devour the Vines . . . God punished the *Egyptians* most, by little things; Hailstones, and Frogs, and Grashoppers; and *Pharaohs* Sorcerers, which did greater, failed in the least, in Lice.[37]

He has a keen eye for illustrations of this theme. On Simon Peter he says:

without any terror from an armed Magistrate, without any surprizall of a subtile Examiner, upon the question of a poor Maide he denied his Master. . . .

As men that rob houses thrust in a child at the window, and he opens greater doores for them, so lesser sins make way for greater.

David is not the man who brought down the giant, but who was brought down himself—

him, whom an Army, and an armed Giant, *Goliah*, neare hand, could not hurt, a weaker person, and naked, and farre off, overthrowes and ruines . . . consider what a dangerous, and slippery station thou art in, if after a victory over Giants, thou mayest be overcome by Pigmees; If after thy soule hath beene Canon proofe against strong tentations, she be slaine at last by a Pistoll; And, after she hath swom

[35] Grierson, I. 210.   [36] *Devotions*, 4, Meditation.   [37] PS, I. 197.

over a tempestuous Sea, shee drowne at last, in a shallow and standing ditch.[38]

Donne contemplated often the experience awaiting the soul after death, and must have reflected upon the sense of surprise on entering upon a new life beyond the grave. Truth's impact as surprising was expressed triumphantly in the tenth of the *Holy Sonnets*:

> Death be not proud, though some have called thee
> Mighty and dreadfull, for, thou art not soe,
> For, those, whom thou think'st, thou dost overthrow,
> Die not, poore death, nor yet canst thou kill mee.
> From rest and sleepe, which but thy pictures bee,
> Much pleasure, then from thee, much more must flow,
> And soonest our best men with thee doe goe,
> Rest of their bones, and soules deliverie.
> Thou art slave to Fate, Chance, kings, and desperate men,
> And dost with poyson, warre, and sicknesse dwell,
> And poppie, or charmes can make us sleepe as well,
> And better then thy stroake; why swell'st thou then?
> One short sleepe past, wee wake eternally,
> And death shall be no more; death, thou shalt die.[39]

There are many examples of the surprise in the course of the argument; sometimes the surprise is in the conclusion; or in the situation (like the name in the window: a looking-glass reflects the person looking, but the window shows him to her). On a first reading 'The Extasie', a 'dialogue of one', presents, as a surprise which shocks, the line 'Else a great Prince in prison lies';[40] the argument is not that the body is the prison from which the soul seeks liberation, but the opposite, that, until the soul resides in the flesh, it is incapable of fulfilment in expression: the body is a book. *Holy Sonnets XVIII* on the Church, the spouse of Christ, ends with the deliberately astonishing lines:

> Who is most trew, and pleasing to thee, then
> When she'is embrac'd and open to most men.[41]

Words written in his *Devotions* which must at first have puzzled many people have seized the attention of our own age—'never

---

[38] IX. 257, 302; V. 300; cf. IV. 171, 183-185; see I. 196f; II. 79, 86, 108; VII. 335; IX. 73.
[39] Grierson, I. 326; see Gardner, pp. 69f.
[40] Grierson, I. 53.   [41] Grierson, I. 330.

send to know for whom the *bell* tolls; It tolls for *thee*.'[42] The instinctive criticism that these words are untrue—surely the bell tolls for someone else—is checked before it is uttered by the suspicion that it is right; this bell announces the burial of literal, superficial meanings; truth is surprising, requiring the drastic alteration of conventional views which have nothing stronger to buttress them than 'of course'.

The poet who awakened by paradox and hyperbole, by shock and surprise, owed much of his effectiveness as a preacher to these same arts. A sermon which, in the opening words, declares:

There is no such unhappiness to a sinner, as to be happy; no such cross, as to have no crosses,[43]

is an invitation, immediately accepted, to look at good fortune from another point of view. An early Lent sermon was on Ezekiel xxxiii.32, a text which changes its course surprisingly with the word 'for' and of which he says:

. . . who can discern, who would suspect any foundation to be laid for an Increpation, any preparation for a Malediction or Curse? God will send good Preachers to the people, and the people shall love their preaching; and yet . . .[44]

In his Easter Day sermon, 1627, he has something to say on miracles:

there is nothing dearer to God then a Miracle. There is nothing that God hath established in a constant course of nature, and which therefore is done every day, but would seeme a Miracle, and exercise our admiration, if it were done but once; Nay, the ordinary things in Nature, would be greater miracles, then the extraordinary, which we admire most, if they were done but once; The standing still of the Sun, for *Iosuahs* use, was not, in it selfe, so wonderfull a thing, as that so vast and immense a body as the Sun, should run so many miles, in a minute; The motion of the Sun were a greater wonder then the standing still, if all were to begin againe; And onely the daily doing takes off the admiration . . . there is in every miracle, a silent chiding of the world, and a tacite reprehension of them, who require, or who need miracles.[45]

He devoted the last of three sermons preached at Lincoln's Inn, on Psalm xxxviii.4, to its application to Christ, and said:

[42] *Devotions*, 17, Meditation.   [43] I. 168.   [44] II. 175.
[45] VII. p. 373f—just as waking is better than dreaming, so the ordinary is more miraculous than the exceptional.

But for that, I shall be short, and rather leave you to *walke with God in the cool of the Evening*, to meditate of the sufferings of Christ, when you are gone, then pretend to expresse them here. The *passion* of Christ Jesus is rather an amazement, an astonishment, an extasie, a consternation, then an instruction.[46]

Sometimes, in more extended passages, he created a sense of crescendo by repetition, with mounting expectation of a dramatic climax ending in surprise:

was it not as easie to believe, that those teares which they saw upon his cheeks, were Pearles; that those drops of Blood, which they saw upon his back, were Rubies: That that spittle, which they saw upon his face, was ennamel: that those hands which they saw buffet him, were reached out to place him in a Throne: And that that Voyce which they heard cry, *Crucifige, Crucifie him*, was a *Vivat Rex, Long live Jesus of Nazareth King of the Jewes*; As to believe, that from that man, that *worm, and no man*, ingloriously traduced as a Conjurer, ingloriously apprehended as a Thief, ingloriously executed as a Traytor; they should look for glory, and all glory, and everlasting glory?[47]

This quotation, from a Lent sermon, on 1 Timothy iii.16, is part of a tremendous paragraph which culminates in the declaration:

Theudas rose up, *dicens se esse aliquem*, he said he was some body; and he prov'd no body. *Simon Magus* rose up, *Dicens se esse aliquem magnum*, saying, he was some great body; and he prov'd as little. Christ Jesus rose up, and said himself not to be some body, nor some great body; but that there was no body else, no other name given under Heaven, whereby we should be saved; and was believ'd.[48]

The course of the passage leads one to expect a reference to humility; the conclusion is surprising, and incontestable.

The conclusion of 'Lovers infinitenesse' presents an idea which runs through Donne's poetry and preaching; instead of the exchange of hearts, considered as something which each can give to the other, each enters upon the fullness of love by union; they no longer have each other (that is, part of each other), they are each other. Donne habitually extended expressions of possession into expressions of being—for example, at the beginning of '*La Corona*':

> *Deigne at my hands this crown of prayer and praise,*
> Weav'd in my low devout melancholie,

[46] II. 132; see Genesis iii.8.   [47] III. 220f.   [48] III. 222.

> Thou which of good, hast, yea art treasury. . . .[49]

Just as the poem is the crown of which it speaks, so Christ is the treasury.

> Let us possesse one world, each hath one, and is one.

> To make, to keep, to use, to be these his Records.

are examples from 'The good-morrow' and 'A Valediction: of the booke'.[50] These passages would not be significant if they stood alone; but they draw to themselves so many parallels, from the poems and the sermons, that they argue their own importance. Let us consider, first, the hint supplied by the offering of the crown. George Herbert gave his poem 'Easter Wings' the shape of the subject—wings.[51] Carlyle, in a letter to John Sterling, said of his famous history: 'It is a wild savage book, itself a kind of French Revolution.'[52] Bengel, in his commentary, wrote on John xiv.26: 'This very discourse (homily) furnishes an instance, as having been a long time afterwards so accurately written out by John.'[53] Apart from 'La Corona', there are numerous examples in Donne of the form embodying the subject. 'Metempsychosis, The Progresse of the Soule', in its fragmentary nature, is a satire on the epic. 'The Canonization', possibly a defiant celebration of his rash marriage, beginning, 'For Godsake hold your tongue, and let me love', is an example of the doctrine it teaches. He turns from the world, where people are concerned only with what is external to themselves—careers, the merchant and his ships, the farmer and his land, the soldier and his warfare, the lawyer and his litigation; all this will go on as before, business will be as usual, leaving him to his renunciation of the world. As for him, his fortune is ruined, but he and his beloved are all the world to each other; 'wee in us finde th'Eagle and the Dove', and they are 'one anothers hermitage'. The great world will pass them by; at their end, no costly funeral, no expensive tomb, no elaborate

---

[49] Grierson, I. 318.   [50] Grierson, I. 7, 30.

[51] See J. H. Summers, *George Herbert, His Religion and Art*, pp. 123-146, reprinted in W. R. Keast, *Seventeenth-Century English Poetry*, under the title 'The Poem as Hieroglyph'.

[52] J. A. Froude, *Carlyle's Life in London*, I. p. 90, letter dated 17th January 1837; see L. P. Smith, *Reperusals and Re-collections*, 'XIII. The Rembrandt of English Prose', especially p. 210, on Carlyle.

[53] J. A. Bengel, *Gnomon of the New Testament*, II. 440.

epitaph, no place in History; truth is not embodied in mere size, however.

> We'll build in sonnets pretty roomes;
> As well a well wrought urne becomes
> The greatest ashes, as half-acre tombes. . . .

They have renounced the world, and, thus qualified, will be canonized, and suppliants will ask them to 'beg from above a patterne' of their love. This poem is itself their memorial, distinguishing the world, which emphasizes possessions, from true religion, which is concerned with being; the lovers, who know what they are, are contrasted with those who know only what they have. Cleanth Brooks says:

The poem is an instance of the doctrine which it asserts; it is both the assertion and the realization of the assertion. The poet has actually before our eyes built within the song the 'pretty room' with which he says the lovers can be content. The poem itself is the well-wrought urn which can hold the lovers' ashes and which will not suffer in comparison with the prince's 'half-acre tomb'.[54]

There are notable examples of the poems containing passages, usually brief, which embody their meaning. Take, for instance, the words in Satyre III:

> . . . On a huge hill,
> Cragged, and steep, Truth stands, and hee that will
> Reach her, about must, and about must goe;
> And what the hills suddennes resists, winne so,[55]

---

[54] Grierson, I. 14f; Cleanth Brooks, *The Well Wrought Urn*, p. 16; see the whole chapter, 'The Language of Paradox', pp. 3-20; see also J. B. Leishman, *The Monarch of Wit*, pp. 241f, and T. Redpath, *The Songs and Sonets of John Donne*, pp. 17-19. Herbert Read, in his essay on 'The Nature of Metaphysical Poetry', *Collected Essays in Literary Criticism*, pp. 69-88, asserts that Milton's thought was apart from his poetic feeling, that he did not think poetically, but expressed his thought in verse; and that the metaphysical poet avoided this dualism by thinking poetically; see H. I' A. Fausset, *The Poet and His Vision*, and F. R. Leavis, 'The Influence of Donne on Modern Poetry', *Bookman* (March 1931), pp. 341, 346; and T. S. Eliot, 'The Metaphysical Poets', *Selected Essays*, pp. 281-291, in which he defends the difficult nature of their verse as faithful to their thought and feeling; and argues that, in our own age, poetry in the context of our complex society must also be difficult, to be veracious. C. S. Lewis, on the other hand ('Donne and Love Poetry in the Seventeenth Century', *Seventeenth-Century Studies presented to Sir Herbert Grierson*, pp. 64-84), regards it as a limitation in Donne that he does not write about, but in, a chaos of passions, which, transitory, cut him off from what is more permanent; see, however, his modification of these earlier views in his *English Literature in the Sixteenth Century*, p. 549.

[55] Grierson, I. 157; Coleridge said, 'If you would teach a scholar in the highest form how to *read*, take Donne, and of Donne this satire . . .' (quoted by T. M. Raysor, *Coleridge's Miscellaneous Criticism*, p. 134).

F

or the description of his beloved, left at home while he is far away
on the Continent, starting up in bed at midnight,

> . . . crying out, oh, oh
> Nurse, ô my love is slaine, I saw him goe
> O'r the white Alpes alone; I saw him I,
> Assail'd, fight, taken, stabb'd, bleed, fall, and die.[56]

The complexity of the embodied thought appealed to his
intricate, subtle mind.

> The Sun it selfe, which makes times, as they passe,
> Is elder by a yeare, now, then it was
> When thou and I first one another saw

—the sun creates time for other people, but itself is a year older.
He and his beloved are Kings; then they must have subjects
—namely, themselves related to each other—

> Here upon earth, we'are Kings, and none but wee
> Can be such Kings, nor of such subjects bee.[57]

The following excerpts show the frequency of the idea:

> She 'is all States, and all Princes, I,
> Nothing else is. . . .'
> Mine owne executor and Legacie . . .
> Thou art so truth. . . .
> For thou thy selfe art thine owne bait . . .
> . . . what a miracle shee was.

(Donne did not expect a miraculous re-ordering of human
circumstances; but people, as this poem shows, could live miraculously.)

> Once I lov'd and dy'd; and am now become
> Mine Epitaph and Tombe . . .
> Each one, his owne Priest, and owne Sacrifice . . .
> . . . farmers of our selves . . .
> I shall be made thy musique; . . .[58]

[56] Grierson, I. pp. 112f; see the essay of William Hazlitt, 'Of Persons One would
wish to have seen' (*The Complete Works of William Hazlitt*, ed. P. P. Howe, XVII,
essay XII), and H. H. Milman, *Annals of St Paul's Cathedral*, pp. 326f.

[57] Grierson, I. 24f, 'The Anniversarie'.

[58] Grierson, I. 11, 20, 37, 47, 63, 70, 178, 186, 368. R. Skelton, 'The Poetry of John
Donne', p. 219 (see Bibliography, p. 245 *infra*), finds this sense of embodiment much
more in the *Songs and Sonets* than the *Holy Sonnets*, which are about something rather

When one looks for examples in the sermons, one finds them in abundance. There are many illustrations of the literary form partaking the nature of the contents. On two occasions he expounds Psalm ci.5 'Him that hath a proud look, and a high heart, I cannot'; when it comes to pride, God the Holy Ghost does not know what to say! There is no need to supply words, like 'work upon him', 'mend him', 'pardon him', 'suffer him', 'stay with him'; abruptly, incapable of speech, God breaks off from the proud man.[59] Preaching on John xi.35, 'Iesus wept', and referring to the verse divisions:

Whoever did it seemes to have stopped in an amazement in this Text, and by making an intire verse of these two words, *Iesus wept*, and no more, to intimate that there needs no more for the exalting of our devotion to a competent heighth, then to consider, how, and where, and when, and why *Iesus wept*.[60]

On the Being of God, he says:

Every thing is His, and therefore every thing is Hee; thy sicknesse is his sword, and therefore it is Hee that strikes thee with it. . . .
Of all things that are, there *was* an *Idea* in God . . . but of Monarchy, of Kingdome, God, who is but one, *is* the *Idea*. . . .

God is our light; not a light which is His, but a light which is He; not a light which flowes from him, no, nor a light which is in him, but that light which is He himself. . . .

not onely the Joy which he gives . . . but the Joy which he is. . . .[61]

On Jesus Christ:

no Grammarian can clear it, whether this name Jesus signifie *salvatorem* or *salutem*, the Instrument that saves us, or the salvation that is afforded us; for it is not only his person, but it is his very righteousness that saves us. . . .

both the Physitian and the Physick.

---

than the something itself. For two passages in the Anniversary poems see *An Anatomie of the World*, line 10; *Of the Progresse of the Soule*, line 442; and the discussion in L. L. Martz, *The Poetry of Meditation*, p. 245; see Grierson, I. 231, 264. The distinction occupies an important place in the closing lines of 'Satyre III', and in the Verse Letter beginning, 'Man to Gods image', Grierson, I. 158, 201-203; see also p. 202, lines 22, 25; p. 216, lines 17f; p. 219, line 45; pp. 221-223.
[59] See PS, I. 215; II. 293; in V. 359 he suggests that the text, Psalm vi.2f ends abruptly because David realizes that he must not enter on an expostulation with God.
[60] IV. 324.   [61] II. 86, IV. 240; VIII. 220; X. 214.

But to those that have, he knocks and he enters, and he sups with them, and he is a supper to them.

he feeds us, and feeds us with himselfe . . .

we cannot say that Christ hath life, but that he is life, and the Life. . . . he is the curse of God, (as it is in the Original) not accursed, but a curse. . . . That which he did was to give; and that which he gave, was himselfe.[62]

On the Holy Ghost:

Since we speak by Him, let us love to speak of Him, and to speak for Him . . . A Comforter; not one amongst others, but the Comforter; not the principall, but the intire, the onely Comforter; and more then all that, The Comfort it selfe.[63]

This emphasis upon the Divine Being, and the communication of the Godhead to mankind, results in an equal emphasis upon the experience of appropriation.

the love of this pureness is part of this pureness it self, and no man hath it, except he love it.

for as a spirit cannot be divided, so they who are thus changed into him, are so much His, so much He, as that nothing can separate them from him. . . .

We may put on Christ so, as we shall be *his*, and we may put him on so, as we shall be *He*.

we shall so appeare before the Father, as that he shall take us for his owne Christ; we shall beare his name and person; and we shall every one be so accepted, as if every one of us were *all Mankind*; yea, as if we were he himselfe.

their conscience, doth not only shew them, but give them, not only declare it to them, but possesse them of it.

Christ himself carries this consideration, beyond all these resemblances, and conformities, not to a *proximity* onely, but to an *identity*, The poore are He.

they are the joy of my heart: It is not *Dant*, but *Sunt*, not that they Bring joy, but that they Are joy.

[62] I. 310, 312; II. 224; IX. 133; II. 321; IV. 296; V. 123.
[63] V. 58; IX. 92.

we are not onely His, but He; To every Persecutor, in every one of our behalfe, he shall say, *Cur me*? Why persecutest thou me?[64]

On Prayer:

Since then every rectified man, is the temple of the Holy Ghost, when he prays; it is the Holy Ghost it selfe that prays; and what can be denyed, where the Asker gives?

That Prayer which our Saviour gave us, (for as he meant to give us all for asking, so he meant to give us the words by which we should ask).[65]

On Preaching:

whilst the Preacher yet spoke, the Holy Ghost spoke. . . .

Thinke not thy selfe well enough preached unto, except thou finde a desire, that thy life and conversation may preach to others. . . .[66]

In conclusion, a number of varied comments may be given—

Your children are you, and your servants are you; and you doe not provide for your salvation, if you provide not for them, who are so much yours, as that they are you.

whilst the heart is under the habits of sin, we are not onely sinful, but we are *all sin*.

Simon Magus . . . not that he had, but that he was the power of God.

John Baptist . . . A Prophet that was prophesied of. . . .

to him that suffers as a Martyr, . . . a crowne is reserved . . . *Stephanus* . . . the first Martyr for Christ . . . a Crown in his name.

the fire in the furnace did not burn the men, but it burnt off those bands, that fettered and manacled them, (for they were loose, and walked in the furnace). . . .

the grave is the Land, and the Tenement, and the Tenant too: He that lies in it, becomes the same earth, that he lies in.

the Testament, in which even the Testator himselfe is bequeathed to you.[67]

---

[64] I. 199, 164; V. 158, 159f; VII. 326; VIII. 286f; IX. 410, 369.
[65] V. 233, 271.   [66] V. 40; II. 271.
[67] IV. 209; I. 192; II. 275; IV. 147; V. 67; VI. 111; IX. 48, 316; see D. Quinn, 'Donne's Christian Eloquence', *ELH*, XXVII (1960) 291, on the first sermon on Psalm xxxviii (PS, II, sermon 1)—David does more than convey and illustrate morality: he *is* moral instruction; *Essayes in Divinity*, p. 75, for the distinction between 'having' and 'being'; *Devotions*—'*We have* the *Phisician*, but we *are not* the *Phisician*'

The reader of Donne's poetry finds that he must slow down to less than walking-pace, that he must retrace his steps, that he must give to its comprehension all the time and attention it requires. Some literature is difficult to read because it is confused, ill-arranged, inconsistent in its terms; the obscurity is a blemish. The difficulty of Donne's poetry is inherent in its nature, and the perception of this at once reduces it, for it yields up its meaning to study. Paradoxical expression is his communication of many-sided truth; packed, involved sentences result from a deliberate attempt to express meaning in the minimum number of words, in the belief that this actually creates an embodiment of meaning not otherwise achieved. As Arthur Symons said: 'Dreading diffuseness, as he dreads the tame sweetness of an easy melody, he will use only the smallest possible number of words to render his thought.'[68] In a letter to Sir Henry Goodyear, Donne said: 'God's mercy is had by asking, and that is asked by having'; and, again, later: 'our accesses to His presence are but His descents into us; and when we get anything by prayer, He gave us beforehand the thing and the petition.'[69] In his sermons he frequently stressed this important doctrine, to which he gave succinct expression in 'A Litanie',

Heare us, weake ecchoes, O thou eare, and cry.[70]

Something positive is achieved by this compression; not when speech is expansive, ample, repetitive, but when it is terse, brief, brought down to minimum dimensions, it apprehends the listener —'A Litanie' is one of his most difficult, involved, poems: the text in Miss Helen Gardner's edition occupies ten pages, the twenty-eight stanzas well spaced; the invaluable notes require twelve pages in small print; the mental discipline involved in appreciating this intricate poem is here richly rewarded. One imagines the poet constructing these intense lines during his sickness, with leisure to meditate, and to improve the expression

(4, Meditation), 'he who was *righteousnes* it selfe,' (5, Expostulation), 'We measure not the *visitations* of great persons, by their *apparel*, by their *equipage*, by the *solemnity* of their comming, but by their very comming . . . him, who speaks thy word, and who is thy word, thy *Son*' (14, Expostulation), and see also, '*his* . . . *Hee himselfe*' (10, Expostulation). See also J. Reeves, *A Short History of English Poetry*, pp. 41f, on the legitimate use of roughness in poetry.

[68] A. Symons, 'John Donne', *The Fortnightly Review* (1899), p. 743.
[69] Gosse, I. 192, 228.   [70] Grierson, I. 347.

of his thoughts—which require the same detachment and unhurried pace from us.[71]

Donne was excited by the emblematic concentration of meaning, by an idea caught up in some conjunction of circumstances, or in some material thing that made thought tangible, apprehensible. His endeavour to compress meaning into the smallest space was not just an exercise in ingenuity, though he could play at this better than most and occasionally did; it was his response to truth, which came to him incarnate, and which he expressed in emblems and images and conceits. We hear the bell because he heard it. Ben Jonson learned by heart 'that passage of the calme, that dust and fethers do not stir, all was so quiet', as he told William Drummond,

> No use of lanthornes; and in one place lay
> Feathers and dust, to day and yesterday.[72]

This passage from 'The Calme' may be compared with words at the beginning of 'The Storme':

> . . . a hand, or eye
> By *Hilliard* drawne, is worth an history,
> By a worse painter made. . . .[73]

His thought centres on the soul's relationship with and communication through the body;

> But since my soule, whose child love is,
> Takes limmes of flesh, and else could nothing doe,
> More subtile then the parent is,
> Love must not be, but take a body too. . . .[74]

The embodiment of the soul in the body is the foundation of his unquestioning acceptance of the Incarnation; further, it brings him, through distinguishing 'being' from 'having', to the acceptance of the Scriptures as being, not only containing, the Word of

[71] Of this poem Edward Dowden said: 'Through this poem we can obtain, perhaps, a clearer insight into Donne's character than through any other that he has written.' (*New Studies in Literature*, p. 97; see pp. 97-99).

[72] H. W. Garrod, *John Donne: Poetry and Prose*, p. xlv; Grierson, I. 178: the poem describes the Islands expedition of 1597 to the Azores, becalmed; the lanterns were suspended from the ships' sterns to keep the fleet together; the Admiral showed the light from his flag-ship and the squadron followed it.

[73] Grierson, I. 175—Hilliard was the first English miniaturist and this reference to him illustrates once again Donne's preference for what is small, compressing more meaning in the lesser space. Artistically he also was a miniaturist.

[74] Grierson, I. 22.

God; to be interpreted by the Author, and their words as serving an embodying as well as expressive function; prayer, he repeatedly stresses, partakes in its exercise of its true end, for it never exists apart from the co-operation of the inspiring Spirit—the life of prayer and the understanding of Holy Scripture are identical in possessing this dual nature. At the death of his sister he, now the last remaining child, wrote to his mother, reviewing her life as 'a sea, under a continual tempest, where one wave hath ever overtaken another', consoling her with these words:

In the meantime, good mother, take heed that no sorrow nor dejection in your heart interrupt or disappoint God's purpose in you; His purpose is to remove out of your heart all such love of this world's happiness as might put Him out of possession of it. He will have you entirely, and as God is comfort enough, so He is inheritance enough. Join with God and make His visitations and afflictions as He intended them, mercies and comforts.[75]

In the same way the Christian Church embodies her message; the end she serves cannot be disconnected from her own nature, she preaches the Gospel and is the Gospel being preached. Her form and discipline are therefore important, and not arbitrary and alterable and merely convenient things. The Christian is involved in this, his whole life is part of the preaching, the setting forth of the truth of Him who said not only 'I am' but 'Ye are' 'the light of the world'. For the Christian preacher the distinction between 'being' and 'having' is all-important. He is not a lecturer, expounding a subject detachable from himself, which, if he is versatile enough, might well be another subject, and possibly one in which he does not believe. He is a communicator, presenting that which is embodied in himself. Donne illustrates this in his life; he returned to Lincoln's Inn, early in his ministry, to preach. In these first days he thus presented the message which became centred on himself, and his ministry there was made the more effectual because he himself was known to be committed and involved. His last sermon was preached in weakness, and in the knowledge of approaching death; it was not simply a sermon on Death, a subject which a young man might legitimately take. It was a sermon on death embodied in a dying man.
His emotions and thoughts were fused and agitated together

[75] Gosse, II. 88-90; cf. 'A Hymne to Christ, at the Authors last going into Germany', line 19, Grierson, I. 353.

by external embodiments of truth, for example a circle, a map, a tolling bell; or by a felt concentration of experience, for example a conjunction of circumstances like travelling westwards on Good Friday. Thus roused, he surrounded the central, activating force, whether physical or mental, with complex paradoxical thoughts expressed in phrases as tightly drawn and compressed as the central image itself. Donne was himself aware of holding together complexity and simplicity, and in the nineteenth Expostulation of his *Devotions* he prayed:

My *God*, my *God*, Thou art a *direct God*, may I not say a *literall God*, a *God* that wouldest bee understood *literally*, and according to the *plaine sense* of all that thou saiest? But thou art also (*Lord* I intend it to thy *glory*, and let no *prophane misinterpreter* abuse it to thy *diminution*) thou art a *figurative*, a *metaphoricall God too*: a *God* in whose words there is such a height of *figures*, such *voyages*, such *peregrinations* to fetch remote and precious *metaphors*, such *extentions*, such *spreadings*, such *Curtaines* of *Allegories*, such *third Heavens* of *Hyperboles*, so *harmonious eloquutions*, so *retired* and so *reserved expressions*, so *commanding perswasions*, so *perswading commandements*, such *sinewes* even in thy *milke*, and such *things* in thy *words*, as all *prophane Authors*, seeme of the seed of the *Serpent*, that *creepes*, thou art the *Dove*, that flies. O, what words but thine, can express the inexpressible *texture*, and *composition* of thy *word*; in which, to one man, that *argument* that binds his faith to beleeve that to bee the Word of *God*, is *the reverent simplicity* of the Word, and to another, the *majesty* of the Word; and in which two men, equally pious, may meet, and one wonder, that all should not understand it, and the other, as much, that any man should.

This association of difficulty, even obscurity, with simplicity, was a felt embodiment of the self-authenticating reality of God Himself, and his endeavour to hold together this 'simplicity' and 'majesty', gives a religious texture to all his work, by which he communicated to others his own awareness of God who was both 'literal' and 'metaphorical'. His nature was deeply passionate, and his influence as a preacher was the consequence of his ability to communicate to others the power, the validity, the supreme importance of that which gripped him. Those who heard him, no more able than we are to focus truth as he did by the power of imagery and words, were as able, as we are, to acknowledge when this has happened. We read in the 17th Meditation of his *Devotions*, 'No man is an *Iland*', and we, like his first readers, apprehend the truth through a physical image.

Donne, like every other preacher, sometimes disappointed; but his hearers, expectant, listened to the text that he announced, as often from the Old Testament as the New, because, with a skill they found in no one else, this preacher gripped it in his hands and made it live again. The word that seized him, preached by him, held them.[76]

[76] On 'The Canonization' Coleridge wrote: 'One of my favourite poems. As late as ten years ago, I used to seek and find out grand lines and fine stanzas; but my delight has been far greater since it has consisted more in tracing the leading thought thr'out the whole. The former is too much like coveting your neighbour's goods; in the latter you merge yourself in the author, you *become He*' (T. M. Raysor, *Coleridge's Miscellaneous Criticism*, p. 137). Writing on the English Divines he said: 'If our old divines, in their homiletic expositions of Scripture, wire-drew their text, in the anxiety to evolve out of the words the fulness of the meaning expressed, implied, or suggested, our modern preachers have erred more dangerously in the opposite extreme, by making their text a mere theme, or motto, for their discourse. . . . It was on God's holy word that our Hookers, Donnes, Andrewses preached; it was Scripture bread that they divided, according to the needs and seasons. The preacher of our days expounds, or appears to expound, his own sentiments and conclusions, and thinks himself evangelic enough if he can make the Scripture seem in conformity with them' (*Notes on English Divines*, ed. Derwent Coleridge, I. 119).

FIVE

CONTRARYES MEET IN ONE
(Holy Sonnets, xix)

THE nineteenth, and last of the *Holy Sonnets,* is suitably placed at the end, for it expresses the characteristic attitude of John Donne to himself throughout his life.

> Oh, to vex me, contraryes meet in one:
> Inconstancy unnaturally hath begott
> A constant habit; that when I would not
> I change in vowes, and in devotione.
> As humorous is my contritione
> As my prophane Love, and as soone forgott:
> As ridlingly distemper'd, cold and hott,
> As praying, as mute; as infinite, as none.
> I durst not view heaven yesterday; and to day
> In prayers, and flattering speaches I court God:
> To morrow I quake with true feare of his rod.
> So my devout fitts come and go away
> Like a fantastique Ague: save that here
> Those are my best dayes, when I shake with feare.[1]

The world, the macrocosm, was composed, it was held, of four elements—fire, air, water, and earth; and the individual, the microcosm, was

> . . . a little world made cunningly
> Of Elements . . .[2]

with four humours, which corresponded to the four elements, based on the phlegm, blood, choler, and black bile; and whichever predominated determined a disposition of personality which was phlegmatic, sanguine, choleric, or melancholy. Donne was a stranger to the serenity of the four humours in balance; 'humorous' in the fifth line is to be understood in relation to the four humours, and he is saying that he knows himself to be changeable, a creature of moods. His reference to this stirs a remembrance of his 'prophane love' when, amazed by his own capacity for diverse experiences,

[1] Grierson, I. 331.   [2] Grierson, I. 324.

astonished by his lack of equilibrium, he exalted Change, Variety in his verse, and now, old enough to know the truth about himself, he resigns himself to what he cannot alter in his nature, investing, almost sanctifying, his discordant spirit with paradox, the sure proof of truth: upon his inconstancy he can depend. The poem closes with the characteristic surprise—a reversal of the conventional view: spiritually he is in best condition when he is trembling with a shivering fit!—the recollection of 'A Litanie', the *Devotions*, and his last sermon, *Deaths Duell*, all written at times of severe sickness, and of his last poem 'Hymne to God my God, in my sicknesse' and the portrait at the time of his 'religious death', reconciles us to the surprise as a statement of fact, and persuades us to take seriously this piece of self-analysis.[3]

The fourteenth of the *Holy Sonnets* describes him, not lying in weakness on his sick-bed, but standing and gripped by an intensity of violence. Torn apart by his own strength, he calls upon God to overwhelm him. He compares himself to a town, seized by a rebel, but divided in allegiance; part of him, reason, has capitulated to the usurper, the other part acknowledges the rightful ruler who is besieging the town. But He is far too gentle. Break me—do not knock; blow, not breathe; burn, not shine; remake, not mend. God must batter down the walls and overthrow the enemy.

> Batter my heart, three person'd God; for, you
> As yet but knocke, breathe, shine, and seeke to mend;
> That I may rise, and stand, o'erthrow mee, 'and bend
> Your force, to breake, blowe, burn and make me new.
> I, like an usurpt towne, to'another due,
> Labour to'admit you, but Oh, to no end,
> Reason your viceroy in mee, mee should defend,
> But is captiv'd, and proves weake or untrue.
> Yet dearely'I love you, 'and would be loved faine,
> But am betroth'd unto your enemie:
> Divorce mee, 'untie, or breake that knot againe,
> Take mee to you, imprison mee, for I
> Except you'enthrall mee, never shall be free,
> Nor ever chast, except you ravish mee.[4]

---

[3] *Devotions*, 15, Prayer, begins: 'O Eternall and most gracious *God*, who art able to make, and dost make the *sicke bed* of thy servants *Chappels* of *ease* to them.'

[4] Grierson, I. 328.

God is addressed as 'three person'd' in a situation of intense awareness of one's divided nature, and, corresponding to the triune nature of the divine Being is the nature of the human being, made in His image, composed of different elements which, in man, are discordant, divisive.

Throughout his life Donne was an assiduous student of himself, performing self-analysis and self-criticism with remarkable detachment, objectively dissecting himself; and there is much to be said for associating him with Psychology and not Metaphysics.[5] His remarkable love poems are essentially studies of his varied reactions to his experiences, self-centred monologues which tell us nothing of the charms and attractions of the beloved. He can stand outside himself, literally 'ecstatically'. He sees himself associating emotion and thought; rebelling against unreal conventions yet, in the moment of self-assertion awakening to his relationship with others; from early days maintaining the liveliest interest in religious beliefs and practices, indulging in life-embracing studies of which those concerning his chosen profession, law, were the least considerable; and when he writes poetry, he impregnates it with the moods and changing arguments which exhibit him propelled by the force of one extreme to its opposite, as he stresses the claims of the body, then of the mind and soul, the very form of his poetry caught up in this tension and capturing the struggle between the spirit and the flesh, in moments of paradoxical insight when thought and feeling, body and soul are fused.

'The Blossome' is a poem of much interest in this connection. He has been staying in the country for a week, and now the time has come to return home to London. Life has been very pleasant in the company of a gracious lady, his hostess, to whom, indirectly, he addresses a subtly complimentary poem on leaving; his admiration and attachment are admitted, and controlled, so that finally the poet vindicates and exalts the unromantic, familiar, ordinary home life to which he is returning. He plays lightly with Petrarchan and Platonic love, the former incapable of anything enduring and the latter incapable of anything; the argument leaves no doubt on the conclusion, yet the two sentiments are so nicely poised, that he reveals himself in his true nature as a self-torturer, whose heart (that is, his mind or soul) is subjected to

---

[5] See *A Garland for John Donne*, p. 182, note 1: 'anatomising' was the term then used for 'psychology'.

rigorous examination. In an early sermon he declared that the
heart itself could be treated effectually, when wounded, if it could
lie still and cease its palpitation and continual motion.[6] He
never attained to this tranquillity, and the tension of body and
soul arrested his whole spirit in the last words that he wrote.

The first and second stanzas are linked by the words 'Little
think'st thou'; he addresses, first, the blossom, and then his own
heart, in comparison; just as the frost kills the spring blossom, so
she, chillingly unresponsive, as indeed she ought to be, checks
his affection for her, and she will even be fast asleep when he
begins his journey at sunrise tomorrow.

> Little think'st thou, poore flower,
> Whom I have watch'd sixe or seaven dayes,
> And seene thy birth, and seene what every houre
> Gave to thy growth, thee to this height to raise,
> And now dost laugh and triumph on this bough,
>   Little think'st thou
> That it will freeze anon, and that I shall
> To morrow finde thee falne, or not at all.
>
> Little think'st thou poore heart
> That labour'st yet to nestle thee,
> And think'st by hovering here to get a part
> In a forbidden or forbidding tree,
> And hop'st her stiffenesse by long siege to bow:
>   Little think'st thou,
> That thou to morrow, ere that Sunne doth wake,
> Must with this Sunne, and mee a journey take.

With the third stanza the mood changes suddenly, as these
romantic notions are considered in the light of reason, which now
stages a disputation between the heart, which stays in the country,
and the body, which travels to London. The heart speaks first,
declaring its sufficiency, apart from the body (which will provide
for itself), to prosper the things of the heart.

> But thou which lov'st to bee
> Subtile to plague thy selfe, wilt say,
> Alas, if you must goe, what's that to mee?
> Here lyes my businesse, and here I will stay:
> You goe to friends, whose love and meanes present
>   Various content

[6] PS, I. 179f.

To your eyes, eares, and tongue, and every part.
If then your body goe, what need you a heart?

In the fourth stanza the body replies. As you will; but you will
find, my heart, that you cannot get far by yourself—the body may
be able to prosper without the heart, as you suggest, but the heart
can get nowhere without the body, which it needs to attain its end.

Well then, stay here; but know,
When thou hast stayd and done thy most;
A naked thinking heart, that makes no show,
Is to a woman, but a kinde of Ghost;
How shall shee know my heart; or having none,
    Know thee for one?
Practise may make her know some other part,
But take my word, shee doth not know a Heart.

The debate ends, in the last stanza, with an emphatic assertion
of the place of the body in life; the references to the precise place
and time and his contacts with men in the workaday world are
deliberate intrusions of realism. Heart and body will be united
as he returns 'to another friend' (his wife?), and to an affection
in which his whole nature is co-ordinated. Thus the conclusion
of the poem is the same as 'The Dreame'—we sleep, to wake.

Meet mee at London, then,
Twenty dayes hence, and thou shalt see
Mee fresher, and more fat, by being with men,
Then if I had staid still with her and thee.
For Gods sake, if you can, be you so too:
    I would give you
There, to another friend, whom wee shall finde
As glad to have my body, as my minde.[7]

This taking of the self to pieces, this analysis of the component
parts of personality, can be illustrated from writings throughout
his life, especially the *Devotions*, and at times one can feel him
coming in full course upon the personal pronoun and pulling
himself up suddenly. One of his letters begins:

Sir,—I hope you are now welcome to London, and well, and well
comforted in your father's health and love, and well contented that
we ask you how you do, and tell you how we are, which yet I cannot
of myself. If I knew that I were ill, I were well; for we consist of three

[7] Grierson, I. 59f, II. 48; see Bibliography, p. 232, *infra*.

parts, a soul, and body, and mind: which I call those thoughts and
affections, and passions, which neither soul nor body hath alone, but
have been begotten by their communication, as music results out of
our breath and a cornet. . . .[8]

In a sermon on Psalm li.7, he says:

but yet Lord, looke more particularly upon me, and appropriate thy
selfe to me, to me, not onely as thy Creature, as a man, as a Christian,
but as I am I, as I am this sinner that confesses now, and as I am this
penitent that begs thy mercy now.[9]

The control of external events is the responsibility of God, and
it is not for man to dispute their course or to try to alter them, a
vain endeavour, for a path and period have been marked out
for everything. But the realist accepts them as the setting for the
dramatic emergence of human personality, linked to existence in
the threefold reality of past, present, future; deeds, decisions
desires; as one is known to others, as one is acquainted with oneself, as one is known to God; and whatever one touches brings to
light man's essentially complex nature, a centre of conflict and
tension, a creature of earth and heaven, of time and of eternity—

> In none but us, are such mixt engines found,
> As hands of double office: for, the ground
> We till with them; and them to heav'n wee raise;
> Who prayer-lesse labours, or, without this, prayes,
> Doth but one halfe, that's none.[10]

In a sermon on John i.8 he says:

Every Christian is a state, a common-wealth to *himselfe*, and in him,
the *Scripture* is his *law*, and the *conscience* is his *Iudge*.[11]

He was trained by reflection and religious meditation, to stand
outside and subject himself to close scrutiny, exercising 'a holy
superintendency'[12] over himself to ensure that, as a preacher, he
heard his own sermons, and, indeed, found material for them in his
own heart, like David, who was his own library and studied himself.[13] 'Let every one of us therefore dissect and cut up himself...'
is his emphatic advice in a passage in which he preaches at length
on the anatomization by which we come to self-knowledge.[14]
Characteristically, he speaks of a man as a murderer of himself,

---

[8] Gosse, I. 183f.   [9] PS, V. 307.   [10] Grierson, I. 197.
[11] PS, IV. 216.   [12] PS, I. 192.   [13] II. 145.   [14] I. 273.

capable, as the toad or spider is not, of poisoning himself by original sin, 'selfe traytor' to his body and his soul, to his thoughts and to his actions, to his whole personality in all its diversity.[15] His awareness of the complexity and subtlety of personality led inevitably in his preaching to a strong emphasis upon temptation and the various ways in which man's nature reacts to it, and to an equal sympathy with the weak and wayward sinner; his self-knowledge made him a preacher with a pastor's heart, and, in his approach to ecclesiastical as well as personal problems, outstanding in his age for the spirit of toleration and forbearance which he showed. The reformed student in the pulpit of Lincoln's Inn guarded himself from the insidious danger of priggishness, the 'purified pureness as makes us *Canonize* our selves, and think others *Reprobates*'[16] and the value of self-knowledge was shown in a Lenten sermon at Whitehall when he said:

It is not safe for a man to expose himself to a tentation, because he hath seen another passe through it. Every man may know his own Byas, and to what sin that diverts him.[17]

This self-analysis was probably no more fashionable then than now, but when undertaken by a master of the spiritual life it established itself by its unquestionable soundness and wisdom, as when, preaching at Lincoln's Inn on Job xix.26, he indicated how much unsuspected meaning was contained in the word 'I', and spoke of the human body perhaps dismembered in different parts of the world, yet reunited at its resurrection; and, taking a familiar phrase, 'all there', showed how divided, and not 'all there', one may be—

I am not all here, I am here now preaching upon this text, and I am at home in my Library considering whether *S. Gregory*, or *S. Hierome*, have said best of this text, before. I am here speaking to you, and yet I consider by the way, in the same instant, what it is likely you will say to one another, when I have done. You are not all here neither; you are here now, hearing me, and yet you are thinking that you have heard a better Sermon somewhere else, of this text before. . . .[18]

The last paragraph of the sermon preached at Lincoln's Inn on Trinity Sunday, 1620, on Genesis xviii.25, begins, 'Descend thou into thy selfe'; the conscience must be searched for evidence of the effect of one's sins upon others, the sins committed against

---

[15] Grierson, I. 28; PS, I. 257, 293; II. 51, 65f, 89, 100.　　[16] I. 206.
[17] IV. 328.　　[18] III. 110.

reason, against one's body, against friendship; appoint oneself as one's judge. Consider oneself, soul and body—the faculties of the former and the sense of the latter; yet judge; discriminate between good and bad, do not be over-rigorous and condemning, and when reconciled to God, rest in this blessed peace and never question it.[19]

His nature was violent and tempestuous, but he had no confidence in himself because he deeply believed that the way of truth and of wisdom always involved the blending and accommodating of diverse elements, and any disposition in him such as a call upon God to exercise Himself with equal violence upon him needed a counterbalancing correction. The *via media* of his ecclesiastical position was established first in his own nature, through his devotional life, and though he never completely attained to the poise of a balanced life he perceived its necessity, and expressed this in the prayers of his 'Litanie'—

> . . . Lord let us runne
> Meane waies . . .
>
> From being anxious, or secure,
> Dead clods of sadnesse, or light squibs of mirth,
> From thinking, that great courts immure
> All, or no happinesse, or that this earth
> Is only for our prison fram'd,
> Or that thou art covetous
> To them whom thou lovest, or that they are maim'd
> From reaching this worlds sweet, who seek thee thus,
> With all their might, Good Lord deliver us . . .
>
> And through thy poore birth, where first thou
> Glorifiedst Povertie,
> And yet soone after riches didst allow,
> By accepting Kings gifts in the Epiphanie,
> Deliver, and make us, to both waies free. . . .[20]

This generation has been made to listen to Donne's bell, tolling, with slow, impressive authority, its message of the unity of mankind. Each of us knows, with him, that we are involved in mankind. Its massive reverberations penetrate as each listener knows

[19] III. 154f. Sidney Godolphin, in his 'Elegie on D.D.', spoke of this aspect of his preaching, ingeniously weaving into his own lines line 54 of 'The Extasie'—see Grierson, I. 393 lines 23-30, and p. 53.
[20] Grierson, I. 343f.

himself to be incorporated in the destiny of the world. But if this were all, the bell would but tell us what we know. And knowledge by itself is not salvation. The message is more than a proclamation of our interlocking indivisibility. The bell is a Church bell, and this young rebellious realist whose poems defy and shatter conventions has made his act of obedience and reconciliation, and if the message of the bell is to be more than a statement of the obvious it must be heard as a call, back to God. Yet more than this is being said. We hear the bell today because the author of the words wrote them in a book of devotions, searched, probed, quested, in the hour of sickness and weakness, took himself seriously, descended into his own soul, found himself face to face with his Maker. After three centuries the youthful poet has come alive again to attack unrealistic conventions, and he has exercised incalculable influence in encouraging openness and daring in the quest for truth and the expression of that quest. His urgent, passionate entreaty is that we shall discover the truth about ourselves, and, in penitence and trust, even though 'contraryes meet in one' and our only offering is confusion and discord, return just as we are, to God. And, perhaps that none should be deterred, this man came with motives mixed and tensions unresolved, and a record of a spiritual pilgrimage with no high moments of unclouded vision, gave himself, and remained loyal to his undertaking, to the end, sure that the outpouring of the self to God is part of the end we seek, and that all the diversity within us, which gives us no peace, is the human counterpart, burdened with infirmity, corresponding to the 'three-person'd God' in whose likeness we were made.

In the year 1610, Elizabeth Drury, the only child and heiress of Sir Robert and Lady Drury (of the family whose name is perpetuated in 'Drury Lane') died, at the age of fifteen. Sir Robert was a man of great wealth, a few years younger than Donne, and he had high ambitions for his daughter. In her honour, though he had never met the girl, Donne composed 'A Funerall Elegie'.[21] The tomb, he says, must not have the last word, not even this magnificent tomb erected in her memory by her grief-stricken parents; nothing, however splendid, can

[21] Grierson, I. 245-248.

compensate for her—the most expensive materials cannot be compared to her. You might well declare that this includes an elegy like this, a mere wrapping of her in paper; truly, but verse will serve to keep her memory while the world lasts, which will not be long, 'for her death wounded it' (line 21). Poets have their contribution to make, no less than princes, counsellors, lawyers, divines, and the rest. Death has won a notable triumph over her, and will proceed to further victory, over the world itself—nothing else is left, for she was unequalled and the death of another individual would be no greater victory:

> For since death will proceed to triumph still,
> He can finde nothing, after her, to kill,
> Except the world it selfe, so great as shee. (Lines 31-33.)

Death is not the last, not the right word; a timepiece, though now lying in pieces, can be reassembled. Yet the loss is real, and we best accept it by remembering her, as now we do, recalling her in her youthful virginity, 'Cloath'd in her virgin white integritie' (line 75), and believing that all subsequent human virtue completes her unfinished life—

> For future vertuous deeds are Legacies,
> Which from the gift of her example rise;
> And 'tis in heav'n part of spirituall mirth,
> To see how well the good play her, on earth. (The closing
>   lines, 103-106.)

One supposes that Sir Robert much approved of the tribute to his daughter, and that Donne was encouraged thereby to undertake a more considerable poem. Lines 84-102 of the poem refer to the book of destiny; Fate; 'Fellow-Commissioner with Destinie' (96), and remind one of the beginning of 'Metempsychosis, The Progresse of the Soule', especially stanzas I and IV. The writing of this brief elegy stirred a recollection of the uncompleted epic, and a desire to endeavour once again to write a poem of such proportions. We do not know the stages of the development, but we do know the result. Soon after composing the elegy, he wrote a poem over four times as long, amplifying the idea of the world as dead through her death; and in this longer poem the dead world is dissected and analysed; determining to commit himself this time to achieve an epic work, in 1611 he published (anonymously) the poem under the title, *An Anatomie of the World. Wherein, By occasion of the untimely death of Mistris Elizabeth Drury, the frailty and the decay of this World is represented.*[22] The poem was prefaced by a commendatory poem, probably by Joseph Hall, a contemporary satirist and wit and later Bishop of Norwich, entitled, 'To the praise of the dead, and the ANATOMIE', and followed by the original elegy. Not only did Donne commit himself by publishing the poem; in it he included a statement of his determination to celebrate the anniversary of her death annually; addressing the 'blessed maid', he says:

> Accept this tribute, and his first yeares rent,
> Who till his darke short tapers end be spent,
> As oft as thy feast sees this widowed earth,
> Will yearely celebrate thy second birth,
> That is, thy death. . . . (Lines 447-451.)

In 1612, faithful to this undertaking, he published (again, anonymously) the second poem, for the title of which he revived the original epic title, with the additional 'of', *Of the Progresse of the Soule. Wherein, By occasion of the Religious death of Mistris Elizabeth Drury, the incommodities of the Soule in this life, and her exaltation in the next, are contemplated.*[23] Joseph Hall introduced it with a poem entitled 'The Harbinger to the Progresse'. All five poems (the two by Hall, the 'Funerall Elegie', the 'Anatomie', and 'Of the Progresse of the Soule') were published together, and the 'Anatomie' became the first Anniversary, and 'Of the Progresse . . .', a slightly longer poem, the second; the poems are usually known as 'The Anniversaries', but there is everything to be said for retaining the original titles which clearly indicate contrasting purposes—the first centres on the death of the world and the girl's untimely death; the second on the girl herself, whose death is no longer untimely, but religious, and whose soul's progress is a subject for contemplation. The two contrasting poems are the most notable example of Donne's use of contrast. The second poem was the last. He encountered adverse criticism, for it seemed to some that he had overpraised the girl outrageously. One wonders what new aspect of the theme would have been treated in subsequent poems; or whether Donne

---

[22] Grierson, I. 229-245.
[23] Grierson, I. 249-266; see Bibliography, pp. 232f, *infra*, for both poems.

would have been forced to abandon once again an enterprise which was too much for him.

Ben Jonson, in his conversations with William Drummond of Hawthornden, declared that Donne's 'Anniversary' (the reference may be to both poems, or either poem) was profane and full of blasphemies; that he told Donne, if it had been written of the Virgin Mary it had been something; to which he answered, that he described the Idea of a Woman, and not as Elizabeth Drury was.[24] Certainly the poems are not much concerned with the personality of the girl, and are not to be interpreted literally, as the first critics supposed, but are to be understood, as Jonson half-guessed, as religious poems, for which the death of Elizabeth Drury provided the occasion. This might have been more evident if, in reviving the idea of the epic, Donne had retained a stanzaic arrangement, or more obviously divided the poems according to the sub-titles provided from time to time at the side, which is the wrong place for them—they are vital to the appreciation of the poems, which are not as continuous as they appear, but present natural pauses of thought based, in part, on the use of a refrain, five times in the first poem and carried over, altered, for use once in the second—

An Anatomie:

1. lines 183f: Shee, shee is dead; shee's dead: when thou knowest this,
   Thou knowest how poore a trifling thing man is.
2. lines 237f: Shee, shee is dead; shee's dead: when thou knowst this,
   Thou knowst how lame a cripple this world is.
3. lines 325f: Shee, shee is dead, shee's dead; when thou knowst this,
   Thou knowst how ugly a monster this world is:
4. lines 369f: Shee, shee, is dead; shee's dead: when thou know'st this,
   Thou knowst how wan a Ghost this our world is:
5. lines 427f: Shee, shee is dead; shee's dead; when thou knowst this,
   Thou knowst how drie a Cinder this world is.

Of the Progresse of the Soule:

1. lines 81f: Shee, shee is gone; she is gone; when thou knowest this,
   What fragmentary rubbidge this world is. . . .

The approach to the refrain is always the same, the word 'she' being repeated a number of times to create a crescendo with the refrain as the climax. On each occasion in the first poem the

[24] Gosse, I. 277.

refrain is followed by the line 'And learn'st thus much by our Anatomie' which introduces a specific, and different, moral. He has abandoned the idea of an anatomy when he writes the second poem, and the form of words is altered and the moral briefly stated. These poems will never win the appreciation they deserve until they are presented differently, the movement of thought indicated by separate sections, and the whole arranged to encourage relaxed and meditative reading.

Professor L. L. Martz has demonstrated that *An Anatomie* and *Of the Progresse of the Soule* were based on the Ignatian method of meditation; the former, negative in character, reproduces the negative aspects of his method, and the latter, much more positive, the positive quest of 'contemplation'—the word used by Ignatius and also in the title. This exposition of the poems is in harmony with modern scholarship which considers that enough, or more than enough, has been said on Donne's originality as a poet, and that the more important, if less obvious, fact is his relation to great religious traditions.[25]

In *An Anatomie* Donne meditates upon the doom that has come upon the world, and, amplifying the brief reference in 'A Funerall Elegie' to astronomy in lines 67-70, considers the impact upon scholasticism and the coherent, co-ordinated world of the middle ages, of new knowledge. As in the great 'Nocturnall', less intensely and personally, he apprehends existence without purpose, and studies the nature of the world from which unity, coherence, meaning have been withdrawn.

1-90: Her death, he says, is a deprivation for the world, on which has descended, unknown to it, a lethargy, that is, forgetfulness—it is we who drink the waters of the river Lethe, not the dead Elizabeth; the world's name and meaning were concentrated in her, and so far the world, forgetting its name, has done nothing about her passing—

> But long she'ath beene away, long, long, yet none
> Offers to tell us who it is that's gone. (41f)

The world is dead, and the only profitable undertaking is to anatomize the corpse, for the benefit of those who, influenced by her virtue, lead a twilight existence still. When a person dies, though the world's life continues, its doom is declared—

[25] See L. L. Martz, *The Poetry of Meditation*, Chapter 6.

> Her death hath taught us dearely, that thou art
> Corrupt and mortall in thy purest part. (61f)

Her influence creates a new world, which

> . . . may be safer, being told
> The dangers and diseases of the old:
> For with due temper men doe then forgoe,
> Or covet things, when they their true worth know. (87-90)

91-190:　After this Introduction he considers the decline of man.

The world is sick, there is no health in us, we do not live as long as the patriarchs, we are not the men who used to be, the race of giants is at an end—not that size is anything of itself, a smaller edition of a book is still the book, but we have deteriorated mentally so much that

> Wee seeme ambitious, Gods whole worke t'undoe;
> Of nothing hee made us, and we strive too,
> To bring our selves to nothing backe; and wee
> Do what wee can, to do't so soone as hee. (155-158)

The opening section ends with the first occurrence of the refrain and the assertion that religion is our only hope; without it man withers and decays.

191-246:　The decline of man has brought division to creation altogether; society is disintegrating through the impact of new knowledge, order exists no more; instead of the concentric arrangement of the four elements of earth, water, air, and fire, man has to adjust himself to the new astronomy—

> And new Philosophy calls all in doubt,
> The Element of fire is quite put out;
> The Sun is lost, and th'earth, and no mans wit
> Can well direct him where to looke for it.
> And freely men confesse that this world's spent,
> When in the Planets, and the Firmament
> They seeke so many new; they see that this
> Is crumbled out againe to his Atomies.
> 'Tis all in peeces, all cohaerence gone;
> All just supply, and all Relation:
> Prince, Subject, Father, Sonne, are things forgot,
> For every man alone thinkes he hath got
> To be a Phœnix, and that then can bee
> None of that kinde, of which he is, but hee. (205-218)

Now the individual is unique, making standards each for himself, private judgement prevails over authority, for there is no other phœnix for comparison. Her death means the withdrawal from life of the unifying influence—

> She that should all parts to reunion bow,
> She that had all Magnetique force alone,
> To draw, and fasten sundred parts in one; (220-222)

She, She is dead, and this world is 'rotten at the heart' (242).

247-338: The third section presents the world grown ugly. The old beauty of the heavens has passed away through new stars appearing and the old vanishing, removing the former round proportion and regular movements; when we consider the earth, especially its morality and administration of justice, 'the worlds proportion disfigured is' (302)—proportion, the essence of beauty, died with her.

339-376: Not only the principal element of beauty, proportion, is removed, but colour and lustre too, without which proportion alone has no value—

> And had the world his just proportion,
> Were it a ring still, yet the stone is gone. (341f)

377-end: The fifth and last section is upon the dissociation of heaven and earth, the last and greatest evidence of the decay of the world; if the heavens influenced earth more, she who has died would influence us more, but they cast no light on earth and the seasons are out of order: the old correspondence of heaven and earth has gone. The poem closes with a reference to the Song of Moses in Deuteronomy xxxii, to which he would refer more than once in his sermons:

> . . . if you
> In reverence to her, do thinke it due,
> That no one should her praises thus rehearse,
> As matter fit for Chronicle, not verse;
> Vouchsafe to call to minde that God did make
> A last, and lasting'st peece, a song. He spake
> To *Moses* to deliver unto all,
> That song, because hee knew they would let fall
> The Law, the Prophets, and the History,
> But keepe the song still in their memory. (457-466)

1-84: The second poem, *Of the Progresse of the Soule*, begins
with Donne saying that a year has passed since her death—truly,
as I said before, the world died in her death, but a ship does not
stop immediately the sails are struck, a decapitated man's body
still twitches, and a sort of life has continued since her death, for
there is motion in corruption—but we have lived oblivious of her,
though I have done my best otherwise, and I intend 'yearely to
bring forth such a child as this' (36); and who knows? these
annual poems may influence poets long after me, to produce
great-grandchildren of these praises,

> And so, though not revive, embalme and spice
> The world, which else would putrifie with vice. (39f)

Such remembrance may create in man a thirst for heavenly
reality. This world is rotten, do not try to salvage anything from
it even by memory, let it go. And so the first section ends with the
refrain from the first poem, altered, and given for the last time,
dying away in distant echoes in lines 247 and 315ff.

85-156: After the last refrain the poet turns away from the
negative meditation of death; his spirit released, he awakens to
the positive creative work impossible without it, the release, the
progress of the soul; and the poem moves on, with ever-gathering
strength, to celebrate the soul's ascent to heaven, and instead of
the sombre reiteration, 'Shee, shee is dead; shee's dead', the word
'Up' is repeated many times, as though he cannot stay to say in
full, 'Lift up your hearts'.[26]

Think about yourself dying, recognize that death is a release;
death's humble service is to lead the soul to the door that leads to
life, and to open it; the friends around, weeping, who seem whole,
are sick, the dying man is about to be cured for ever—

> Thinke then, my soule, that death is but a Groome,
> Which brings a Taper to the outward roome,
> Whence thou spiest first a little glimmering light,
> And after brings it nearer to thy sight:
> For such approaches doth heaven make in death.
> Thinke thy selfe labouring now with broken breath,
> And thinke those broken and soft Notes to bee
> Division, and thy happyest Harmonie.

[26] See D. C. Allen, 'The Double Journey of John Donne,' *A Tribute to George Coffin Taylor*, p. 99.

Thinke thee laid on thy death-bed, loose and slacke;
And thinke that, but unbinding of a packe,
To take one precious thing, thy soule from thence. (85-95)[27]

157-250: Think how the body has caused the degradation
of the soul, imprisoning it; but the body, like a rusty pistol,
discharges the bullet, the soul; death is the beginning of life,
the soul is liberated from the restrictions of the body and flies
at great speed through the air—

Dispatches in a minute all the way
Twixt heaven, and earth. . . . (188f)

251-320: The contrast between earth and heaven, seen in the
slowness of earth set against the soul's flight to heaven, is seen
also in the contrast of human ignorance with immediate knowledge gained in heaven. 'Poore soule, in this thy flesh what dost
thou know?' (254), and there is no end to our ignorance—after
a long catalogue of examples he bursts out impatiently:

. . . But up unto the watch-towre get,
And see all things despoyl'd of fallacies: . . .
In heaven thou straight know'st all, concerning it,
And what concernes it not, shalt straight forget. (294-300)

321-382: But this contrast is most vividly perceived by the
consideration of human society and conversation, so corrupting
and debasing on earth, so enriching and ennobling in heaven,
where we shall be with Mary the Virgin, the Patriarchs, Apostles,
Martyrs and Virgins—

Up, up, my drowsie Soule, where thy new eare
Shall in the Angels songs no discord heare; . . .
Up to those Patriarchs, which did longer sit
Expecting Christ, then they'have enjoy'd him yet.
Up to those Prophets, which now gladly see
Their Prophesies growne to be Historie.
Up to th'Apostles . . .
Up to those Martyrs . .
Up to those Virgins . . .
Up, up, for in that squadron there doth live
She . . . (339-357)

27 J. Hollander (*The Untuning of the Sky*, pp. 282f) discusses the musical significance
of lines 91f and the terms 'breaking' and 'division'. The 'broken', laboured breathing
of a dying person, because of the approaching release, becomes 'division', a melodic
sequence of notes (see Grierson, II. 197).

383-470:   Think of the greatest earthly joys to their disadvantage, set against the incidental joys of heaven. All earthly things change, and deceive, and die, like human beauty and love—

> . . . *that* she, and *that* thou,
> Which did begin to love, are neither now;
> . . . whilst you think you be
> Constant, you'are hourely in inconstancie. (391-400)

This earth cannot be the basis of happiness any more than it can be the basis, or provide the materials for, a tower to reach to heaven. Felicity must be sought only in that which is enduring—

> This is essentiall joy, where neither hee
> Can suffer diminution, nor wee;
> 'Tis such a full, and such a filling good;
> Had th'Angels once look'd on him, they had stood. (443-446)

471-end: So, in the seventh and last section, it is asserted that even the least joys of heaven exceed the greatest joys of earth—

> But could this low world joyes essentiall touch,
> Heavens accidentall joyes would passe them much. (471f)

For the most part Donne's poetry is self-centred, and reference to himself is characteristic; yet, writing three poems on Elizabeth Drury, in all over a thousand lines, he refers only occasionally to himself, and this new discipline prepared him for the absorption of his whole nature in the source of his preaching, which emerges briefly in these lines from *An Anatomie of the World*—

> When nature was most busie, the first weeke,
> Swadling the new borne earth, God seem'd to like
> That she should sport her selfe sometimes, and play,
> To mingle, and vary colours every day: (347-350)

and these from *Of the Progresse of the Soule*—

> As some daies are at the Creation nam'd,
> Before the Sunne, the which fram'd daies, was fram'd . . . (23f)

In these poems his major concern is with the world, and release from it; yet they brought him considerable worldly advantage in the patronage of Sir Robert, an inconsistency which Donne himself was too introspective to overlook. These relatively long poems, with their hyperbolic praise of a young woman, contained an altogether exaggerated contempt of the world, which he had to express in order to outgrow. The poems are sincere expressions of a mood which changed, and were essential to the progress of his own soul.

At the time of their composition contraries met in one, for his studies and thoughts were convincing him of the positive nature of creation, of the sinfulness of nihilism (and probably suicide, which he later condemned, departing from the position in *Biathanatos*) and of the need to construct a religious position in positive terms. The tensions of Donne's experience required violent expression, and the picture of the death of the world was dark, exaggerated, reiterated with power, not because he believed intensely what he wrote, but because there existed in his consciousness an opposite position challenging it. Fortunately we are able to study his own record of this experience, for he has left a revealing document, not prepared for publication, which discloses the nature of the struggle.

In the year 1651, John Donne junior published, for the first time, a volume by his father, which the son entitled *Essayes in Divinity; being several Disquisitions, interwoven with Meditations and Prayers: before he entred into Holy Orders.* In an address to Sir Harry Vane junior, to whom he dedicated the book, the son declared that the contents of the volume were 'writ when the Author was obliged in Civill business, and had no ingagement in that of the Church'; and in an accompanying address to the reader he said:

It is thought fit to let thee know, that these *Essayes* were printed from an exact Copy, under the Authors own hand: and, that they were the voluntary sacrifices of severall hours, when he had many debates betwixt God and himself, whether he were worthy, and competently learned to enter into Holy Orders. They are now publish'd, both to testifie his modest Valuation of himself, and to shew his great abilities; and, they may serve to inform thee in many Holy Curiosities.[28]

The father did not use the word 'essay' in the course of the volume. In 1652 it was published along with *Paradoxes and Problemes* and 'An Essay of Valour' and the son observed that the new volume contained 'the *Essays* of *two Ages*, where you may see the *quicknesse* of the *first*, and the *firmness* of the *latter*',[29] and one

[28] *Essayes in Divinity*, pp. 3f.   [29] p.xxviii.

wonders if the son gave the title of 'essays' to the book, a vague
word which wrongly suggests short pieces and fails to indicate
their elaborate character, and unity of theme. It would be more
appropriate to use the word 'meditation', as in the opening sentence,[30] and to this extent the poems inspired by Elizabeth Drury
and this book have a similar nature: both are acts of meditation.
But he did use of these prose writings the word 'sermon', and due
significance must be given to this.

Upon this confidence, and conscience of purposing good, I proceed
in these Sermons; for they are such, in the allowance of him whom
they have stiled *resolutissimum et Christianissimum Doctorem*; for he says
Scriptor manu prædicat. And that to write books, though one gain and
profit temporally by it, yet if the finall respect be the glory of God, is
latriæ veneratio, and more honorable to the Church, then the multiplication of vocal prayers. . . . Did the Author of that book, the
Preacher, make vocal Sermons? Though these lack thus much of Sermons, that they have no Auditory, yet as Saint *Bernard* did almost
glory, that Okes and Beeches were his Masters, I shall be content that
Okes and Beeches be my schollers, and witnesses of my solitary Meditations.[31]

There is nothing imprecise about 'sermon'. It is a technical term
for Christian preaching, and was so used by him. As he
approached the prospect of becoming a Christian minister he
thought seriously of the preaching office, and put all his emphasis
upon it. The *Essayes in Divinity* are private trial sermons. Had he
prepared them for publication their form would have been
improved. But their character as first efforts at sermons is self-
evident. It is unthinkable that he would have used the word
'sermon' if this were not so. If, as the son says, they were written
at a time of inward 'debate', the issue undecided, he would
understandably avoid the word in a title, but this does not alter
the fact that we have here a picture of the future preacher testing
himself out in the art of sermon-writing, to discover if he was
'worthy, and competently learned to enter into Holy Orders'.
It is not to be expected that these first efforts will show the
author firmly controlling and ordering his learning in relation to
his text, and for this reason the arrangement of the material

---

[30] Also, e.g., on p. 39.
[31] p. 41—see notes on p. 124: he is referring (1) possibly to Johannes Gerson, *De
Laude Scriptorum Considerati*; (2) to Ecclesiastes i.1.

is sometimes discursive and tedious; but their sermon-nature is
confirmed by the presentation of a passage of Scripture which
serves as text, followed by an indication of what he intends to
say.

Gosse expressed his disappointment with the *Essayes*.

There is no revelation here of the writer's personal experience; nothing
is for edification. These short homilies are more like the notes of a
theological professor who is lecturing on Genesis and the early chapters
of Exodus, than the outpourings of a man who is trembling on the
threshold of the Holy of Holies.[32]

Inevitably, the later sermons contain occasional personal references, but they are very few in number. His preaching is objective
and scriptural, with little personal comment and allusion, and
one service performed by the poems on Elizabeth Drury, as we
have seen, was to liberate him from writing about himself. Gosse
wrongly imagined that the *Essayes* were the introspective meditations and confessions of an ordinand at vigil.

It was assumed by Gosse that the *Essayes* were written on the
eve of Donne's ordination, on the authority of the son's words to
the reader; but they refer, not to the conclusion, but to the course,
of the debate, and in the dedication he stated clearly that his
father was engaged in some (unstated) secular activity. An
ordinand cannot be said to have 'no ingagement in that of the
Church'. Even if the date of composition is thought to be near
1615, which is quite unlikely (the use throughout of the Geneva
Bible, not the Authorized Version, suggests a date earlier than
that), the contents of the *Essayes* must be the result of study spread
over a considerable period, probably continuing during the time
represented by the Anniversary poems, and finding expression
in this form some time afterwards, when the debate about the
Ministry was proceeding; we know that he had expressed an
intention to enter Holy Orders some years before 1615,[33] and that
the hope of a secular appointment remained almost to his ordination, so it is not surprising that the *Essayes*, though written during
the debate, indicate a strong inclination to the Ministry, by their
sermon-character, by a fit sense of the sacred nature of the
Ministry—

[32] Gosse, II. 63; the *Essayes* are discussed on pp. 62-64, 102f, 321f.
[33] Gosse, II. 20.

So, though every one should watch his own steps, and serve God in his vocation; yet there should be some, whose Vocation it should be to serve God; as all should do it, so some should do nothing else—

and by the admission that his secular hopes have been thwarted by God—

Thou hast delivered me, O God, from the Egypt of confidence and presumption, by interrupting my fortunes, and intercepting my hopes. . . .[34]

Yet he makes it clear that he is a layman still. The debate is not over, as surely it would have been if the *Essayes* were written just before ordination. Apart from the questionable word 'essay', the much-criticized son has told us the truth of the matter.

Donne intended to write an 'Anniversary' annually, and in fact wrote only two poems. A little later, we believe, he began the enterprise represented by the *Essayes*. He turned from verse to prose. He turned from the death of the world and the progress of the soul after death, to the positive subject of the Creation, which now gripped his attention so much that he determined to discover for himself what he could make of it in sermon-form. In addition, having decided to begin this exercise with the first verse of Holy Scripture, perhaps still influenced by the discarded idea of an annual poem, he determined to write a series of sermons on the first verse of each book of Holy Scripture: he speaks of 'my first purpose of taking the beginning of every book', shortly before his use of the word 'sermon'.[35] In fact he wrote only two, the *Essayes* consisting of sermons on Genesis i.1 and Exodus i.1, and this book no less than the Anniversary poems belongs to his unfinished work. The conclusion is dull and unimpressive, and his interest in continuing the course ended for a good reason. To write on the first verse of each book was not his true purpose. His interest now was in the beginning of Genesis, and, for inspiration, he never needed to go beyond its opening chapters.

Book I begins with the announcement of the text, Genesis i.1; an introductory section on the Bible is followed by a reference to Moses, and the book of Genesis; Part I follows, a consideration of the time, namely In the Beginning; Part II continues the study of the text, the Person, namely God, and the significance of His Name; Part III reflects upon the action: He created, and

[34] pp. 71, 75.   [35] p. 41.

discusses the subject Nothing; Part IV, the last, declares the work: Heaven and earth. Book I ends with a Prayer.

Book II also begins with the announcement of the text, Exodus i.1, and is considerably longer. Part I shows the significance of the diversity of the names of the children of Israel, justifying diversity in the Church of God; and of the number seventy; Part II is a consideration of the four 'elements', the Mercy, Power, Justice, and Judgement of God; he writes of the supremacy of Mercy and its exercise in human life by people toward one another and all living things, and of God's Mercy toward the Israelites in delivering them from famine by bringing them into Egypt, in their propagation, the exodus from Egypt and their preservation in the desert; and of God's Power shown in His miracles, His mercy, justice, judgements, and law. This second and last Book closes with four Prayers.

Three times as he expounds the Scriptures and the Faith he stresses his lay position: ' . . . to strangers they open but a little wicket, and he that will enter, must stoop and humble himselfe. To reverend Divines, who by an ordinary calling are Officers and Commissioners from God, the great Doors are open;' 'what treasure of saving mysteries do his Priests see, when we on the threshold see enough to instruct and secure us?' 'such as I, who are but Interlopers, not staple Merchants, nor of the company, nor within the commission of Expositors of the Scriptures.'[36] That it is the poet rather than the academic student who is approaching the Bible, one who, while obedient to the discipline of the Word of God will not interpret it only literally, may be seen from the first words, in which his mind flashes from the first to the last book and, holding two ends together makes his circle, the symbol where his mind is at peace—

I do not therefore sit at the door, and meditate upon the threshold, because I may not enter further; For he which is *holy and true, and hath the key of David, and openeth and no man shutteth, and shutteth and no man openeth*; hath said to all the humble in one person, *I have set before thee an open door, and no man can shut it, for thou hast a little strength.*[37]

His consideration of the opening verse of Exodus shows first, his close study of the subject, and then, the freedom with which he would apply the Scriptures to himself—

[36] pp. 5, 6, 32.　　[37] p. 5.

H

Only to paraphrase the History of this Delivery, without amplifying, were furniture and food enough for a meditation of the best perseverence, and appetite, and digestion; yea, the least word in the History would serve a long rumination. If this be in the bark, what is in the tree? . . . Dig a little deeper, O my poor lazy soul, and thou shalt see that thou, and all mankind are delivered from an Egypt; and more miraculously then these . . . Go one step lower, that is higher, and nearer to God, O my soul, in this Meditation, and thou shalt see, that even in this moment, when he affords thee these thoughts, he delivers thee from an Egypt of dulness and stupiditie. . . .[38]

Interest in the Creation story is emphatic and sustained. He notices the similarity with St John's Gospel—

This word, *In the beginning*, is the beginning of this book, which we finde first placed of all the holy books; And also of the Gospel by Saint *John*, which we know to be last written of all. But that *last* beginning was the *first*; for *the Word was with God*, before God created Heaven and Earth.[39]

The Latin words *faciamus hominem* ('let us make man', Genesis i.26), to be found often in the sermons, make their appearance, and of man he says, 'And wast made by Gods hands, not his commandment', another familiar observation on the same verse; man's divine appointment to subdue the earth, and rule over all creatures is mentioned. His meditation on the Genesis story causes him to say: 'I marke, that the first which ever pronounced the name, *God*, was the Divell. . . .' He quotes words from St Augustine which we meet again in his sermons.[40]

Already in the *Essayes* we find a strong insistence upon the Christian community, the Church. He is firmly Protestant, critical of Rome for its uniformity, prayers for the departed, undue emphasis upon our Lord's mother; and emphatic on the positive duty of Christians 'to keep the world in reparation, and leave it as well as we found it', and to do this by following a calling, and not withdrawing from the world into monastic seclusion; yet he looks forward to the reunion of Christendom in order that Christ might be seen by all, 'clearly and uniformly'. In a long discussion prompted by the diversity of names in Exodus i.1, with the words written in the margin, '*Difference* in things not

[38] pp. 74f.
[39] p. 16; see PS, I. 306; III. 348; IV. 89 for references to this link between Genesis and St John's Gospel.
[40] pp. 26, 30, 36, 71, 23, 15f, (see p. 129f *infra*).

essentiall', he opposes uniformity in exterior worship and Church polity, and defends a measure of diversity from the variety of names and their spelling in the Bible; and he concludes 'That an unity and consonance in things not essentiall, is not so necessarily requisite as is imagined'; he separates himself from Rome, yet acknowledges that 'that Church concurs with us in the root', and he 'dare not pronounce that she is not our Sister'.

Thus much was to my understanding naturally occasioned and presented by this variety of Names in the Scriptures: For, if *Esau*, *Edom*, and *Seir* were but one man; . . . so Synagogue and Church is the same thing, and of the Church, *Roman* and *Reformed*, and all other distinctions of place, Discipline, or Person, but one Church, journying to one *Hierusalem*, and directed by one guide, Christ Jesus; In which, though this Unity of things not fundamentall, be not absolutely necessary, yet it were so comely and proportionall with the foundation itself, if it were at Unity in these things also, that though in my poor opinion, the form of Gods worship, established in the Church of *England* be more convenient, and advantageous then of any other Kingdome, both to provoke and kindle devotion, and also to fix it, that it stray not into infinite expansions and Subdivisions; (into the former of which, Churches utterly despoyl'd of Ceremonies, seem to me to have fallen; and the *Roman* Church, by presenting innumerable objects, into the later). And though to all my thanksgivings to God, I ever humbly acknowledg, as one of his greatest Mercies to me, that he gave me my Pasture in this Park, and my milk from the brests of this Church, yet out of a fervent, and (I hope) not inordinate affection, even to such an Unity, I do zealously wish, that the whole catholick Church, were reduced to such Unity and agreement, in the form and profession Established, in any one of these Churches (though ours were principally to be wished) which have not by any additions destroyed the foundation and possibility of salvation in Christ Jesus; That then the Church, discharged of disputations, and misapprehensions, and this defensive warr, might contemplate Christ clearly and uniformely. For now he appears to her, as in *Cant. 2 9. He standeth behind a wall, looking forth of the window, shewing himself through the grate.* But then, when all had one appetite, and one food, one nostrill and one perfume, the Church had obtained that which she then asked, *Arise ô North, and come ô South, and blow on my garden, that the spices thereof may flow out.* For then, that *savour of life unto life* might allure and draw those to us, whom our dissentions, more then their own stubborness with-hold from us.[41]

[41] pp. 70, 49, 50, 51f, and see PS, II. 111f for the reproduction of part of pp. 51f in a sermon at Lincoln's Inn.

We find in the *Essayes* the same approach to the place of miracles in religion which we find in the sermons (p. 84f), and a similar view to the sermons on faith and reason—

For Reason is our Sword, Faith our Target [i.e. shield]. With that we prevail against others, with this we defend our selves: And old, well disciplined Armies punished more severely the loss of this, then that.[42]

He would not have been pleased with his son's promise of 'curiosities', even holy ones; 'curiosity', like 'singularity', was a word used for something much disliked by him (pp. 5, 7, 13). A vigorous element of his religion was the discouraging of undue speculation and enquiry, because life is mysterious, and in these first attempts at sermons there are at least four passages contending for a place to be given to mystery (pp. 13, 27, 49, 87f). The subject of Mercy, which occurs so notably in the sermons, has a large place here (pp. 63, 86); the ubiquitous word 'conscience', in most sermons, is found (pp. 49, 59, 100); the occasional direct address to God in an ejaculation (p. 15); the use of proper terms in a religious connection, like 'park' (p. 51), 'Common Law' (p. 81), 'Prerogative' (p. 81), 'matriculated' (p. 44); favourite words like 'intirely' (p. 44), 'rags' (pp. 14, 39); the play on words, 'onely', 'own', 'spacious and specious' (pp. 97, 49); the much used reference to Wisdom xvi.20 (p. 38); the distinction between God's action and being, between having and being—'No garment is so neer God as his word: which is so much his, as it is *he*' (p. 39; see p. 17 [did/was]); the reference to the Song of Moses in Deuteronomy xxxii (p. 92), the story of the general and the walls of the besieged town (p. 40), the illustration of the Spanish King with dominions so vast and extended that the sun cannot hide himself from his eye, or shine out of his dominions (p. 35), the idea that men make greater sacrifices for hell than for heaven—'He made us travell more for hell, then would have purchased Heaven' (p. 75), the repeated exhortation to descend farther, to penetrate more deeply (p. 74f), the apprehension of truth by comparison —'But alas, what are these' (i.e. men with the most grandiloquent titles) 'our fellow-ants, our fellow-durt, our fellow-nothings, compared to that God whom they make but their pattern?' (p. 35f) —the *Essayes* are full of illustration of ideas, references, expressions, like these, found repeatedly in the sermons.

[42] p. 16; see pp. 20f, 54.

The prayers at the close of each Book deserve close study, for they apply the sermon to his own condition. They show how firmly the practice of meditation was established in his religious life, and, in particular, how this discipline had revealed to him the need to practise the philosophy of the *via media*. The prayer at the end of Book I includes the following:

. . . *as thou didst so make Heaven, as thou didst not neglect Earth, and madest them answerable and agreeable to one another, so let my Soul's Creatures have that temper and Harmony, that they be not by a misdevout consideration of the next life, stupidly and trecherously negligent of the offices and duties which thou enjoynest amongst us in this life; nor so anxious in these, that the other (which is our better business, though this also must be attended) be the less endeavoured . . . And that for fame, . . . I so esteem opinion, (that I despise not others thoughts of me, since most men are such, as most men think they be: nor so reverence it, that I make it always the rule of my Actions. . . .*[43]

Just as he was much opposed to the singularity of the individual dissociated from society, so he was suspicious of 'truth' in the singular. Faith and reason, body and soul: in such ways he expressed his understanding; at the beginning of the *Essayes* he links humility with studiousness (which is not 'curiosity') to promote the activity of our understanding to search out those secrets of God which are accessible (p. 5). Humility and studiousness, he says, are so near of kin, that they are both agreed to be limbs and members of one virtue, Temperance; a little later he asserts that all mankind is naturally one flock feeding upon one common, but, though this is so, equality does not mean interchangeability, and for the peace of society, property, and magistracy are necessary. The recorded devotions of John Donne disclose the fact of the *via media* as a personal discipline, an exercise in charity, and a recognition of one's place in society. Behind a succinct statement such as this, 'none is to be accused, that every one doth not all, so all do all' (p. 70) lies a view of humanity and one's place in it which is the rich reward of incorporation into Christ, the Son of man.

The experience of creating the two poems on the destruction of the world was paradoxical to the point of absurdity, and in the full maturity of his years he now dedicated himself to the presentation, through Christian preaching, of the goodness of God in

[43] pp. 37f; cf. *An Anatomie of the World*, line 335, in brackets, 'Since most men be such as most thinke they bee', Grierson, I. 241.

the creation of His world. His first endeavours assured him that
the written prose sermon was a medium that he could use. Once
or twice in the *Essayes*, notably in the passage on the unity of the
Church, and in contemplation of the Egypt from which we have
been delivered, or in that magnificent line, 'the building of this
great patriarchal Catholick Church, of which every one of us is a
little chappel' (p. 41) he must have known that he had in him the
power to celebrate this theme worthily; to use prose to exalt the
Mercy of God.

Perhaps a new spirit came even into the writing of poetry as
he awakened to the glory of God's handiwork, and while the
debate to which his son referred proceeded, there came a day in
1613, when the Lady Elizabeth, daughter of King James, was to
be married—St Valentine's Day—

> Haile Bishop Valentine, whose day this is,
> All the Aire is thy Diocis,
> And all the chirping Choristers
> And other birds are thy Parishioners. . . .[44]

The idea of Nothing horrified him. To desire to return to
Nothing, from which Creation proceeded, was the supreme sin,
from which he had himself been saved.

> . . . we must return again to our strong hold, *faith*, and end with this,
> *That this Beginning was, and before it, Nothing* . . . And, oh ye chief of
> men, ye Princes of the earth . . . know ye by how few descents ye are
> derived from Nothing? . . . For to be Nothing, is so deep a curse, and
> high degree of punishment, that Hell and the prisoners there, not only
> have it not, but cannot wish so great a loss to themselves, nor such a
> frustrating of Gods purposes . . . In Hell, none is ever said to have
> wished himself Nothing . . . it is impossible that any man should wish
> himself Nothing: for we can desire nothing but that which seems
> satisfactory, and better to us at that time; and whatsoever is better,
> is something. Doth, or can any man wish that, of which, if it were
> granted, he should, even by his wishing it, have no sense, nor
> benefit? . . .[45]

So he prepared himself, so he prepares us, in his *Essayes*, for the
first sermon, with the subject 'Sold for Nothing'.

---

[44] Grierson, I. 127.   [45] pp. 19, 30f.

SIX

I LAUNCH AT PARADISE, AND I SAILE
TOWARDS HOME

('Metempsychosis, The Progresse of the Soule', Stanza VI)

IN the evening of Christmas Day, 1624, at St Paul's Cathedral, John Donne preached on the text Isaiah vii.14, from the first lesson. The long opening paragraph of the first part, on the mercy of God, is the most frequently quoted of all passages from his sermons. Of the closing section, beginning with the words 'God made Sun and Moon', George Saintsbury wrote:

A passage than which I hardly know anything more exquisitely rhythmed in the whole range of English from Ælfric to Pater. . . . The Shakespearian magnificence of the diction, such as the throng of kindred but never tautological phrase in 'wintered and frozen', etc., and the absolute perfection of rhythmical—never metrical—movement, could not be better wedded. It has, I have said, never been surpassed. I sometimes doubt whether it has ever been equalled.[1]

The paragraph is, substantially, as follows:

We begin with that which is elder then our beginning, and shall over-live our end, The mercy of God. *I will sing of thy mercy and judgement*, sayes *David*; when we fixe our selves upon the meditation and modulation of the mercy of God, even his judgements cannot put us out of tune, but we shall sing, and be chearefull, even in them. As God made grasse for beasts, before he made beasts, and beasts for man, before he made man: As in that first generation, the Creation, so in the regeneration, our re-creating, he begins with that which was necessary for that which followes, Mercy before Judgement. Nay, to say that mercy was first, is but to post-date mercy; to preferre mercy but so, is to diminish mercy; The names of first or last derogate from it, for first and last are but ragges of time, and his mercy hath no relation to time, no limitation in time, it is not first, nor last, but eternall, everlasting; Let the Devill make me so far desperate as to conceive a time when there was no mercy, and he hath made me so far an Atheist, as to conceive a time when there was no God; if I despoile him of his mercy, any one minute, and say, now God hath

---

[1] *A History of English Prose Rhythm*, pp. 162f.

no mercy, for that minute I discontinue his very Godhead, and his beeing. Later Grammarians have wrung the name of mercy out of misery; *Misericordia præsumit miseriam,* say these, there could be no subsequent mercy, if there were no precedent misery; But the true roote of the word mercy, through all the Prophets, is *Racham,* and *Racham* is *diligere,* to love; as long as there hath been love (and *God is love*) there hath been mercy: And mercy considered externally, and in the practise and in the effect, began not at the helping of man, when man was fallen and become miserable, but at the making of man, when man was nothing. So then, here we consider not mercy as it is radically in God, and an essentiall attribute of his, but productively in us, as it is an action, a working upon us, and that more especially, as God takes all occasions to exercise that action, and to shed that mercy upon us: for particular mercies are feathers of his wings, and that prayer, *Lord let thy mercy lighten upon us, as our trust is in thee,* is our birdlime; particular mercies are that cloud of Quailes which hovered over the host of Israel, and that prayer, *Lord let thy mercy lighten upon us,* is our net to catch, our Gomer to fill of those Quailes.

The aire is not so full of Moats, of Atomes, as the Church is of Mercies; and as we can suck in no part of aire, but we take in those Moats, those Atomes; so here in the Congregation we cannot suck in a word from the preacher, we cannot speak, we cannot sigh a prayer to God, but that that whole breath and aire is made of mercy. But we call not upon you from this Text, to consider Gods ordinary mercy, that which he exhibites to all in the ministery of his Church; nor his miraculous mercy, his extraordinary deliverances of States and Churches; but we call upon particular Consciences, by occasion of this Text, to call to minde Gods occasionall mercies to them; such mercies as a regenerate man will call mercies, though a naturall man would call them accidents, or occurrences, or contingencies; A man wakes at midnight full of unclean thoughts, and he heares a passing Bell; this is an occasionall mercy, if he call that his own knell, and consider how unfit he was to be called out of the world then, how unready to receive that voice, *Foole, this night they shall fetch away thy soule.* The adulterer, whose eye waites for the twy-light, goes forth, and casts his eyes upon forbidden houses, and would enter, and sees a *Lord have mercy upon us* upon the doore; this is an occasionall mercy, if this bring him to know that they who lie sick of the plague within, passe through a furnace, but by Gods grace, to heaven; and hee without, carries his own furnace to hell, his lustful loines to everlasting perdition ... If I should declare what God hath done (done occasionally) for my soule, where he instructed me for feare of falling, where he raised me when I was fallen, perchance you would rather fixe your thoughts upon my illnesse, and wonder at that, then at Gods goodnesse, and glorifie him in that; rather wonder at my sins, then at his mercies, rather consider how ill a man I was, then how good a God he is. If I should inquire upon what occasion God elected me, and writ my name in the book of Life, I should sooner be afraid that it were not so, then finde a reason why it should be so. God made Sun and Moon to distinguish seasons, and day, and night, and we cannot have the fruits of the earth but in their seasons: But God hath made no decree to distinguish the seasons of his mercies; In paradise, the fruits were ripe, the first minute, and in heaven it is alwaies Autumne, his mercies are ever in their maturity. We ask *panem quotidianum*, our daily bread, and God never sayes you should have come yesterday, he never sayes you must againe to morrow, but *to day if you will heare his voice*, to day he will heare you. If some King of the earth have so large an extent of Dominion, in North, and South, as that he hath Winter and Summer together in his Dominions, so large an extent East and West, as that he hath day and night together in his Dominions, much more hath God mercy and judgement together: He brought light out of darknesse, not out of a lesser light; he can bring thy Summer out of Winter, though thou have no Spring; though in the wayes of fortune, or understanding, or conscience, thou have been benighted till now, wintred and frozen, clouded and eclypsed, damped and benummed, smothered and stupified till now, now God comes to thee, not as in the dawning of the day, not as in the bud of the spring, but as the Sun at noon to illustrate all shadowes, as the sheaves in harvest, to fill all penuries, all occasions invite his mercies, and all times are his seasons.[2]

This is, and is called in the second sentence, a meditation, enriched by his habitual reflection on the story of Creation. He reminds himself of pre-existent Nothing, and of Light out of darkness; he dwells, as he often did, upon the wonder of immediate completeness in the first Creation. In a sermon on Genesis i.2 on Whitsunday, 1629, he observed that the Spirit of God, not a power in the water or earth, enabled the earth to produce trees with ripe fruits immediately; in a sermon preached at Lincoln's Inn on Ascension Day, 1622, he stated that all things were created perfect in the beginning, when all was summer; and in his first sermon at St Paul's Cross he spoke of a sin of relapse which revives former sins which then have all the age of those former sins, born like Adam full-grown.[3] He attaches importance to the discipline

[2] PS, VI. 170-172; see the analysis on pp. 14f.
[3] See PS, IX. 100; IV. 136; I. 194; see p. 37 *supra*, and note 31.

of the first week of Creation, the purposeful sequence of days, grass for beasts, and beasts for man, a familiar emphasis in other sermons, and refers to sun and moon, and their purpose. When it is remembered that the sermon was preached at the darkest time of the year, the contrast with the 'Nocturnall' is impressive, for it is now that the Light is most appreciated. Here in this passage are many characteristic touches—the use of 'conscience', an essential word in his religious vocabulary; human reason cut down to size; the bell; the touch of realism in the vivid picture of the plague-stricken house and the reference to himself; and the strong injection of scriptural allusion and the sense of the Church. Much of the typical Donne is concentrated in this paragraph; the subject, the Mercy of God, may be said to be over all *his* works.

In its attitude to Time it reiterates the central conviction of his poetry. The apprehension of truth came to Donne in many ways—through the tensions of his nature, engaged in active struggle; through comparison; through paradox; through the concentration of truth in an emblem; and through the experience of the Return. In a sermon he used the picture of a person bouncing a ball on the ground or against a wall, intending that the ball shall return, as an illustration of God restoring man to Himself—

> Therfore that he may raise the Lord throws down. . . .
> That I may rise, and stand, o'erthrow mee. . . . [4]

The idea of a Return is one of the great, sustained themes of the Bible, [5] and the supreme place given to the parable of the prodigal son the world over indicates the unerring human instinct to seize truth in this form. The return journey is the theme of 'The Blossome', which narrates Donne's return to London, where his temporarily excited heart settles down again. The developing, changing argument of many of his poems has the effect of staging an excursion only to present a more satisfying return; often the subject is the subtle relationship of body and soul, and the consistently held conclusion, repeated in different forms, is that one returns, in the end, to this life, and its corporeal, temporal nature. However unsatisfying it is, whatever the problems its nature raises for the questing spirit which can stand outside the body

---

[4] PS, III. 193, and see IV. 126; Grierson, I. 369, 328.　　[5] See PS, I. 281.

and time, one comes back to the created order which God in His goodness has prepared for us. This may be studied in 'Aire and Angels', 'Elegie X', 'The Dreame', 'A Valediction: forbidding mourning' with its picture of the compasses and the return home,[6] and in three other poems to which longer reference is now made. In 'The Primrose' we picture him at Montgomery Castle, 'upon the hill, on which it is situate', searching for an unusual primrose which was the token of true love in his day; normally a primrose has five petals, but sometimes four, or six, and for one of these he seeks.

> Vpon this Primrose hill . . .
> I walke to find a true Love; and I see
> That 'tis not a mere woman, that is shee,
> But must, or more, or lesse then woman bee.
> Yet know I not, which flower
> I wish; a sixe, or foure;
> For should my true-Love lesse then woman bee,
> She were scarce any thing; and then, should she
> Be more then woman, shee would get above
> All thought of sexe, and think to move
> My heart to study her, and not to love;
> Both these were monsters. . . .

and he ends by abandoning the search for the exceptional primrose and returning to the normal (that is, the normal woman):

> Live Primrose then, and thrive
> With thy true number five. . . .[7]

'The Extasie' is the second poem.[8] Donne attached significance to the literal meaning of this word, as we know from a letter beginning,

Sir,—I make account that the writing of letters, when it is with any seriousness, is a kind of ecstasy, and a departure and secession and suspension of the soul, which doth then communicate itself to two bodies. . . .[9]

---

[6] Grierson, I. 22, 95, 37f, 49-51; see also 'Elegie V. His Picture', 'Good Friday, 1613. Riding Westward', Grierson, I. 86f, 336f, and pp. 200, 216f, *infra*.

[7] Grierson, I. 61f, II. 48f; see Bibliography, p. 232f, *infra*.

[8] Described by Rupert Brooke as 'Donne's greatest poem' (*The Prose of Rupert Brooke*, ed. C. Hassall, p. 90), and similarly by John Sparrow in his introduction to his edition of the *Devotions*, p.xii.

[9] Gosse, I. 173.

But it does not follow that the title indicates a normal view of the subject, and the poem argues that the important part of this particular ecstasy was the return to the normal integrated life of body and soul. Just as the poem is said to be a dialogue, but of a most unusual nature, of one, so this ecstasy is unlike any other, because it leads to a heightened awareness of the value of this present life. The word 'ecstasy' occurs occasionally in the sermons, but one does not feel that he gives it much respect.[10]

In the second sermon preached at St Dunstan's, he allows the point, with no enthusiasm, that there are people who maintain, from tales that are, he supposes, credible—the word 'some' is used four times in twelve words: 'some men draw some reasons, out of some stories of some credit'—that in a state of ecstasy or rapture, the soul, leaving the body on the floor or in the bed, may go out to contemplate heavenly things. But he immediately turns from this unimportant and dubious possibility, to the reverse, suggesting the perverse ecstasy of the person whose body is in the house of God but whose soul has gone out to contemplate worldly pleasure or profit.[11] This twist of meaning is characteristic of him. Reading the poem in the light of this passage, one concludes that his attitude to the subject was consistent throughout his life. Significantly, unusually, it is in the past tense; the return to the body, for which it argues, has already taken place.

Two lovers recline upon a bank, hand in hand, gazing at each other; their bodies are in repose, and their souls go forth from their separate bodies, to meet and become one in an ecstasy (not the usual highly individual experience, but the ecstasy of two persons).

---

[10] Except in the famous passage on a 'death of rapture, and extasie', PS, II. 210f —see J. B. Leishman, *The Metaphysical Poets*, p. 204.

[11] PS, VI. 101; see p. 353; VIII. 119; *Ignatius his Conclave* begins: 'I was in an *Extasie . . .*', and ends: 'And I returned to my body; which

> As a flower wet with last nights dew, and then
> Warm'd with the new Sunne, doth shake off agen
> All drowsinesse and raise his trembling Crowne,
> Which crookedly did languish, and stoope downe
> To kisse the earth, and panted now to finde
> Those beames return'd, which had not long time shin'd,

was with this returne of my soule sufficiently refreshed' (J. Hayward, *John Donne Dean of St Paul's: Complete Poetry and Selected Prose*, pp. 359, 407f).

> Our soules, (which to advance their state,
> Were gone out,) hung 'twixt her, and mee.
> And whil'st our soules negotiate there,
> Wee like sepulchrall statues lay;
> All day, the same our postures were,
> And wee said nothing, all the day.

The experience clarifies for both souls the meaning of their love. The climax of the poem is contained in the conclusion, beginning at line 49, enjoining upon the souls the need to return to their bodies—it is not, for example, because, for some unexplained purpose the soul must be disciplined by the body but because without the body the soul cannot express itself to others, who will learn the true meaning of love by reading this 'book'—

> As our blood labours to beget
> Spirits, as like soules as it can,
> Because such fingers need to knit
> That subtile knot, which makes us man:
> So must pure lovers soules descend
> T'affections, and to faculties,
> Which sense may reach and apprehend,
> Else a great Prince in prison lies.
> To'our bodies turne wee then, that so
> Weake men on love reveal'd may looke;
> Loves mysteries in soules doe grow,
> But yet the body is his booke.
> And if some lover, such as wee,
> Have heard this dialogue of one,
> Let him still marke us, he shall see
> Small change, when we'are to bodies gone. (61-end.) [12]

(The spirits were believed to be vapour-like, rarefied substances in the blood, through which the brain exerted its will over the body, and which united soul and body: cf. the expression 'animal spirits'.)

Donne was a realist who, consistently, included in his poetry the ugly and discordant elements of experience, dissonantly expressed; and who refused to present an escape from the created order, the proper scene of man's activity. These souls advanced their state by going out, in order to return.

[12] Grierson, I. 51-53, II. 41-45; see Bibliography, p. 233, *infra*.

Finally, the theme of the Return is presented in the thought of
'The Anniversarie'.

> All Kings, and all their favorites,
> All glory of honors, beauties, wits,
> The Sun it selfe, which makes times, as they passe,
> Is elder by a yeare, now, then it was
> When thou and I first one another saw:
> All other things, to their destruction draw,
> Only our love hath no decay;
> This, no to morrow hath, nor yesterday,
> Running it never runs from us away,
> But truly keepes his first, last, everlasting day.
>
> Two graves must hide thine and my coarse,
> If one might, death were no divorce.
> Alas, as well as other Princes, wee,
> (Who Prince enough in one another bee,)
> Must leave at last in death, these eyes, and eares,
> Oft fed with true oathes, and with sweet salt teares;
> But soules where nothing dwells but love
> (All other thoughts being inmates) then shall prove
> This, or a love increased there above,
> When bodies to their graves, soules from their graves remove.
>
> And then wee shall be throughly blest,
> But wee no more, then all the rest;
> Here upon earth, we'are Kings, and none but wee
> Can be such Kings, nor of such subjects bee.
> Who is so safe as wee? where none can doe
> Treason to us, except one of us two.
> True and false feares let us refraine,
> Let us love nobly, and live, and adde againe
> Yeares and yeares unto yeares, till we attaine
> To write threescore: this is the second of our raigne.[13]

This poem studies the relationship of love and time. The first
stanza asserts the freedom of their love from the law of destruction,
but the next admits that their bodies are destroyed by death,
though their souls, released by it, remain. The argument swings
back in the last stanza to assert that human life now is the scene
of their reign, for in heaven they will be no more blessed than
others. Time is not the scene of the discipline of the soul, but of its
triumph.

[13] Grierson, I. 24f, II. 23f; see G. Williamson, *The Proper Wit of Poetry*, p. 36.

In 'The Sunne Rising' he asserts:

> Love, all alike, no season knowes, nor clyme,
> Nor houres, dayes, moneths, which are the rags of time.[14]

'Rags' was a word which he used with great effect—in the first of the Elizabeth Drury poems, 'A Funerall Elegie', he spoke of his poem as 'these memorials, ragges of paper',[15] and he used it in the Christmas sermon to diminish the significance of time. 'The Sunne Rising' sustains to the end his contempt for time, and a tired sun, an 'old foole'. But the sermon, though it begins with a touch of his old imperious disdain—'we begin with that which is elder then our beginning, and shall over-live our end . . . first and last are but ragges of time . . .'—returns to time, and the created order, to establish the sovereignty of God in time: ' . . . to day he will heare you . . . now God comes to thee . . . all times are his seasons'. No day of the year was more appropriate for this meditation on the everlasting mercy of God, in whom time is reinvested with its native dignity.

John Donne was more fortunate than some. The understanding that had come to him through the poems that grappled with his experience, to make sense of it, was richly confirmed in actuality by the writing of *Pseudo-Martyr* through which he came back to Oxford University to receive the degree of M.A., and by the appointment which caused him to return, a preacher of the Gospel, to Lincoln's Inn. Here, earlier, he had thrown off the encumbering discipline of professional studies; here, home again, he gave meaning to time and providence. The theme of the Return was embodied in his experience.[16]

The long quotation from the Christmas sermon of 1624 is the noblest example of the influence of the Creation story, but it is significant because it is not isolated, but, rather, typical. In the pages that follow an attempt will be made to set forth the signs of this inspiration in the sermons that have come down to us. But in order to appreciate their importance it is necessary to set the source of his inspiration in its contemporary context. A preacher must be acquainted with the trends of current literature; he must

---

[14] Grierson, I. 11.   [15] Grierson, I. 246; see p. 49.

[16] His return to Christian teaching on sex, in the establishment of his own home, is stressed by Robert Lynd, *The Art of Letters*, p. 41, and C. S. Lewis, 'Donne and Love Poetry in the Seventeenth Century', in *Seventeenth-Century Studies presented to Sir Herbert Grierson*, p. 73.

endeavour to understand, and assess, the books that his hearers
are likely to read. The thesis that Donne's principal source for
his preaching was the opening chapters of Holy Scripture, that,
to use his own words, he launched at paradise, must be sustained
by evidence from his own words. It is not enough to seek to
establish a thesis, however. Fundamentally one needs to be
persuaded, not so much of the soundness, as of the importance, of
the claim. Some attempt is now made to suggest reasons for the
view that Donne was strongly influenced, by a particular religious
and literary tradition, to emphasize this theme; and that his
hearers, no less, were aware of, and responsive to it; and, further,
that thereby Donne's sermons are set in this tradition which links
him with great preachers and commentators of the past, and
with Milton.

It was necessary in the earlier years of the Donne revival
to stress the originality of John Donne the poet, in his rebellion
against poetic convention. He was regarded as an innovator,
creating a fresh poetic style and form, separating himself from
classical inspiration and boldly presenting himself in his self-
sufficiency. There was much in what he wrote to encourage and
justify this view. In the Epistle introducing 'Metempsychosis,
The Progresse of the Soule' he said: 'Now when I beginne this
booke, I have no purpose to come into any mans debt.'[17] He
would be influenced as little as must be by others. Yet the
picture that he has left us of himself noting the Spanish authors in
his library[18] and the recollection of his famous phrase on his
'hydroptic, immoderate desire of human learning and languages'[19]
persuades us that the influence of other writers on him must have
been immense. His Satires, his earliest writing, were influenced
by the realism of Juvenal, and the rugged obscurity of Persius
whose fame was revived by Casaubon in Geneva. Ovid influenced
the Elegies, and Martial the Paradoxes and Problems, and
Epigrams. Occasional references to contemporaries and others
show that he read the literature and science of his own times.
Modern scholarship has relieved Donne of his splendid isolation
and demonstrated that the sources of his inspiration were
numerous, and his dependence much greater than had been
supposed. It may be that Donne was less ready than others to
admit dependence—Fausset speaks of his calculated taciturnity

[17] Grierson, I. 293.   [18] See p. 278, *supra*.   [19] See p. 13, *supra*.

on other writers[20] but probable sources and influences have been suggested for 'Metempsychosis, The Progresse of the Soule' (Philo), for 'The Extasie' (e.g. Leone Ebreo's *Dialoghi d'Amore*), and for the Anniversary poems (Ignatian meditation).[21]

Nothing so precise is suggested for one hundred and sixty sermons, yet in a consideration of the influence of the Creation story on them the work of the Huguenot poet du Bartas and its possible effect upon Donne and his hearers must be noted. When Ben Jonson stayed with the Scottish poet William Drummond at Hawthornden (near Edinburgh) for some weeks in 1619 they spoke together on many literary matters. His views on 'Metempsychosis, The Progresse of the Soule' and 'The Anniversaries' have been quoted.[22] The record of these conversations states, with reference to Joshua Sylvester, the principal translator of the Huguenot poet Du Bartas into English:

(1) Of Silvester—that Silvester's translation of Du Bartas was not well done, and that he wrote his Verses befor it err he understood to confer.

(Jonson had written commendatory verses at the front of Sylvester's translation ('before it'), admitting his ignorance of French and his inability to judge the merits of the translation by Sylvester.)

(2) Of Du Bartas—that he thought not Bartas a Poet but a Verser, because he wrote not Fiction.[23]

Grierson in his introduction to and commentary on his edition of the Poems refers to the French poet in the opening paragraph of the introduction, and quotes extensively from his works in the course of the commentary, in the original, or, more frequently, in Sylvester's version.[24] At the beginning of the commentary, pp. 3f, discussing metaphysical poetry and Donne's learning, he considers the contention that Donne was indebted to Du Bartas

[20] *John Donne, A Study in Discord*, p. 45.

[21] See pp. 378 *supra*, 233 *infra*, 89 *supra*; Merritt Y. Hughes, 'Kidnapping Donne', *Essays in Criticism, 2nd Series*, suggests that Donne took the figure of the compasses in 'A Valediction: forbidding mourning' from the title-page of Justus Lipsius' *De Constantia* (1584), reproduced as a frontispiece to the volume in which this essay appears; and see p. 80.

[22] See pp. 35, 88, *supra*.

[23] *Ben Jonson's Works*, ed. C. H. Herford and P. Simpson, I, Appendix 1, 'Contemporary Notes and Records', Introduction pp. 128-131 and Notes pp. 152-178 to 'Ben Jonson's Conversations with William Drummond of Hawthornden', on pp. 132-151; see especially p. 133.

[24] See II. v; 3f, 44, 65, 79, 81, 106, 124, 135, 190, 193f, 198; see also Grierson's essay, 'The Metaphysical Poets', *The Background of English Literature*, p. 129.

I

and influenced by him in his verse; and though he comes to a largely negative conclusion it is sufficient to note at this stage that Donne and Du Bartas are names that occur in Ben Jonson's conversations, and are at least associated for purposes of illustration in a monumental commentary.[25] Donne's 'Elegie upon the untimely death of the incomparable Prince Henry'[26] was published in *Lachrymae Lachrymarum*, an anthology of poems on the subject edited by Joshua Sylvester.

Grierson, who is inclined to regard Donne as Catholic or pro-Catholic to a much later date than more recent study suggests, holds that Donne, a Catholic, would not have been as attracted to the work of the Huguenot as were Protestant poets,[27] but his reference in 'Elegie VIII' and in a sermon to 'Sanserra's starved men', to illustrate deliverance from famine, suggests sympathy for the Huguenot cause, for the Protestants in Sancerra were besieged by the Catholics for nine months in 1573, and suffered severe privations, their sufferings and resistance and deliverance providing the point of the allusion—in the sermon it is mentioned with Goshen, Jewry and Geneva;[28] a man with Catholic sympathies would not have written in this way, in the poem or the sermon.

William of Salust, Lord of Bartas, as he was styled in English, a Gascon, was born at Monfort near Auch, in 1544, and died in 1590 of wounds received while fighting for the Protestant cause at the battle of Ivry. He was a son of a Treasurer of France, and until early middle life followed the pursuits of a country gentleman and scholar, but then enlisted in the ranks of the Huguenots under Henri de Navarre, and was his envoy to England, Scotland and Denmark. He won general respect for his Christian convictions and occupied a position of distinction as a poet, though he flourished much more outside France than in his own country. He was regarded as an originator, initiating a new form of epic style for revolutionary subject-matter. In 1574 he published *La Muse Chrétienne*, which included three works, (1) 'La Judit' (Judith), (2) 'L'Uranie, ou Muse Celeste', (3) 'Le Triomphe de la Foi'. The first of these, in epic style, was based on the story of Judith in the Apocrypha and presented the novel idea of epic poetry dedicated to the presentation of the Scriptures. This

---

[25] II. 3f.   [26] Grierson, I. 267-270.   [27] Grierson, II. 4.
[28] Grierson, I. 91, II. 74; PS, V. 71.

innovation was justified in the second poem, which told how Urania, the classical goddess of astronomy, came to the poet in a vision, begging that he would make her his muse for divine poetry, dedicating to her a religious theme. Poets, she urged, would be revered if they sang of holy things, like David, and Judith. So Urania became the Christian Muse; she stood sometimes for the Holy Spirit, and was the Heavenly Muse in the mind of Milton when he began *Paradise Lost*. In 1578 he published the first of two major epic poems which established his renown. This was *La Sepmaine, ou Création du Monde* (the full title was *Commentaires et Annotations sur la Sepmaine de la Création du monde*), a work of didactic as well as epic character, written in Alexandrine couplets, recounting the seven days of the creation of the world. Perhaps without being aware of it, he had revived an early Christian practice of giving poetic expression to the scriptural drama of Creation. This was followed in 1584 by *La Seconde Semaine, ou Enfance du Monde*. He planned once again a poem in seven major sections, each subdivided into four parts, presenting the history of mankind through biblical to much later times. He did not complete this work, but four of the seven days were narrated, and in this second work particularly he amplified the story with information of an encyclopedic character, with the result that his work became, not only an edifying poem on a scriptural subject, but also a store of scientific and other information of a varied kind, a treasury of devotion and knowledge which would readily establish itself in the homes of pious Protestants—though it was not at all a divisive work and it was read by Catholics as well. To the framework of the sacred drama he added knowledge of natural history, contemporary life, geographical discoveries. He quickly became known for his style, its neologisms, compound adjectives, dialect terms, onomatopoeic words and imitative harmonies, diminutives, and various novelties of expression, conceits, fantastic imagery, verbal displays, puns, sudden pauses, all of which showed the domination of thought over language, and which in this made him a recognizable adherent of the Pléiade and the metaphysical style. Protestant literature, hitherto confined to sermons, commentaries and treatises of various kinds, now found a new and more compelling form of expression of much wider appeal, and while critics were not slow to express themselves on some of his literary devices, his fame and influence grew rapidly, he was translated into many languages, his works began to be widely circulated, he was honoured by French, Italian, and Spanish imitators, and the scriptural epic had arrived to stay. With reference to his first venture, 'Judith', he had written: 'Yet in so much as I am the first in *Fraunce*, who in a just *Poeme* hath treated in our toung of sacred things, I hope of thy favour to receive some excuse, seeing that things of so great weight cannot be both perfectly begunne and ended together.'[29] Criticism of his work must be balanced by appreciation of its novelty and of the importance of the new conception of poetry at the service of religion and human knowledge.

Du Bartas was admired by a number of contemporary English writers, and his work was well known to Spenser, Ben Jonson, William Browne, Lodge, Marston, Drayton, John Davies of Hereford. The French poet was translated into English, as into many other languages (Latin, Italian, Dutch, Spanish, German, Polish, Danish), and Sir Philip Sidney, Robert Ashley, William L'Isle, Thomas Winter, and Lodge were among those who undertook this work in the years of his mounting influence. The close political relationship of France and Scotland, and the strongly Protestant sympathies of the latter, promoted Scottish interest in him at a time when the monarch was a young man of pedantic erudition. James VI, later James I of England, to whom Donne owed much, was well read in theological and literary matters, and conversed on them with his guests at meals; and, further, he was a writer and poet, and much of his time was spent with a group of versifiers, including Alexander Montgomerie, Thomas and Robert Hudson—musicians in his household since his childhood —William Fowler, who was an uncle of William Drummond of Hawthornden, and others. It is said that at one of the royal table conversations Thomas Hudson, contrary to the king, maintained the possibility of translating Du Bartas into English, and that James assigned to him the poem on Judith as a test piece. The translation was made, and a little later James himself translated 'L'Uranie', with the original printed at the side. Addressing 'the favorable Reader', he said:

Having oft revolved, and red over (favorable Reader) the booke and Poems of the devine and Illuster Poëte, *Salust du Bartas*, I was moved

[29] Translated by Thomas Hudson; see Lily B. Campbell, *Divine Poetry and Drama in Sixteenth-Century England*, p. 76.

by the oft reading & perusing of them with a restles and lofty desire, to preas to attaine to the like vertue. . . . I was constrained to . . . doe what lay in me, to set forth his praise . . . which I thought, I could not do so well, as by publishing some worke of his, to this yle of Brittain . . . aswell as they ar made manifest already to Fraunce.

He hoped that someone 'borne under the same, or as happie a Planet, as *Du Bartas* was, might by the reading of it, bee moved to translate it well, and best, where I have both evill, and worst broyled it'.[30] In the year 1587 Du Bartas came in person to the Scottish court, as envoy from Henry of Navarre, was treated with great honour and reluctantly permitted to depart, James addressing to Henry the following:

Monseiur mon frère, je n'ay voulu laissé passer l'occasion du partement du sieur du Bartas sans par la présente vous tesmoigner le grand contentment que j'ay reçu par sa compagnie ce temps passé et combien son absence me seroit desplaisante sy autre-ment se pourroit faire. Vous avez certes grande occasion de louer Dieu, et vous estime tres-heureux d'avoir le service et conseil d'un si rare et vertueux personnage.[31]

In 1585 James had written a poem on the overthrow of the Turks at the sea battle of Lepanto of 1571, a religious work in epic style modelled on the Huguenot's writings, and Du Bartas on returning home translated this into French and wrote a poem on King James. In 1591 James translated 'Les Furies', the third part of the first day of *La Seconde Semaine* together with the Exord, or Preface to the Second Week. James also translated the second day of the first 'Week', and 'Eden' the first part of the first day of the second. He often quoted Du Bartas in his prose writings. Behind the Authorized Version of the Scriptures, by which 'the most high and mighty prince James' is especially remembered, were many years of Bible reading and consideration of sacred themes, and the place of the Huguenot poet in his personal history must be remembered in estimating those influences which made him a champion of the new translation. James, with his royal authority did as much as anyone to introduce and commend Du Bartas to English readers, and the French poet was acknowledged to be a true adherent of Protestant, scriptural religion, combining its expression in the native language and the contemporary scene

[30] *The Poems of James VI of Scotland*, ed. James Craigie, The Scottish Text Society, I. p. 16.
[31] A. H. Upham, *The French Influence in English Literature*, p. 151.

with a most exalted sense of the epic nature of God's creative act.

Joshua Sylvester was the most successful and popular translator of Du Bartas into English, and through his version of the two major poems the drama of Creation was established in the homes of the people, not simply as Scripture, but as an event linked with the great struggle in France, and with the development of new literary forms. Sylvester dedicated his *Du Bartas His Divine Weekes and Workes* to King James, and the first complete edition appeared in 1608, a version in decasyllabic heroic couplets, reproducing the original with fidelity yet presenting a lively version and not a dull, literal rendering.

Alexander B. Grosart, who, by his edition of Donne's poems did much to encourage the revival of the metaphysical poets, among many other literary labours edited in the Chertsey Worthies' Library a two-volume edition, in 1880, of the complete works of Joshuah Sylvester. The contents of the two poems were as follows:

1. The First Week

Du Bartas his first weeke: or, birth of the world. Wherein, in seven dayes the glorious Worke of the Creation is divinely handled; In the

1 Day	The Chaos
2 Day	The Elements
3 Day	The Sea and Earth
4 Day	The Heavens, Sun, Moon, etc.
5 Day	The Fishes and Fowles
6 Day	The Beasts and Man
7 Day	The Sabbath

2. The Second Week (four days only completed)

1 Day Adam	1. Eden
	2. The Imposture
	3. The Furies
	4. The Handycrafts

2 Day Noah	1. The Arke
	2. Babylon
	3. The Colonies
	4. The Columnes

3 Day Abraham	1. The Vocation
	2. The Fathers
	3. The Law
	4. The Captains

4 Day   1. The Tropheis
David   2. The Magnificence
           3. The Schisme
           4. The Decay

In other words, *the First Day* had for its subject (1) Adam and
Eve; (2) Eve's temptations; (3) the expulsion from Paradise
and the ill consequences for man, and (4) the later history of
Adam and Eve;

   the second Day, (1) Noah and the ark; (2) the tower of Babel;
(3) the dispersion; and (4) a treatise on mathematics and astronomy;

   the third Day, (1) the story of Abraham; (2) the story of Isaac;
(3) Moses and the lawgivers; (4) the earlier history of the Jewish
state;

   the fourth Day, (1) David; (2) Solomon; (3) Judah and Israel;
(4) the fall of Jerusalem. (The 5th, 6th, and 7th Days were
intended to be 5. Zedechias 6. Messias 7. Th'eternall Sabbath.) [32]
The following passage from the sixth day of the first week, lines
456-505, is offered as an example of Sylvester's style, and for the
reader's consideration, in the light of a passage from one of
Donne's sermons, which follows.

> Now of all Creatures which his Word did make,
> MAN was the last that living breath did take:
> Not that he was the least; or that God durst
> Not undertake so noble a Work at first:
> Rather, because he should have made in vain
> So great a Prince, without on whom to Reign.
> All th'admirable Creatures made beforn,
> Which Heav'n, and Earth, and Ocean doe adorn,
> Are but Essays, compar'd in every part,
> To this divinest Master-Piece of Art.
> Therefore the supreme peer-less Architect,
> When (of meer nothing) he did first erect
> Heav'n, Earth, and Aire, and Seas; at once his Thought,
> His Word, and Deed, all in an instant wrought:
> But, when he would his own self's Type create,
> Th'honour of Nature, th'Earth's sole Potentate;
> As if he would a Councell hold, he citeth
> His sacred Power; his Prudence he inviteth,

[32] See Grosart's edition; also S. Lee, *The French Renaissance in England*, p. 335.

> Summons his Love; his Justice he adjourns,
> Calleth his Goodness, and his Grace returns;
> To (as it were) consult about the birth
> And building of a second God, of Earth;
> And each (a-part) with liberall hand to bring
> Some excellence unto so rare a thing.
> Or rather, he consults with's onely Son
> (His own true Pourtrait) what proportion,
> What gifts, what grace, what soule he shoulde bestow
> Upon his *Vice-Roy* of this Realm below.
> When th'other things God fashion'd in their kind,
> The Sea t'abound in Fishes he assign'd;
> The Earth in flocks: but having Man in hand
> His very self he seeméd to command.
> He both at-once both life and body lent
> To other things; but when in Man he meant
> In mortall limbs immortall life to place,
> He seem'd to pawse, as in a weighty case:
> And so at sundry moments finishéd
> The Soule and Body of Earth's glorious Head. . . .[33]

On 26th April 1625, John Donne preached a sermon at Denmark House, Westminster, 'some few days before the body of King James, was removed from thence, to his buriall', as the heading states. The text, the last verse of the third chapter of the Song of Solomon, 'Goe forth ye daughters of Sion, and behold King Solomon, with the crown, wherewith his mother crowned him, in the day of his espousals, and in the day of the gladnesse of his heart' was a subtle allusion to the British Solomon, and begins with a reference to Genesis i.26 in which he introduces a favourite word, 'Faciamus'—

In the Creation of man, in that one word, *Faciamus, let Vs make man*, God gave such an intimation of the *Trinity*, as that we may well enlarge, and spread, and paraphrase that one word, so farre, as to heare therein, a councell of all the *three Persons*, agreeing in this gracious designe upon Man, *faciamus*, let us make him; *make* him, and *mend* him, and make him *sure*: I, the Father, will make him by my power; if he should fall, Thou the Sonne shalt repayr him, re-edify him, *redeem* him; if he should distrust, that this Redemption belonged not to him, Thou, the *Holy Ghost*, shalt apply to his particular soule, and conscience, this *mercy* of mine, and this *merit* of the Sonnes; and so let *us make him*.[34]

[33] Grosart, I. 76.   [34] PS, VI. 280.

This quotation, an example of the significant place given by Donne to the Creation theme at the beginning of a sermon on a historic occasion, at the time of the King's death, showing its influence on his treatment of one of the great doctrines, suggests the possibility of another cryptic allusion to the monarch who, in his earlier days, had delighted to welcome Du Bartas to his court, and by his own exertions introduced his poems to his subjects. Whether deliberate or not, it is a singularly fortunate opening, for there was good reason, when thinking of King James, to recall the epic theme of the world's Creation.

That Donne knew of the king's interest in Du Bartas may be assumed. There is, however, no sure evidence that he was himself interested in him or his translator. Gosse says, 'He had doubtless read, without advantage to his style, Sylvester's popular version of the *Divine Weeks and Works*',[35] but this amounts to no more than the assertion of T. S. Eliot that Donne would have read what the scholar of his time, with his interests, might have been expected to read.[36]

We know the titles of some of the books possessed by Donne, and Du Bartas and Sylvester are not represented. It is possible to find examples in his verse of similarities to the novelties of style in the French writer. A. H. Upham advanced a detailed presentation of evidence in support of this.

Even in the case of John Donne, the great leader in the use of daring figures drawn from the material things of life, there seems ample reason to consider the possible influence of the *Semaines*. . . . practically all the peculiarities of Donne had already appeared in Du Bartas, lacking there only the mastery of genius to make them vital and impressive instead of vapid and commonplace. . . . The poetry of Du Bartas was before him; he had every reason to know it. Even as he experimented and composed, Sylvester's translations were coming into circulation. Elaborate figures, complicated figures, comparisons drawn from all the minutiæ of contemporary science and hardly pausing at the threshold of men's sense of taste and proportion: all these were spread out before him, and he had only to approve them and give them power.[37]

'First, last, everlasting', 'through-shine', 'on both sides written',

[35] Gosse, I. 264.
[36] See T. S. Eliot, 'Donne in our Time', in *A Garland for John Donne*, p. 8.
[37] *The French Influence in English Literature*, pp. 178-185.

'three person'd' were given as examples of compounds, and linked words, a frequent usage in Du Bartas; the two senses in 'whose insides meete, meate comes', the three different ideas in 'all formes, uniforme deformity' were among examples given of verbal echoes and conceits; Upham urged that the two 'Anniversaries' 'seem in a number of ways subject to the direct influence of Du Bartas', being in ten-syllable couplets, like Sylvester's translation, and containing two specific references[38] to the world's creation; noted the emphasis in both writers on man the microcosm; and suggested that 'Metempsychosis, The Progresse of the Soule' 'is a daring narrative development of the idea of metempsychosis, looking remarkably like a parody of such sacred epic as that of Du Bartas'.[39] Sir Sydney Lee made a similar contention, declaring 'Virile Donne's debt to Du Bartas is the most interesting fact about the French poet in the history of English poetry'; 'The Huguenot poet or his English translator was clearly one of the influences at work on Donne's somewhat crabbed muse. The uncouth metaphor, the harsh epithet, the varying pause in the line, which are characteristic of Donne's rhyming decasyllables, all seem to mirror irregularities which dominate Du Bartas's or Sylvester's achievement'.[40]   The statements by both these authors are confidently made, but rest on meagre evidence which hardly bears the strain, and the criticisms of both writers by Grierson[41] are reasonable.   There is a great difference between the works of the two poets, and those of Donne are immeasurably superior, especially in the use of simile—whereas Du Bartas is often forced, arbitrary, Donne justifies his choice of images which are, finally, self-commending. Nevertheless, though the final results are very different, the influence may still be admitted, and Grierson goes far to concede this in the commentary, with its occasional references to Du Bartas or his translator. Certainly, on reading 'Metempsychosis, The Progresse of the Soule', one has the feeling that the epic style is parodied, and if one turns to the French poems there is a similarity in allowing the Creation story to attract all manner of allusions; and, one can believe

---

[38] Quoted on page 94, *supra*.

[39] See Upham, pp. 178, 179, 183, 185; and, for his references here quoted, Grierson, I. 24, 26, 266, 328; 175, 177, 241f, 252.

[40] S. Lee, *The French Renaissance in England*—an account of the literary relations of England and France in the sixteenth century, pp. 351, 353; see pp. 333-355.

[41] II. 3f.

the younger writer to be quite capable, while allowing the Frenchman to influence him, of caricaturing an undertaking which admittedly was beyond Du Bartas' powers.

The theory advanced by Upham and Lee has been disregarded rather than disproved in the intervening years. In their consideration of the subject, in their search for evidence, both writers turned only to Donne's poetry; but if the argument is that Du Bartas influenced Donne, the evidence may be as much in the prose as in the verse. Once the *Essayes in Divinity* and the sermons are related to the theory it becomes much more readily tenable, for they provide sufficient evidence, in theme and thought, of a sustained concern to present the inner, timeless, spiritual meaning of the Genesis narrative. Further, to open up the discussion to include the prose involves the hearers of the sermons as well as the preacher. Du Bartas, translated by Sylvester, was much more popular in England than France, and reflection upon the theme of the Divine Weeks and Works was an established element of Protestant devotion, easily stirred by a preacher emphasizing the Creation theme.

Many readers of Du Bartas who would not be especially interested in new poetic and verbal forms were deeply satisfied by the endeavour of the Huguenot to link man's increasing knowledge of the world to the drama of the first seven days, and Donne's sermons demonstrate the excitement he himself experienced in returning repeatedly to this Biblical source of inspiration.

The place of the theme in the religious mind of the age may be seen in Sir Walter Raleigh's *The History of the World*, in five books, a work belonging to the age of Donne. It begins by 'Intreating of the Beginning and first Ages of the same, from the Creation unto Abraham'. The first chapter, 'Of the Creation, and Preservation of the World', affirms 'That the Invisible God is seen in his Creatures', and the opening sentence of the work is, 'God, Whom the wisest men acknowledge to be a Power uneffable, and Virtue infinite . . .' He discusses the meaning of 'In principio', 'heaven and earth',

how it is to be understood, that the spirit of God moved upon the waters; and that this is not to be searched curiously—

a passage follows to which Donne would have assented, for he too was much opposed to the exercise of 'curiosity'—

There would be no difference between God and man, if man's understanding could conceive the counsels and disposing of that eternal majesty; and therefore to be over-curious in searching how the all-powerful word of God wrought in the creation of the world, or his all-piercing and operative Spirit distinguishing, gave form to the matter of the universal, is a labour and search like unto his, who, not contented with a known and safe ford, will presume to pass over the greatest river in all parts, where he is ignorant of their depths: for so doth the one love his life, and the other his understanding. We behold the sun, and enjoy his light, as long as we look towards it, but tenderly, and circumspectly: we warm ourselves safely, while we stand near the fire; but if we seek to out-face the one, or enter into the other, we forthwith become blind or burnt.

He proceeds to consider fate, the influence of the stars, prescience, providence, predestination, fortune. In the second chapter, 'Of Man's estate in his first Creation, and of God's rest', there are numerous conventional references to Ambrose, Basil, Chrysostom, Augustine. He writes

Of the image of God, according to which man was first created. . . . Of the intellectual mind of man, in which there is much of the image of God; and that this image is much deformed by sin. . . . Of our base and frail bodies: and that the care thereof should yield to the immortal soul. . . . Of the spirit of life, which God breathed into man in his creation. . . . That man is (as it were) a little world: with a digression touching our mortality. . . . Of the free power, which man had in his first creation, to dispose of himself. . . . Of God's ceasing to create any more: and of the cause thereof, because the universal created was exceeding good.

In this way the history of the world began.

John Donne was one of a succession of commentators and preachers who returned expectantly to the Creation story for inspiration. His contribution is less specific and particular than some to be mentioned. His sermons cannot be presented as a course on this subject, and his references are allusive, occasional, brief, in relation to his total output. But his spiritual insight is notable, compared, for example, with Raleigh, and on this subject he is an instructed scribe, like unto a man that is an householder, bringing forth out of this treasure things new and old.

F. E. Robbins, in his book *The Hexaemeral Literature*, reviewed the tradition of commentary on the six days of creation as narrated in Genesis. The word 'hexaemeral' conflates the Greek 'ἕξ' (six)

and 'ἡμέρα' (day) (cf. 'ephemeral'). In the first chapter he considers the influence of Greek philosophy on the early commentaries on Genesis, notably Plato, with his doctrine of an 'idea' of the world preconceived in the divine mind and underlying the foundation of the material universe, and the Stoics, with their doctrine of the '*spermatikos logos*', a force in matter which developed it in the same way that seeds grow. This doctrine influenced Basil, who argued that the commands of God created the nature of things which retain these commands in their structure; and Gregory of Nyssa, who held that heaven, earth, ether, air, stars, fire, sea, animals, plants, were developed from beginnings, causes, powers set in the world from its creation; potentially all things existed at that moment; the world's development is not automatic, but the working within each created thing of its '*logos*', and the sequence of the six days is due to God in His wisdom so creating one thing in relation to another. He then turns in the second chapter to Philo Judæus and Jewish Hexaemeral writings— one element in non-canonical Hebrew writings was the farther study of the story of creation, retelling it with a view to stressing points not mentioned, or only briefly, in Genesis; Philo,[42] in his *De opificio mundi*, the first extant work in Greek on this subject, interpreted the Genesis story, stating that though God had no need of time, and could have created everything immediately, He made the world in six days because of the need for order in created things; and He made it so that His goodness should be shared. A study of early Christian Hexaemera in chapter 3, suggests that the Church took great interest in the subject, which was firmly established by the *Hexaemeron* of Basil the Great, Bishop of Cæsarea (370-379), who in it devoted himself exclusively to this subject for the first time, though probably there were earlier writings, now lost, on it (see chapter 4). Gregory of Nyssa and Ambrose are important names in this connection, subsequent to Basil (see chapter 5). In Augustine the consideration received further impetus, as he sought to interpret the six days, with the aid of allegory, as containing Christian significance; in him the great spiritual content of Genesis is affirmed and vindicated (see chapter 6). In the final (7th) chapter, the history of the tradition is brought forward to the Renaissance, the *De divisione naturæ* of

---

[42] See p. 37f, *supra*, for his suggested influence on 'Metempsychosis, The Progresse the of Soule'.

Johannes Scotus Erigena being of particular interest. 'The
Premiere semaine of Du Bartas, the first chapters of Sir Walter
Raleigh's *History of the World*, Tasso's *Le sette giornate del mondo
creato*, and the seventh book of Milton's *Paradise Lost* may be taken
as representative Hexaemera of this final period of the history
of the tradition.' The author concludes: 'Doubtless a thorough
examination of the philosophers, encyclopaedists, and historians
of the late Middle Ages, the Renaissance, and the post-Renais-
sance period would demonstrate that a surprisingly large number
made use of topics derived from the Hexaemera, and inherited
through many intermediate hands from Plato, Philo, Basil, and
Augustine. The recognition of the existence of this long line of
writings, whose subject-matter tended to arrange itself under a
limited number of topics common to all, is important for the
complete understanding of many literary works, not only Milton,
Raleigh, and Du Bartas, but also passages in many authors not
directly connected with the tradition.'[43] The Bibliography lists
twelve pages of authors and titles, but Donne is not mentioned.
This is not surprising; but it is suggested that he is one of the
writers to whom the last paragraph properly refers. He belongs
to the tradition of the hexaemeral literature, a tradition which is
established within the Bible itself, which, in passages like Job
xxxviiif, Proverbs iii.19, viii.22ff, and in 2 Esdras vi.38ff, Wisdom
of Solomon ix.9, 2 Maccabees vii.28 and Ecclesiasticus xxiv in
the Apocrypha, turns back to its own beginning. He refers to the
sermons of St Basil on the beginning of Genesis.[44] He refers
elsewhere to other contributors to the tradition, and especially,
as in his *Essayes in Divinity*, to Augustine, and in one sermon in
particular establishes himself firmly in it, with a wealth of allusion
to early writers. On Whitsunday 1629 he preached in St Paul's
from the text Genesis i.2, and stressed the significance of water in
Holy Scripture, maintaining that the text refers to God the Holy
Spirit, comparing the reference to Him after that made to the
Trinity in the previous verse to the Church's remembrance of St
Andrew after All Saints. In the text, he says, is the first reference
to a distinct Person of the Godhead; the previous verse, with its

[43] It is probable that Sylvester's translation of Du Bartas influenced Milton as a
youth, and in his choice of the theme and the epic conception of *Paradise Lost*. Sylvester, popular throughout the first half of the century, helped to create sympathy and
expectation toward the theme of the poem. See Bibliography, pp. 234-236, *infra*.
[44] PS, I. 260; V. 42.

plural 'Gods' (*Bara Elohim*) refers to the Trinity; and then Moses gives us his first intimation of the Holy Ghost. Man was not created when He moved upon the waters, and His activity was extended to man only in his re-creation in Christ and in baptism. Donne rejects the Jewish explanation that the text signifies a very strong wind, because the wind had not been created; nor will he allow that the reference is to the spirit of God but not God the Spirit. He considers, first, the work of the Spirit in creation, and then applies these thoughts to His work in man's baptism, in the same way as, in the *Essayes in Divinity*, he studied the historical deliverance from Egypt and then interpreted it as a picture of man's spiritual experience. God works upon unpromising material; the waters upon which the Spirit moved had no inherent creative power; in the first creation, the Spirit of God did not move upon nothing, which was before creation, but upon the waters—they had nothing in themselves to respond, nevertheless He had waters to move upon; so it is with us: our faculties have nothing in themselves to respond to the motions of the Spirit of God, nevertheless He works upon them; and just as creatures proceeded out of but not from the waters, so good actions proceed out of, but not from our faculties (Donne seems here deliberately to oppose the idea of *spermatikos logos*). A perceptive suggestion from St Basil is that the Spirit of God wrought upon the waters prophetically, because He intended to do so later, in man's regeneration (an activating thought, each day in its creation implying the days to follow, the six days being crowned by the Sabbath; the creation of time implying a purpose beyond, and a dominion over it). The sermon refers to Basil, Ambrose, Jerome, Tertullian, Cyprian, and, especially, to Augustine. In this sermon of 1629, in an earlier sermon preached at St Paul's in 1622, in a sermon on the Sunday after the conversion of St Paul, 1625, in the *Devotions*, 7, Expostulation and in the *Essayes in Divinity*, he quotes from Augustine's *Confessions*, Book XI, ch.3, in which, as Donne says, Augustine meditates upon the Word of God.[45] The passage in full, clearly a favourite recollection of Donne's, is as follows:

I would hear and understand, how, 'In the Beginning Thou madest the heaven and earth'. Moses wrote this, wrote and departed, passed hence from Thee to Thee; nor is he now before me. For if he were, I

[45] PS, IX. 94; IV. 215; VI. 218, *Essayes in Divinity*, pp. 15f.

would hold him and ask him, and beseech him by Thee to open these things unto me, and would lay the ears of my body to the sounds bursting out of his mouth. And should he speak Hebrew, in vain will it strike on my senses, nor would aught of it touch my mind; but if Latin, I should know what he said. But whence should I know, whether he spake truth? Yea, and if I knew this also, should I know it from him? Truly within me, within, in the chamber of my thoughts, Truth, neither Hebrew, nor Greek, nor Latin, nor barbarian, without organs of voice or tongue, or sound of syllables, would say 'It is truth', and I forthwith should say confidently to that man of Thine, 'thou sayest truly'. Whereas then I cannot enquire of him, Thee, Thee I beseech, O Truth, full of Whom he spake truth, Thee, my God, I beseech, forgive my sins; and Thou, who gavest him Thy servant to speak these things, give to me also to understand them.[46]

If Moses were here, Donne, no less than Augustine, would hold him fast until he had received an exposition of his words. And to Donne, as to Augustine, came the understanding that in meditation, in the chamber of one's thoughts, Truth speaks. And as Augustine prayed, he prayed, that the Author of the words would interpret them to him. A substantial part of his preaching is the answer to his supplication.[47]

This discussion of Donne and Du Bartas has disclosed a traditional, conventional element in Donne's preaching (though his treatment of it was far from ordinary). He was in full harmony with popular, Bible-based devotion, and the reality of his reconciliation to life may be measured by this fact. His success as a preacher was due in part to his sympathy with the religious convictions of his hearers, especially as these related to the beginning of the Scriptures. The effective preacher is rarely original; his power resides in his ability to make momentous what is already familiar, and Donne invested with memorable distinction the almost commonplace hexaemeral theme, improving upon the traditional exegesis in refreshing ways. Arnold Williams, in his book *The Common Expositor: An Account of the Commentaries on Genesis 1527-1633*, makes numerous references to Du Bartas, and to the writings of Donne, including 'Metempsychosis, The Progresse of the Soule', and *Essayes in Divinity*. Ample evidence is

---

[46] Translation by E. B. Pusey.
[47] See PS, IX. 92-108, and the notes on pp. 5-7; see also IV. 251; V. 61, 146, 173; VII. 70; VIII. 267f for further references to the text; he reflects that the first thing that produced any living sensible creature was water.

here given of the prominent place occupied by the Genesis theme in popular religion before, and during, Donne's life. Thirty-nine names of Catholic and Protestant authors of commentaries on Genesis from 1525 to 1633, are given, arguing a demand for such a considerable, varied and sustained supply; a number were contemporary with Donne, and the most important was Benedictus Pererius, a Spanish Jesuit of Valencia (c.1535-1610), whose commentary made conveniently accessible the views of the Church Fathers and medieval Doctors on the first book of Holy Scripture. Of many ideas and reflections in Donne which we find embedded in traditional commentary upon Genesis, the following six may be mentioned:

(a) Adam naming the creatures interpreted as a sign of man's dominion, and of his wisdom in choosing names appropriate to their natures;

(b) the plural name of God in the first verse (*bara elohim*; *creavit dii*) intimating the Trinity;

(c) human labour a necessity for positive and creative living, and not a regrettable consequence of sin;

(d) the six days of Creation divisible into (i) creation from nothing, (ii) works of distinction, and division, and localization with specific functions, (iii) the ornamentation of the created order—planets, stars, plants, animals, man;

(e) man essentially a social being;

(f) man, a social being, created through an act of fellowship and agreement.[48]

As we today, through the revival of the metaphysical poets, hear again the strong, confident Jacobean preachers, we shall find ourselves reflecting that there is no need to turn from the opening chapters of Holy Scripture when a literal interpretation is no longer credible. This is not all that men like Du Bartas and Donne believed. They were poets at heart (as the writer of the beginning of Genesis must have been) who, through these words, penetrated to what is ultimate and enduring. Donne was supreme as an interpreter because he was supreme as a poet; but he had many companions who prized the Creation story even as he did, and who, with him, returned, never disappointed, to its great simplicities, for corroboration of all that is important for belief.

[48] Pp. 81, 244, 110, 51f, 216, 68.

SEVEN

ANCHORS LAID IN THAMES

('Metempsychosis, The Progresse of the Soule', stanza VI)

JOHN DONNE, born in London, was a London preacher all his ministry, and most of the sermons which we possess were preached there. Paddington, Camberwell, and other places then just outside the City provided opportunity for him to practise the art of preaching, which he was soon called upon to exercise before important City congregations.

He began to preach comparatively late in life. In his Verse Letter to 'B.B.' he urges his friend to wean himself from Cambridge and enter upon his life's work—

> And begin soone, lest my griefe grieve thee too,
> Which is, that that which I should have begun
> In my youthes morning, now late must be done;
> And I as Giddy Travellers must doe,
> Which stray or sleepe all day, and having lost
> Light and strength, darke and tir'd must then ride post.[1]

His late start gave to his preaching a sense of urgency, and an intensity of zeal concentrated on the great, central themes of Christianity and life. Remorse, despair, bereavement, were realities of his own experience. His texts were varied, and not by any means confined to the classical statements of doctrine, but the substance of his preaching was never peripheral. He returned repeatedly to the great subjects—the incarnation, the relationship of body and soul, the unity of mankind in death, life's essential mystery and wonder—these and other massive themes were presented with majesty and power, and made so prominent that religious and political controversies were kept firmly in a subordinate place. His priorities were right.

One of the *Elegies* upon him stated:

> It was his Fate (I know't) to be envy'd
> As much by Clerkes, as lay men magnifi'd;

[1] Grierson, I. 212f.

And why? but 'cause he came late in the day,
And yet his Penny earn'd, and had as they[2].

The call came late to one who had stood idle all too long; but
there was advantage in it. The compression which gave quality
to his finest verse was required for his preaching too. The youthful
satirist had grasped long ago that the ascent of the hill on which
Truth stands would be a race against time, against the gathering
darkness—

Yet strive so, that before age, deaths twilight,
Thy Soule rest, for none can worke in that night[3].

More of his life lay behind than ahead, and he vividly
remembered his past sins and mistakes, through which, nevertheless, he had become familiar with the weakness and duplicity
of the human heart; as life advanced, he had discovered it to be
an insoluble mystery, and man's increasing knowledge a delusion;
marriage, the responsibilities of parenthood, sickness, bereavement, the disappointments of unfulfilled ambition, tempered his
rebellious nature and brought to the surface hidden virtues of
patience and forbearance as he became reconciled to God's
created order. A man of middle years is not likely to change his
fundamental position, and though Donne's sermons show development of thought as well as, certainly, improvement in its
expression, they mostly reiterate earlier themes, and his first
sermons are as important for study as the later ones. This would
not be the case with one who began in the early twenties, with
most of his life still before him, perhaps unmarried, un-
acquainted with illness or bereavement, his enthusiasm as yet
largely untested, still to discover how it will go with him in 'the
long day of this world'[4] when 'my moisture is turned into the
drought of summer'.[5]

The first of the sermons which have come down to us was
preached at Greenwich on 30th April 1615, and although Gosse
says that it 'has nothing in it of great importance'[6] it is worthy of
close study, for several characteristic features of later preaching

[2] Grierson, I. 387.   [3] Grierson, I. 157; see p. 67 *supra*.
[4] *Essayes in Divinity*, p. 19.
[5] Psalm xxxii.4—see PS IX, sermon 12.   [6] II. 8of.

may be found in it, and it is intentionally autobiographical. The text was from Isaiah lii.3, following the Authorized Version, recently published, 'Ye have sold yourselves for nought; and ye shall be redeemed without money'. He deliberately used the version which suggests a free, responsible act, instead of the Geneva Bible, 'Ye were sold for nought', but in the sermon he brought out the significance of 'therefore' in the Geneva version which continued, 'therefore shall ye be redeemed without money': a characteristically eclectic use of his material.

The text of this first dated sermon is in the past tense, and suitably so, for a man beginning to preach in the middle forties, unlike a youth, must look back. It may be regarded as his verdict upon himself, and the significance of the words of Isaiah for him is indicated by the fact that ten years later, preaching before King Charles at Whitehall on Isaiah l.1, which contains the words, 'for your iniquities have ye sold yourselves', he returned to the subject of this first sermon.[7]

The idea of a bargain, or exchange, was used by Donne in his poems 'Lovers infinitenesse', 'Loves Vsury', and 'Loves exchange',[8] and is developed in the sermon, which introduces legal considerations. The bargain, he argues, is illegal, and therefore void, for the devil has no rights over us; the bargain made by the sinner is a fraudulent conveyance, rightly cancelled, because in the exchange not even half the value (the legal minimum) has been given. The effect of this sinful act of prodigality is to reduce the sinner to the state of 'nothing'. In the opening stanza of 'Loves exchange' the two ideas of 'bargain' and 'nothing' are linked—

> *Love*, any devill else but you,
> Would for a given Soule give something too.
> At Court your fellowes every day,
> Give th'art of Riming, Huntsmanship, or Play,
> For them which were their owne before;
> Onely I have nothing which gave more,
> But am, alas, by being lowly, lower.

At the side of one of the most important paragraphs of the sermon the word '*Nihil*' is printed.

. . . as we have prodigally sold our selves, so we have inconsiderately

---

[7] See PS, VII. 79; this was one of the few sermons published during his lifetime.
[8] Grierson, I. 17f; 13f; 34f; see G. Williamson, *The Proper Wit of Poetry*, pp. 41f.

sold our selves for nothing; we have in our bargain, diseases, and we have poverty, and we have unsensibleness of our miseries; but diseases are but privations of health, and poverty but a privation of wealth, and unsensibleness but a privation of tenderness of Conscience; all are privations, and privations are nothing. If a man had got nothing by a bargain but repentance, he would think, and justly, he had got little: but if thou hadst repentance in this bargain, thy bargain were the better; if thou couldst come to think thy bargain bad, it were a good bargain; but the height of the misery is in this, that one of those nothings, for which we have sold our selves is a stupidity, and unsensibleness of our own wretchedness.[9]

Donne's sermons, especially in their emphasis on the Creation narrative of Genesis, are a sustained condemnation of nihilism, and the word '*Nihil*' is exposed to attack in this first sermon. The subject 'nothing' fascinated him. It is the motif of 'A nocturnall upon S. Lucies day', and references to it may be studied in many poems—e.g. 'Aire and Angels', 'A Valediction: of weeping', the last two stanzas of 'A Litanie'.[10] He alluded to it, spoke about it, and repeated himself upon it, in the sermons throughout his ministry, and they would not be misrepresented by the words 'From nothing to something'. He put the matter thus. The distance between nothing and something is infinitely greater than the distance between something and something else. The distance between 0 and 1 is infinitely greater than that between 1 and 2 or any other number.[11] The idea is to be found frequently in different forms. (It is familiar to every cricketer.) We may put it by saying that there is a bigger difference between a childless couple and parents with an only child than between the latter and parents with a large family; between not starting a task and making the first attempt than between this and continuing it. Donne had hold of something widely and deeply experienced in life: it may be true that it is not the beginning but the continuing of the same unto the end, until it be thoroughly finished, which yieldeth the true glory, but many a person finds the beginning of the task essentially more difficult than the continuing. Certainly Donne's life suggests that; once he became a preacher his difficulties were resolved *ambulando*, but he took a long, long time, to

9 PS, I. 158f.

10 Grierson I. 44f, 22, 38f, 347f. See also 'The Calme' lines 1f, 51-3, pp. 178-80; 'To the Countesse of Bedford' lines 7f, p. 195; and pp. 14-20, 48, 90, *supra*.

11 See PS, II. 247; III. 50; IV. 100f: to repair the world after the Flood was less wonderful than to create it from Nothing; see *Devotions*, 2, Expostulation.

come to a decision. His reiterated emphasis on this greater distance between nothing and one derived from his own experience. He introduces this thought in varying ways. In one sermon he observes that the wise men of the east by the lesser light found a greater—Jesus, but by darkness would have found nothing.[12] If you are on the ladder, your feet are off the ground, whatever the step you are on; a great fire grows from a spark; to touch His hem is sufficient—but the beginning of our regeneration is often the most difficult part of all.[13]

He drives a wedge between nothing and something; an absolute distinction must be made between them, whereas one thing can be compared with another. This establishes a distinction between God and man. Men may be compared with one another, but all mankind together must be contrasted with God. He expresses this through the image of balances. It would be easier for a grain of sand, a speck of dust, an atom in the air, to weigh down the whole world than for the world itself to counter-balance, 'counterpose' the Almighty; there is no creature so poor, childish, impotent, compared to others as man is compared to God; eternity is set over against time: the oldest and the youngest, the first Fiat at Adam's creation and the last note of the trumpets at the judgement have all more in relation to one another than to the eternal; clocks and sun-dials have more affinity with the sun, and the sun with them, than they have with eternity; what we regard as size is a comparative measurement and the greatest creations are insignificant set over against the Creator: ant and elephant, mustard seed and cedar, earth and the heavens together must be seen against God's creation out of nothing; the cloud and the sun, the beggar and the king, all are one, and their relative size and importance disappear when considered as creatures; Moses and Paul, great compared to others, together cannot be compared to Jesus. This idea of the balances, and the setting of all created things over against the Creator, is found in Psalm lxii.9, and this was one of the five psalms on which he meditated daily, and on which he preached a sermon, contending that men may be compared with one another, but all mankind together, when laid in the balance, is lighter than vanity over against God.[14]

Though pride expresses itself comparatively in human relations,

[12] III. 270.   [13] V. 342f.
[14] See III. 95; V. 79; VI. 331, 363; IV. 89f; III. 156; VI, sermon 15.

its essence is not that a person thinks himself better than another, but that he sets himself as an equal over against God, like the rebellious angels; the basis, therefore, of his religion is not the idea of Creation, of great importance though this is, but the absolute separation of the Creator from his work.[15]

'God found me nothing, and of that nothing made me';[16] this declaration is basic to the sermons. He distinguishes non-existence from the nothing that is the negative of a positive like sickness and death; sin is essentially negative, or it would be created by God, which is impossible.[17]

He refers frequently to the Nullani, less than minorities, less than minims, less than Ignorantes, in the Roman monastic orders, who, suitably, he observes, came to nothing.[18] Donne is consistently hostile to the monastic life, and strongly emphasizes the need to fulfil a calling; in his first sermon preached at St Dunstan's he declared that every man should follow a calling— 'God hath brought him from being *nothing*, by creating him, but he resolves himselfe into nothing againe, if he take no calling upon him'.[19]

Again, he condemns passing through the world as though one were not part of it; God created everything of nothing, to be something, but not to follow a calling is to be good for nothing. In a sermon preached at St Paul's on Midsummer day 1622 is a passage which is closely reproduced in a sermon preached at Whitehall in 1628. It is unusual for Donne to repeat himself so exactly and for so long; the inference is obvious, that it was a satisfying statement of something fundamental. He seeks to awaken the hearer, unconcerned that he has been created, to the truth that he has a function to fulfil, by reminding him that God spent six days' labour for the creation and provision of man, that He might have left this hearer to whom he addresses himself uncreated; or a stone; or a toad; or a heathen; or a Jew; or a Papist. The man who brings all this to nothing passes through the world like a lightning-flash: none knows its beginning or end, and though light it gives none and has no significance; or like the hand in the wash-basin, leaving no trace, save dirt, in the water. Adam was placed in the world to fill it, subdue it, rule

---

[15] On pride, see II. 288, 290, 294, 296.   [16] VII. 136.
[17] II. 99, 88; V. 80, VI. 238; see *Essayes in Divinity*, p. 69.
[18] I. 209; II. 298; IV. 119f; VI. 308.   [19] VI. 84f.

it; paradise was entrusted to him to dress and keep it. A comparison of the two passages shows not only almost identical wording, but the conviction strengthened with the passing of time; one would expect the earlier passage to be pruned, but it is amplified with the emphatic statement that God's way is positive, and that the world is one body, and the individual should be associated with it; underlying this is the distinction between nothing and something, however small, being infinitely greater than any distinction between created things. His emphatic, reiterated declaration of the unity of the race, a notable feature of his sermons and *Devotions*, springs from this basic contention.[20]

The creation of something out of nothing involved the abolition of nothing, and it is impossible to return to nothing—even the desire to do so is something, not nothing; therefore, argues Donne, the sinner cannot hope to escape judgement, by self-annihilation, and hell is not to be understood as negation. The declaration in 'The broken heart',

> Yet nothing can to nothing fall[21]

controls his views on death, the destiny of the body, and hell; and it is not surprising that he proclaimed intensely his belief in the body's resurrection. In his preaching, in addition to awakening men to the duty of positive living, he seeks, by means of this emphasis on nothing and something, to urge the impossibility of extinction and the certainty of survival to blessedness or punishment, which to him is separation from God. We have been created in God's image, and though that image burns in us in hell, it will never be burnt out of us. His constant endeavour is, by repeated emphasis upon the significance of Creation, to arouse an awareness of the tremendous import of these subjects. Words and arguments will never suffice. In passages of great power he tries, as he had done in the 'Nocturnall', to penetrate to the nothingness before existence, countering the insanity of man's nihilism with the poet's sense of wonder. In the course of an argument on God the Creator, creating out of nothing, and contrasting this with the creative acts of human beings, who have something to work

[20] IV. 148f and VIII. 177f. Some of the many references to the duty of undertaking a profession are: I. 208f, 222; II. 227, 246; III. 67, 329; IV. 109, 160; VI. 47, 100, 299, 355; VII. 104, 273, 282f; VIII. 198f; IX. 63, 102, 340; X. 216.
[21] Grierson, I. 49.

upon, he suddenly exclaims: 'my Creation is a holy wonder, and a mysterious amazement.'[22]

Under the discipline of his central conviction he does not flinch from the conclusion that the redemptive work of Christ is less wonderful than the Creation in the beginning, for it also takes its place, though a supreme place, in the events that follow upon the Creation. Before his ordination, in a letter to Viscount Rochester, he wrote:

It is easier for God to unite the principles and elements of our bodies, howsoever they be scattered, than it was at first to create them of nothing.[23]

All that follows upon Creation is less difficult than the first act itself; we have seen that he certainly would hold this view of individual enterprises—to begin is harder than to continue; and he applies this even to God Himself. This conclusion needs to be balanced with Donne's conviction that the Second Person of the blessed Trinity was as intimately involved in the work of creation as of redemption. To reinforce his contention that a proper understanding of Creation is the beginning of all sound teaching, Donne boldly asserts what to many hearers must have been very surprising, that our redemption was easier to God than our creation.[24]

Donne believed that this life and the next are inextricably connected, that one's choices, priorities, principles in this life affect the nature of life after death. The life to come is part of the something that has been created. Heaven is a multiplication, not a creation, beginning in this life—Christ can infinitely enrich it, as He multiplied the loaves, but He worked upon them, not upon nothing; the joy we take with us from this world He will multiply inexpressibly, but if we take none with us, there is nothing to multiply. A man going to a far country would first study the map, the manners and language of the people; so he that proceeds to the joys of heaven will have a foretaste and insight before he goes.[25]

John Donne held orthodox views on the great Christian themes. His distinction was to invest them with authority, and

[22] VIII. 283. See, for this paragraph, I. 160; II. 236, 247; IV. 85; V. 336; VI. 227, 363; VII. 368; IX. 64, 81f.
[23] Gosse, II. 23.   [24] See III. 96; I. 249; IV. 85, 183.
[25] III. 339f.

to present them as credible and of overwhelming importance. The sustained, repeated, habitual method of approach was to present the triune God as Creator, whose work of Creation from nothing is so wonderful that if this is believed of Him all else can be believed. By the help of this doctrine he presented life as purposeful, significant, responsible, and he called men to live creatively in the expectation that to him that hath shall be given, and the life to come will crown God's glorious work and vindicate it for ever.

There cannot be a greater unthankfulnesse to God then to desire to be *Nothing* at all, rather then to be that, that God would have thee to be; To desire to be out of the world, rather then to glorifie him, by thy patience in it.

To this statement, which summarizes the message so fittingly introduced to us in his first sermon, it may be permitted to add, in conclusion, the prayer which he offered before his 'Sermon of Commemoration of the lady Danvers' (Magdalen Herbert):

Suffer us not therefore, *O Lord*, so to undervalue our selves, nay, so to impoverish thee, as to give away those soules, thy soules, thy deare and precious soules, for nothing. . . .[26]

Specific references to the biblical account of Creation are as plentiful as allusions to the theme of nothing and something. First, we note his repeated emphasis upon the word for 'God', in Genesis i.1, *Elohim*. This, he observes, is a plural word, and on this foundation he erects a considerable superstructure. With only the occasional exception[27] he approves of what is plural, and suspects what is singular as odd and unusual.[28] In a sermon for All Saints' Day, on Revelation vii.2f, he underlines that the angel cried with a loud voice, '. . . till we have sealed . . .', the singular speaking in the plural, through the Church, 'which is no singular person'. In another he observes that often, in the Scriptures, a man does evil, walking in the way of his father, not 'fathers'—God's blessings were bestowed on their fathers, who were brought out of Egypt, and it is a blessed thing to sleep at last with one's fathers—

[26] II. 53; VIII. 61.   [27] E.g. III. 228.   [28] E.g. IX. 75, 87.

Good ways, and good ends are in the *plurall*, and have many examples; else they are not good; but sins are in the *singular*. . . .

One should do nothing for which there is not an example, for there is nothing worse in religion than singularity, which is the essence of sectarianism; in the beginning Christ provided against singularity by calling two brethren, even as in the beginning 'God created man in his own image, in the image of God created he him; male and female created he them' (Genesis i.27)—

God loves not singularity; The very name of Church implies company; It is *Concio, Congregatio, Cœtus*; It is a Congregation, a Meeting, an assembly. . . .

The Holy Ghost Himself is a dove, and that implies couples, pairs, not a solitary, but a sociable creature. A sermon preached at a christening begins with the declaration that God loves unity but not singularity; ever alone, He is never singular, for He is Three Persons. His first sermon preached at St Dunstan's, in which he sets forth his idea of the parish priest, opens with the words:

From the beginning God intimated a detestation, a dislike of *singularity*; of beeing *Alone*. The first time that God himselfe is named in the Bible, in the first verse of *Genesis*, hee is named *Plurally, Creavit Dii, Gods*, Gods in the plurall, Created Heaven and Earth. God, which is but *one*, would not appeare, nor bee presented so *alone*, but that hee would also manifest more persons. As the *Creator* was not *Singular*, so neither were the *creatures*; First, he created *heaven and earth*; both together; which were to be the generall parents, and out of which were to bee produced all other creatures; and then, he made all those other creatures plurally too; *Male, and Female created hee them*; And when he came to make *him*, for whose sake (next to his own glory) he made the whole world, *Adam*, he left not *Adam alone*, but joyned an *Eve* to him; Now, when they were *maried*, we know, but wee know not when they were *divorced*; we heare when *Eve* was made, but not when shee *dyed*; The husbands death is recorded at last, the wives is not at all. So much detestation hath God himselfe, and so little memory would hee have kept of any singularity, of being alone. . . .[29]

Among many fine sermon passages two stand out as memorable:

. . . the *sociablenesse*, the *communicablenesse* of God; He loves holy meetings, he loves the *communion of Saints*, the *houshold of the faithfull: Deliciæ*

[29] See Gosse, II. 202-4 on this sermon.

ejus, says *Solomon*, *his delight is to be with the Sons of men*, and that the Sons of men should be with him: Religion is not a *melancholy*; the spirit of God is not a *dampe*; the Church is not a *grave*: it is a *fold*, it is an *Arke*, it is a *net*, it is a *city*, it is a *kingdome*, not onely a house, but a house that hath *many mansions* in it: still it is a *plurall* thing, consisting of *many*: and very good *grammarians* amongst the *Hebrews*, have thought, and said, that that *name*, by which God notifies himself to the world, in the very beginning of *Genesis*, which is *Elohim*, as it is a *plurall word* there, so it hath no *singular*: they say we cannot name God, but *plurally*: so sociable, so communicable, so extensive, so derivative of himself, is God, and so manifold are the beames, and the emanations that flow out from him.

The Key of *David* openeth and no man shutteth; the Spirit of Comfort shineth upon us, and would not be blown out. Monasterie, and Ermitage, and Anchorate, and such words of singularitie are not *Synonyma* with those plurall words *Concio*, *Cœtus*, *Ecclesia*, *Synagoga & Congregatio*, in which words God delivereth himselfe to us. A Church is a company, Religion is Religation, a binding of men together in one manner of Worship; and Worship is an exteriour service; and that exteriour service is the *Venite exultemus*, to come and rejoyce in the presence of God.

The infinite distance of nothing from something, and the relation of all the created order, including judgement and the life to come, is the basis of his thinking; under the influence of the plural *Elohim* he urges the significance of the relationship of all created things to one another; instead of the comparison of things, by which such a useless category as size is established, and by which valueless distinctions of class and birth flourish among men, he asserts the interrelationship of all things, and his reiterated emphases, on the social nature of the Church, and the solidarity of the human race, find their logical place in the development of his thought. 'In the beginning, *Elohim* . . .': as he himself said, it is a garden worthy of our walking in it.[30]

As poet, letter-writer, controversialist, preacher, Donne was well

[30] X. 44, 49 (cf. V. 141f); II. 102f; IX. 278; III. 87f (cf. II. 280, 297, 299; VIII. 227; X. 84 on sects); II. 270, 279; IV. 349 (cf. V. 63f); V. 113; VI. 81f, 152; X. 219; and again VI. 152; and see also I. 235; VI. 107; VII. 66 on the meaning of Elohim; III. 143; VI. 141f on this subject in relation to the Trinity; also VIII. 155; IX. 75, 314; see *Devotions*, 5, Meditation, 7, Expostulation, and note that occasionally he addresses God in the plural 'you', 21, 23, Expostulations.

practised in the use of words, and aware of their power. Fair speaking, he said, though not doing, prepares an acceptation before, and puts a value after, upon the best actions. Speech is the glue, the cement of conversation and religion, and God not only made all things good, He blessed His deed with words, and this is part of the religious significance of the seventh day. The power of God was shown in speech—He spoke, and it was done, His speech was imperative, and His saying that He would do it could not be separated from accomplishing it; man's words and deeds can be disconnected, but not His. Donne, under the discipline of his source, regards human speech religiously and speaks frequently against the sin of blasphemy, and one recalls

> The grim eight-foot-high iron-bound serving-man,
> That oft names God in oathes, and onely than.

Speech is a divine attribute, of the essence of the Triune God, whose creative work involved Him in speaking, though there were no creatures to hear, because He is a sociable Being, whose deeds express His speech within the relationship of the blessed Trinity. The three Persons are associated together in the declaration of the Word, and man, endowed with the gift of speech, should express in all his words his relationship with God, for, even as God made us with His word, with our words we make up the character, humanly speaking, of the mystical body of Christ, by our prayers and worship, and words of consecration in the Sacrament, and preaching. The Christian has a duty to speak of God; inward consideration, meditation, speculation, contemplation, have their function, but must not be substitutes for speech. God Himself did more than conceive in Himself from all eternity certain ideas, which by themselves could not produce any created thing; it was when He spoke that all things were made. God will listen most willingly to us when men are listening to our words. The whole first week of Creation was spent by God in speaking for the good, and the place of speech in the work of Creation establishes its importance in the Church—hearing His word preached, reading His Scriptures, believing the words of His Son. Under the compulsion of Genesis Donne gives priority to preaching: this is the contribution he must make, and the intensity of his zeal to proclaim Christ derived from the profound influence upon him of the familiar, but to him ever remarkable words with which the Scriptures begin.[31]

His mind played often upon the significance of the sequence of the six days, in which he traced an unfolding purpose, and a causal relationship. God made the Firmament, Heaven, after the division of the waters, and when we have separated our tears, natural from spiritual, worldly from heavenly, a Firmament is opened to us. Man is the emblem of God's perseverance; in the Creation, if God had given up His work on the third or fifth day, where would man have been?

The beginning of the prayer ending section 19 of the *Devotions*, when his grievous illness had taken a turn for the better, and 'at last the physicians, after a long and stormy voyage, see land . . .', is an example of the theme in his devotional life—

O Eternall and most gracious *God*, who though thou passedst over infinite millions of generations, before thou camest to a *Creation* of this *world*, yet when thou beganst, didst never intermit that *worke*, but continuedst *day* to *day*, till thou hadst perfited all the *worke*, and deposed it in the hands and rest of a *Sabbath*, though thou have beene pleased to *glorifie* thy selfe in a long exercise of my *patience*, with an *expectation* of thy *declaration* of thy selfe in this my *sicknesse*, yet since thou hast now of thy goodnesse afforded that, which affords us some hope, if that bee still *the way* of thy *glory*, proceed in *that way*, and perfit *that worke*, and establish me in a *Sabbath*, and *rest* in *thee*, by this thy *seale* of *bodily restitution*.

In two of his earlier sermons the sequence is explored at length. He preached two connected sermons on 19th April 1618 on 1 Timothy i.15, to which might be given the title, 'He hath been in a pilgrimage towards thee long', from the second sermon. In the whole range of the sermons there is none more satisfying, more impressive than these two, to be regarded as one sermon, and in the course of the first he studies closely the events of the first week in relation to one another. This was much extended a year later in one of his most famous sermons, 'A Sermon of Valediction at my going into Germany, at Lincolns-Inne, April 18 1619'. Encouraged by the word 'dayes' in the text (Ecclesiastes xii.1), he reflects upon the succession of days.

[31] VIII. 338, 342 (cf. III. 94); IX. 304; on blasphemy: I. 262, 308; II. 315; V. 82; Grierson, I. 85; VIII. 52 (cf. IX. 282; II. 228); III. 259f; VIII. 119f; II. 233; VII. 368; IV. 101; VI. 216.

The first day of Creation brought light into the world, and so all creatures would be visible—a purpose was thus written into the first day, and light, beyond itself. Our Christian life begins with the Light of the world, in whom all things are seen in their true nature; God made light first, that His other works might appear, and that He, as an example to us, might do all His other works in the light, separating them from darkness. The significance of the second day is the acceptance of limits to human knowledge and understanding, for God separated the waters above from those below the firmament. On the third day, following on this, the assembling of the waters together took place, signifying the establishment in the Church of a body of doctrine sufficient for this present life, in preparation for the life to come—here in this world are produced all herbs and fruits necessary for us, seminal doctrines to last until the end of time. The fourth day brought the creation of sun and moon, reminding the Christian that adversity, no less than prosperity, is the scene of his service of God. The fifth day's work, the creation of creeping and flying things, reminds man of the need to be humble and to flee from worldly enticements, at the same time avoiding self-despising. The sixth day and the Sabbath are given a more significant place in other sermons, which will be noted. Not only did each day carry its own message, each day was linked to the other days in growth and development, and what was created had meaning for what was yet to come; the week creates a sense of purpose, part of the creation itself, and a gathering excitement as events move forward to the making of man; no day was complete in itself, each looked to the morrow to expound and interpret its yesterday; God had made light in vain if He had made no creatures to see, and to be seen by, that light, and He had made them to no purpose without man to use and enjoy them. Man may be called every creature, for all created things have meaning in relation to him. The great, purposive work was begun, continued, ended, and the Sabbath confirms and concludes the creative task; that which God intended to do, He did, perfectly.[32]

John Donne's first sermon at St Paul's, on Christmas Day, 1621,

[32] IV. 340; VI. 93; I, sermons 8, 9, and esp. pp. 289-91, II, sermon 11 and esp. pp. 240-243 (cf. IV. 210); VII. 144f; V. 253; see also, on God's patience, II. 233; IV. 76, 295.

on John i.8, was a magnificent utterance on the theme of Light.[33]
We have no warmth in ourselves, he declared; but Christ came
in the winter; we have no light in ourselves, but He, the Light,
came in the night. And as John, the author of the text, was
inspired by Genesis in his first chapter, so Donne was inspired.[34]
He often stressed the significance for him that darkness preceded
light, and that in Genesis evening and morning make up the day
(see Genesis i.5, 8, 13, 19, 23, 31). The ecclesiastical usage of
including the previous eve in the twenty-four hours of a day,
like turning to the East, was a liturgical recollection of the biblical
story of Creation, and the frequency of reference to the evening
and the morning of the first days, in the sermons, shows the
importance which Donne attached to this.[35] He also made much
of the creation of the sun, moon and stars on the fourth day, not
the first, as a declaration of God's will that there should be light,
which they fulfil: but they have no inherent power of illumination,
no sovereignty, and were made to take their place in the sequence
of ordered events—God made the earth and its fruits before He
made the sun, whose task was to work upon the earth and its
fruits, giving heat as well as light, but He made the sun before
He made paradise, so that the sun might shine upon the two trees
of life and knowledge—and the place of the sun is presented as an
analogy of the place of the Son in man's salvation: reason is the
original light, faith the greater light which includes reason
within itself. In the same way Scripture teaching supersedes
natural knowledge.[36] In his first St Paul's sermon Light was
presented as a striking emblem of spiritual truth; the sun is the
most evident thing to be seen, yet the hardest to look upon—
nothing clearer, nothing darker; nothing nearer, nothing more
remote; nothing easier, nothing harder; nothing more apprehensible, or more incomprehensible.[37] This extraordinarily impressive sermon owes much to the inspiration of Genesis. Not less
must be said of the longest of all his utterances. On Easter
Monday morning, 1622, his first Easter as Dean, he preached his
longest recorded sermon, lasting well over two hours, in the open

[33] For confirmation of this, see the opening sentence, PS, IV. 145.
[34] III. 374, 348.
[35] See I. 217; II. 354; III. 206, 353; X. 183; and Grierson, I. 177.
[36] III. 362; see V. 248; IV. 47; V. 362, 367; VIII. 232, X. 220 on the creation of
light, and of the sun.
[37] III. 356.

air at Spital Cross by the Hospital of St Mary, in the Churchyard of St Mary's-without-Bishopgate. Despite his undertaking not to extend himself to an unnecessary length, he spoke amply and magnificently, until his voice began to fail, on Light.

This Easter Monday occasion was notable. Special accommodation was provided for the Lord Mayor, Aldermen and Sheriffs and other distinguished persons who attended. The text, 2 Corinthians iv.6, refers immediately to Genesis i.3, and the sermon begins with a contrasting reference to Genesis i.1 and John i.1, the first part of the text referring to the former, and the second part to the latter. But it is easy to link creation and redemption, for Jesus is the light of both. The purpose of light is to illumine—God commanded light out of darkness, that man might see the creature; light, in the Scriptures, is never used in an ill sense—Christ is the light of the world, and no ill thing is ever called light; there was light from light before, very God of very God, an eternal Son of an eternal Father; but light out of darkness is like music out of silence. The Creation story exalts man as the crown and consummation of God's work, and the text links man's creation and re-creation; the gifts of light and of spiritual illumination are both supremely for man, in whom all creatures are included; man is not a microcosm, he is greater than the world, possessing the light, greater than natural light, the light of reason, of the Law, the Prophets and the Gospel, and this is an all-sufficient light, needing no supplementation and incapable of improvement, for man can add nothing to light to improve it (and the light shining in England needs no 'improvement' from Rome!). The reference in the text to the heart prompts a quotation from St Ambrose and this in turn awakens in Donne the most memorable single reflection of the many that he made on the Creation story—

Fecit Deus Cœlum & Terram, Non lego quod requieverit, says that Father; God made heaven and earth, but I do not read that he rested, when he had done that: *Fecit Solem & Lunam*, (as he pursues that Meditation;) He made the Sun and Moon, and all the host of heaven, but yet he rested not: *Fecit hominem, & Requievit*; When God had made man, then he rested: for, when God had made man, he had made his bed, the heart of man, to rest in. God asks nothing of man, but his heart; and nothing, but man, can give the heart to God.[38]

[38] IV. 108.

L

Light has a purpose beyond itself, to illuminate, and God is glorified when we see His good works, His creatures, and glorify Him; in His creation of light as His first work God wrote a purpose to be fulfilled, for God would have made light to no purpose, if He had not made creatures to show by that light. So His spiritual illumination serves a purpose beyond itself, and our lives must be lit up for all the world to see, and the world should glorify God when it sees our lives; the purpose of light is to establish what it reveals; and as God commanded light for the manifestation of His creatures, so He has shined in our hearts that our actions might appear by that light. And just as light was created by the Word, so our illumination is through preaching. Light involves separation from darkness, it takes from darkness its totality; before light was created darkness was complete, but it has never since been total, and when the light of the Gospel illuminates a man, he never returns to total darkness.

Light is one of the great emblems of his sermons. To him, Light was God's signature by which He set His hand to the creation; His eldest child, the first born of His creatures, heir to the world as the first born and in fact possessing it, yet in so far as it is true to itself, diffusive, communicative, self-giving.[39]

The Latin phrase *Faciamus hominem*, or, simply, *Faciamus*, the Vulgate version in Genesis i.26 of 'Let us make man', found repeatedly in Donne's sermons, was familiar to seventeenth-century listeners. Bishop Andrewes, in his 'Sermon on the Gunpowder Plot, November 5, 1606,' declared that God made 'with *Faciamus*, with more ado, greater forecast and framing, as man, that masterpiece of His works'. Bishop Hall, whose commendatory verses were attached to *An Anatomie of the World* and *Of the Progresse of the Soule*, expounded the significance of the word when he declared:

All thy creation hath not more wonder in it, than one of us: other creatures thou madst by a simple command; man, not without a divine consultation: others at once; man thou didst first form, then inspire: others in several shapes like to none but themselves; man, after thine own image: others with qualities fit for service; man, for domination. Man had his name from thee; they had their names from man.[40]

[39] IV. 103; II. 294; VIII. 240; VII. 396; see E. Hardy, *John Donne: a spirit in conflict*, pp. 151f.

[40] Bishop Andrewes, *Sermons* IV. 207; Bishop Hall, 'Contemplation II' (*Works*, ed. D. A. Talboys, I. 9), quoted by Arnold Williams, *The Common Expositor*, p. 68.

Faciamus hominem was one of the Latin words and phrases of traditional religion, like *Pater noster, Ave, In principio,* by which a preacher could allude to the whole range of a prayer or a doctrine, and assume in his hearers an understanding of his meaning. Donne preached in an age which showed its spiritual intelligence by the widespread reading of Du Bartas and commentaries on Genesis; he preached to people who knew themselves to be involved in the drama of the world's Creation and who could be called to think about it by an allusive *Faciamus.* A study of the principal passages of the sermons in which the word occurs reveals both his conventional and his original use of a familiar phrase.

1. PS, I, sermon 8, pp. 289-291, (1618): He discerns three stages in Creation: (1) creation of matter without speaking (*sine verbo*) in Genesis i.1—matter without form, heaven without light; (2) creation of lesser creatures by a mandatory word (*in verbo*) in verses 3-25; (3) creation of man by a conference, a counsel, a consultation (*in sermone*); and here, for the first time occurs the phrase '*faciamus hominem*', by which he asserts that man was made, not by a simple decree, but after a consultation resulting in an agreement. Similarly, in the regeneration of mankind, God comes to man without speech in the created order, in the words of Holy Scripture, and in the incarnation, which is another *faciamus hominem.*

2. II, sermon 2, pp. 72f, (1618): In the opening paragraph he says that, as the Trinity is implied in the plural *faciamus,* so also man's plural nature, the divine image, is implied—one soul, for God is one, but understanding, will and memory are three elements of its nature, for God, in whose image man is made, is three Persons.

3. II, sermon 11, p. 249, (1619): In the moving conclusion to the 'Sermon of Valediction', in which he says farewell to his friends at Lincoln's Inn, speaking of the eternal Kingdom, he says, almost at the end: 'We shall agree as fully and perfectly in our *Allelujah,* and *gloria in excelsis,* as God the Father, Son, and Holy Ghost agreed in the *faciamus hominem* at first. . . .' Here the words are given almost a liturgical use; the brief allusion presupposes in his hearers an understanding of their religious meaning, and the words *faciamus hominem* are made to appear as familiar as *sursum corda* to us. The peroration is emotional and deeply stirring, and the importance to Donne of these two Latin words is revealed by their use in this prose valediction which shares the greatness of his valedictory poems.

4. *III*, *sermon 12, p. 265, (1621)*: A brief reference.

5. *IV*, *sermon 7, p. 185, (1622)* (published): In the first creation from nothing there was a concurrence, a co-operation of persons, a *Faciamus*.

6. *IV*, *sermon 15, p. 367, (1623)* (published): In the sermon preached at the dedication of the new Chapel at Lincoln's Inn, he says that at first, God the Trinity said *Faciamus*, alone, apart from man, but His 'let us', Donne implies, was destined to over-flow to include man, in the Church.

7. *V*, *sermon 7, p. 157*: In this christening sermon, he quotes the Latin *Faciamus hominem ad Imaginem nostrûm* and says that in the first creation, when God seems to have held a consultation about the creation of man, man put on all God; in the redemption God put on all man, all mankind, every man.

8. V, sermon 14, p. 278f:

when God bestowed upon man, his first and greatest benefit, his making, it is expressed so, *Faciamus hominem*, *Let us*, All us, *make man*; God seems to summon himselfe, to assemble himselfe, to muster himselfe, all himselfe, all the persons of the Trinity, to doe what he could in the favour of man.

Here, as in the previous example, the words excite other thoughts, and he turns to Genesis xi.7, where, in contrast, God altogether acts against the Tower of Babel—'*Venite*, *Let us*, All us come together, And *Descendamus*, & *confundamus*, *Let us*, all us, *goe down, and confound their language*.' It was not Donne's habit simply to quote Scripture; its effect upon him was dynamic, causing him sometimes to add to or alter the wording to bring out some new idea.[41] Now he takes the words *faciamus hominem* and applies them to man's attitude to his fellows, and puts God's words at the Creation into man's mouth (just as we take these words of Holy Scripture and speak of man making God in his own image):

. . . when we see others in distresse, whether nationall, or personall calamities, whether Princes be dispossest of their naturall patrimony,

[41] E.g.

. . . He which said, *Plough*
And looke not back, to looke up doth allow. (Grierson, I. 197.)

and inheritance, or private persons afflicted with sicknesse, or penury, or banishment, let us goe Gods way, all the way; First, *Faciamus hominem ad imaginem nostram*, Let us make that Man according unto our image, let us consider our selves in him, and make our case his, and remember how lately he was as well as we, and how soone we may be as ill as he, and then *Descendamus & confundamus*, Let us, us, with all the power we have, remove or slacken those calamities that lie upon them.

In the next paragraph he calls men to prayer, to answer God's *Faciamus* with man's *Dicamus*, God's *Descendamus* with man's *Ascendamus*—once again the words have almost a liturgical, and here an antiphonal, use. This passage takes us far from the original meaning of the words, and illustrates the poetic temperament of the preacher at work upon his principal source. His sense of the unity of the race and the solidarity of mankind is traced here to its origin in Genesis.

9. *V, sermon 17, p. 362:* A passage which shows Donne's devotional use of the first chapter of Genesis—

that which God did by way of Commandement, in the first Creation, doe thou by way of prayer, in this thy second Creation; First he said, *Fiat lux, Let there be light*: Pray thou, that he would enlighten thy darknesse. God was satisfied with that light for three daies, and then he said, *Fiant luminaria, Let there be great lights*; Blesse God for his present light, but yet pray that hee will inlarge that light which he hath given thee; And turne all those his Commandments into prayers, till thou come to his *Faciamus hominem, Let us make man according to our own Image*; Pray that he will restore his Image in thee, and conforme thee to him, who is *the Image of the invisible God*, our Lord and Saviour Christ Jesus.

10. *VI, sermon 7, p. 154, (1624:)*

God would not be without man, nor he would not come single, not alone to the making of man; but it is *Faciamus hominem, Let us, us, make man*; God, in his whole counsail, in his whole Colledge, in his whole society, in the whole Trinity, makes man, in whom the whole nature of all the world should meet.

11. *VI, sermon 13, p. 266 (Easter Day, 1625):* He asserts that, in *Faciamus hominem* the whole Trinity consulted even to make the lower part of man, his body—Let us, all us: this is his emphatic insistence upon the activity of the whole Godhead.

12. VI, sermon 14 (1625): This has been discussed on page 122 *supra.*

13. VI, sermon 15, p. 296 (1625) (the first Prebend sermon)—

Of what creature did God ever say, *Faciamus,* Let us, us make it, All, all, the Persons together, and to imploy, and exercise, not onely Power, but Counsaile in the making of that Creature?

All God's work, he says, on the other days was a laying-in of materials to make man, made in the image of Father, Son, Spirit; see the whole page.

14. VII, sermon 1, p. 61 (1626) (the second Prebend sermon)*:* Another passage stressing the concurrence of the whole Trinity, and man created according to an Idea.

15. VIII, sermon 1, p. 55 (Trinity Sunday, 1627): Another reference, emphasizing the significance of the plural.

16. VIII, sermon 10, p. 241 (1628): From the sermon considered on pp. 207-211 *infra*; on the earnestness of God, as though He thought it nothing to have worked a whole week, who comes to His *faciamus hominem*, '*Now* let us make man', as to the climax of His work.

17. X, sermon 4, p. 108: Another reference to the whole Trinity, 'us'. On page 134 the Latin is not used, but there is a reference to 'Let us make man', the word that stands between man and non-existence.

18. In *II, sermon 17 (p. 344) faciamus* and *faciam* are contrasted (see p. 164 *infra*); in *IX, sermon 1, pp. 48* (English only), *49, 70* are further references; see pp. 164-166 *infra*; also *Devotions*, 9, Expostulation and Prayer, repeatedly stressing the divine consultation before man's creation, and the prayer, 'Yet take me again, into your *Consultation, O blessed* and *glorious Trinitie*'; 20, Meditation, on counsel, involving action, or it is illusion.

God did much before creating man, yet all was for him; the creation of light was good, He was glad because of the sea, the earth, the sun, the moon, the stars; but when all was completed with the creation of man, all was very good.[42]

Reference to verse 28 of the first chapter of Genesis is also frequent, and the words *Subjicite & dominamini* ('subdue and rule

[42] See V. 362 (cf. IV. 148); VI. 153f.

all Creatures'—see Genesis i.28, in the Vulgate) occur frequently as an allusive summary; he expects his hearers to understand, without more detailed exposition, that these Latin words establish authoritatively man's dominion in the world. He must be on intimate terms with his subject, and with his audience about it, to be able to abbreviate his reference to an important element of the doctrine of man by simply saying 'the *Subjicite*, and *Dominamini*', to which he refers as 'that Donation'.[43]

Three consequences of this command are noted:

(1) *Elohim*, the name of God in the Creation, was a name of Power, in the plural, all Power; we read that God was angry, sorry, weary, but not that He was ever afraid. Nor should man be. This command would have been impossible if man were afraid of that which he must subdue and govern. In his innocence Adam heard the roaring of lions, created before himself, but he was not afraid—until his sin, when in fear he hid from God (Genesis iii.10).

(2) Obedience to this command involved man in labour. He must till, subdue and rule the earth; he must dress, and keep paradise; he must keep the world in reparation.

(3) Obedience would mean also avoiding a creaturely love. Rule and government are impossible if the ruler is indistinguishable from the governed. Sin, as Augustine said, is a turning of man to the creature, and all inordinate love is an abandonment of the dignity with which man was invested when he shared the Creator's nature of ruling; everything, save God Himself, should be inferior to man; the sin of idolatry is man's abasement before that which should be obedient to him.

Of particular interest is one of the christening sermons, which begins with the statement that God's Being is one of relationship, Three Persons, to be distinguished, but not separated, for the Father involves the Son and the Son the Father, and the Spirit the Father and the Son. This relationship, without which the idea of counsel, consent, agreement, could not be held, was expressed first in the relation of ruler and subject; later in the relation of husband and wife, and parents and children. A christening was a suitable occasion to stress the importance of

---

[43] IX. 378; II. 82; and see II. 291; VI. 272, 296; VII. 418: in giving this command God allowed man to share in His own nature as Creator; VIII. 274, contrasting Genesis i. 28, a positive commandment with ii. 17, which is negative.

relationship—of parents to child and child to parents, of children to God. The reference to ruler and subject is followed by the words, '*Subjicite & dominamini*', and the insistence that they involve a special and delicate responsibility; they do not invest master, husband or father with such supremacy that they may disregard the other part which is coupled to them and without which 'master', 'husband', 'father' have no meaning. They depend upon one another. Man's nature is, naturally, impregnated with this divine relationship of Persons; and right relations, agreement, consent, are as natural, proper, attainable, for man as for God; and even as all truth is in God, in whom are relationships, our apprehension of truth involves for us right relationships. Man came late in the week in the sequence of God's creative acts. If he had been created first, all that was created subsequently might well have seemed to him, with such a command, merely subordinate and inferior. But other creatures, of whom he is appointed overlord, were created before him, with their own inherent rights and status.

Donne, a royal Chaplain, preached many sermons at Court, and alluded occasionally to the monarchy. These were days when the divine right of kings and the duty of passive obedience to them was seriously urged, and James himself believed that Holy Scripture associated kingship and divinity and protected him from rebellion by subjects and the obligation to give an account of himself to them. In the sermon preached by Donne at Paul's Cross in 1617, when James was on his way to Scotland, on the anniversary of his accession to the English throne, a very important occasion with a great many notable people present, he chose for his text Proverbs xxii.11, 'he that loveth pureness of heart, for the grace of his lips, the king shall be his friend', and laid much stress on this idea of relationship, declaring:

King and subjects are Relatives, and cannot be considered in execution of their duties, but together. The greatest Mystery in Earth, or Heaven, which is *the Trinity*, is conveyed to our understanding, no other way then so, as they have reference to one another *by Relation*. . . . As in Divinity, so in Humanity too, *Relations* constitute one another, King and subject come at once and together into consideration. Neither is it so pertinent a consideration, which of them was made for others sake, as that they were both made for Gods sake, and equally bound to advance his glory.

Donne was troubled by the contemporary loss of a sense of relationship. His poems have numerous positive references to the subject, in words like 'inter-assured', 'interinanimate', 'enter-graft', and in the opening lines of 'The Dissolution':

> Shee'is dead; And all which die
> To their first Elements resolve;
> And wee were mutuall Elements to us,
> And made of one another.
> My body then doth hers involve. . . .

The modern Church is speaking of its 'involvement', and is borrowing from Donne a word employed by him not only in his verse but in the *Devotions* in a passage which has penetrated the modern mind, and in which, beginning significantly with Baptism, he asserts the fact of relationship—

17. Nunc lento sonitu dicunt, Morieris.

> Now, this Bell tolling softly for another, saies to me,
> Thou must die.

17. Meditation.

Perchance hee for whom this *Bell* tolls, may be so ill, as that he knowes not it tolls for him; And perchance I may thinke my selfe so much better than I am, as that they who are about mee, and see my state, may have caused it to toll for mee, and I know not that. The *Church* is *Catholike, universall,* so are all her *Actions; All* that she does, belongs to *all.* When she *baptizes a child,* that action concernes mee; for that child is thereby connected to that *Head* which is my *Head* too, and engraffed into that *body,* whereof I am a *member.* And when she *buries a Man,* that action concernes me: all *mankinde* is of one *Author,* and is one *volume;* when one Man dies, one *Chapter* is not *torne* out of the *booke,* but *translated* into a better *language;* and every *Chapter* must be so *translated; God* emploies several *translators;* some peeces are translated by *age,* some by *sicknesse,* some by *warre,* some by *justice;* but *Gods* hand is in every *translation;* and his hand shall binde up all our scattered leaves againe, for that *Librarie* where every *booke* shall lie open to one another: As therefore the *Bell* that rings to a *Sermon,* calls not upon the Preacher onely, but upon the *Congregation* to come; so this *Bell* calls us all: but how much more mee, who am brought so neere the *doore* by this *sicknesse.* There was a *contention* as farre as a *suite,* (in which both *pietie* and *dignitie, religion,* and *estimation,* were mingled) which of the religious *Orders* should ring to *praiers* first in the *Morning;* and it was *determined,* that *they should ring first that rose earliest.* If we understand aright the *dignitie* of this *Bell* that tolls for our *evening prayer*, wee would bee glad to make it ours, by rising early, in that *application*, that it might bee ours, as wel as his, whose indeed it is. The *Bell* doth toll for him that *thinkes* it doth; and though it *intermit* againe, yet from that *minute*, that that occasion wrought upon him, hee is united to *God*. Who casts not up his *Eie* to the *Sunne* when it rises? but who takes off his *Eie* from a *Comet* when that breakes out? Who bends not his *eare* to any *bell*, which upon any occasion rings? but who can remove it from that *bell*, which is passing a *peece of himselfe* out of this *world*? No man is an *Iland*, intire of it selfe; every man is a peece of the *Continent*, a part of the *maine*; if a *Clod* bee washed away by the *Sea*, *Europe* is the lesse, as well as if a *Promontorie* were, as well as if a *Mannor* of thy *friends* or of *thine owne* were; any mans *death* diminishes *me*, because I am involved in *Mankinde*; And therefore never send to know for whom the *bell* tolls; It tolls for *thee*.

To conclude, God does not work alone in heaven; man does not live alone on earth; there is a conversation, a correspondence and a commerce between God and man, a mutual interest in one another. His lifelong study of the relationship of body and soul, severed by death, against which life in its essential nature of relationships, protests, his conviction that this life and the life to come are connected, his emphasis upon man's relationship in community, his statement of divine grace co-operating with man's natural faculties so that God never forsakes us and never allows us to forsake ourselves, are all important aspects of his teaching derived from insights that came to him through pondering the divine command to man to 'subdue and have dominion'. One must not leave this subject without noting the free, independent application of the theme to man's own nature. Donne was too fond of giving his text a twist of meaning, and of presenting it in a fresh light, to resist the opportunity to turn it upon man himself—

God spake not onely of the beasts of the forest, but of those beasts, that is, those brutish affections, that are in us, when he said, *Subjicite & dominamini*, subdue, and govern the world; and in sinning we lose this dominion over our selves, and forfeit our dominion over the creature too.

Man is a *king* in his Creation; he hath that Commission, *Subjicite, & dominamini*; the world, and himselfe, (which is a lesse world, but a greater dominion) are within his Jurisdiction. . . .

This is not the academic exposition likely to win the approval of
scholars; but it is the fertile interpretation, even adaptation,
of Holy Scripture, natural to the poet-preacher, which gained
him the immediate attention of great audiences, and if his
relevance to the torn and tortured soul of our century needs farther
illustration, it is here. Our failure in self-government keeps the
rich and rightful blessings of man's conquest of his world for ever
out of reach; and in our torment we endure the mockery of
almost touching what is so near, yet, being beyond us, is farther
than what we know is unattainable.[44]

References to the Sabbath are less numerous, though, as we have
seen, one of his most notable reflections relates to it, and is echoed
in his declaration that God Himself has a Sabbath in our Sabbath,
a fullness in our fullness, a satisfaction in ours.[45] The basis of his
preaching was the goodness of God manifested in His Creation,
and the sinfulness of man; it is quite unfair to him to detach his
sermons on the latter from that basic conviction. One of his most
memorable utterances, on St Matthew xxi.44, ends with a volcanic
passage on the impenitent sinner in which the stone truly grinds
him to powder, but it begins with a positive assertion that God
made us for His glory which He fulfils, not in our destruction, but
our happiness, which He served by the Creation. Another sermon,
on Amos v.18, has in brackets, in the second paragraph, the statement that God loves this world as the work of His own hands, the
subject of His providence, the scene of His glory, the garden-plot
watered by the blood of His Son. God has displayed His goodness
in the created order, which He declared to be good before any
man existed to say so; indeed man himself was created through
the goodness of God and set in the context of His good works. This
goodness manifests itself in a certain extravagance, like the rain
falling on the sea; He planted a garden, though it served man for
so short a time, the sixth day being the day of man's fall—what
a dwelling God provided for man, though He knew he would
not pass a day in it; or one could go farther back and see the goodness of God in creating Light when there was nothing to illumine

[44] See VI. 107f; on man's labour in the world: IV. 149; VI. 140; VII. 167, 424;
VIII. p. 101; X. 219; II. 132f; V. 113f; I. 184; Grierson, I. 50, 52, 51, 64, and see
p. 90 *supra*; VIII. 194; on Grace: V. 316f, 379; VII. 63; II. 100; V. 202.
[45] See V. 207, 278; and see also VIII. 157f; VII. 300; see Devotions, 19, Prayer.

and no creature to behold it. This goodness is expressed in the variety of His created order, creatures in the heavens, in the earth, in the sea, in divers stations, yet all sharing in the verdict of God upon His work, that it was very good.[46]

The sermons are enriched with numerous interesting ideas generated by the story of Creation.

1. Genesis i.9, the gathering together of the waters into one place: the heats and lusts of youth overflow, as the waters overflowed in the beginning, when the earth was barren with nothing growing, and the waters were barren too, with no fishes or fowls —the scattering of affections leads to barrenness, their concentration in marriage is fruitful. Productive growth, in other words, requires discipline.

2. Man alone, of all the creatures, has departed from his natural dignity; they all preserve those degrees of goodness imparted to them in the beginning, and the ancient declaration can still be made, that they are good; but God was distrustful of man from the beginning, for He did not say, when man was created, that man was good—as light was good; man's goodness could not be established so simply, being dependent upon the future use of his free will. When a King goes in state, he is preceded by Lords, Earls and other persons of rank. When man was created, he was preceded by Light, Firmament, Earth, Sea, Sun, Moon, to dignify man in the same way, yet man, the principal in the procession, by losing his appointed place of supreme dignity, had disordered all. The heavens and the earth were finished, and all the host of them—this great host is disciplined, except for the general. Instead of governing the beasts, we have become beasts ourselves.

3. Adam, we are told in Genesis ii.19, named every living creature; all creatures were brought to him, and because he understood their nature, he was able to name them. But he gave no name to himself, because he understood himself less than he understood the other creatures. This is a characteristic attitude to man, as expressed in a long passage in *Of the Progresse of the Soule*:

> Poore soule, in this thy flesh what dost thou know?
> Thou know'st thy selfe so little, as thou know'st not,
> How thou didst die, nor how thou wast begot.
> Thou neither know'st, how thou at first cam'st in,

[46] II. 196, 180, 349; VI. 230, 232; X. 48; VI. 237; VII. 417.

Nor how thou took'st the poyson of man's sinne.
Nor dost thou, (though thou know'st, that thou art so)
By what way thou art made immortall, know.
Thou art too narrow, wretch, to comprehend
Even thy selfe. . . .

It occurs in the sermons and is a constant attitude throughout
his life. No study is so necessary as to know ourselves, but sin
plunges us into ignorance, even of the nature of sin itself—it is
the work of grace upon us to open our eyes to the true nature of
our actions, to see our sinful pleasure as adultery and incest,
frugality as oppression and covetousness; through grace a sinner
is brought into company with himself, he sees his sins with other
faces and hears them speak with other voices and call to one
another by other names.

4. Man destroys more quickly than he creates. The exact
opposite is true of God. He created the world in six days, but
needed eight days to destroy Jericho. Speed is a sign of God's
activity, and when a person falls into some act of sin, the corruption, though suddenly evident, has been proceeding for a long
time.

5. In a sermon on confession, he observed that God knew where
Adam was, yet He asked him where he was, because He would
know it from Adam himself.

6. As many preachers have done, he referred to the earth
without form and void, and the darkness upon the face of the
deep; and the Spirit of God moving on the face of the waters.
These waters, he said, had no power in themselves and awaited
the action of God upon them. As at the first creation the Holy
Spirit, the only Person of the Trinity to be mentioned in the
opening verses of Holy Scripture, moved on the face of the waters,
and the first creatures were then produced, so He moves over all
our tribulations, bringing to us spiritual comforts.[47]

There are many allusions to the Genesis account of Creation
scattered through the sermons to illustrate themes of quite a
diverse nature; there are also numerous sermons specifically and
directly upon the subject. In any list of the principal sermons
illustrating the influence of Genesis, those mentioned already

[47] For (*1*) see V. 116; (*2*) IX. 373f; (*3*) IX. 256f, 299f; Grierson, I. 258f; see V.
248; II. 74, 84; III. 98; IX. 129; (*4*) I. 275, III. 153; V. 307; cf. II. 148—it was late
when God corrected Adam, but He satisfies us early with His mercy; (*5*) II. 160f;
(*6*) I. 217; VIII. 211; VI. 129.

must be given a significant place—the first sermon of all, 'Sold for nothing', preached on 30th April 1615, on the subject of Nothing; the great evangelical utterance in two linked sermons at Whitehall on 19th April 1618; the 'Sermon of Valediction' on 18th April 1619; the first sermon preached as Dean of St Paul's on Christmas Day 1621; the immense sermon preached on Easter Monday, 1622; the first sermon preached as Vicar of St Dunstan's on 11th April 1624; and the Whitsunday sermon, 1629. These sermons, many of which were on notable occasions, have all been mentioned in earlier discussion.[48]

In addition, there are several others to be considered, if the influence of this source upon him is to be seen in some completeness.

1. PS, II, sermon 9 on Psalm lxxxix.48, 'What man is he that liveth, and shall not see death?', 'preached to the Lords upon Easter-day, at the Communion, the King being then dangerously sick at New-Market.'

It is fitting to recall, as Donne reminds us at the beginning of his first Prebend sermon, that our Lord, on the first Easter Day, mentioned the Psalms, together with the Law and the Prophets, as the Scriptures which spoke of Him and must be fulfilled (Luke xxiv.44). The first Easter sermon by Donne which has survived, was preached in 1619. Queen Anne had died recently; and the King was dangerously ill. The reflection that death comes to the greatest may have prompted the choice of subject, and the text from the Psalms. The word 'man' in the text is not *ishe* (which signifies a man, not a woman), nor *Adam* (signifying mankind), nor *Enos* (that is, a wretched and miserable creature) but *Gheber*, signifying a strong man, contrasted with women, children, non-combatants, a man, as Donne says, accomplished in all excellencies, a man accompanied with all advantages, a great man, and a good man, a happy man, and a holy man— which would serve to describe the King (a later sermon refers this text to a monarch, even a monarch to whom, Donne says, Psalm lxxxii.6 might apply—and certainly James applied those words, 'Yee are gods', to consecrated kings).

The sermon is dramatic, making effective use of Latin. Three different expressions are presented, sensationally, in contrast—

---

[48] See (1) pp. 133-140, (2) p. 144, (3) pp. 144f, (4) pp. 145f, (5) pp. 146-148, (6) p. 141, (7) pp. 128f *infra*.

Quis homo? Ecce homo! Ego homo. What man can hope to avoid death? the Psalm leaves the question unanswered, for it answers itself (*Quis homo?*); yet the New Testament says, Behold one man of whom it is true that he shall not see death (*Ecce homo!*); and at the end of the sermon Christ Himself answers the question in the text, speaking in the believer, in his spiritual death and resurrection (*Ego homo*).

The consideration of death takes his mind back immediately, in the opening paragraph, to Adam. The divine judgement on disobedience, he says, was absolute—'Thou shalt surely die' (Genesis ii.17); this was somewhat toned down by Eve in her words with the serpent—'perchance, if we eate, we may die' (iii.3); the serpent removed the danger altogether—'surely you shall not die' (iii.4). This reflection, based on the Vulgate, provides the structure of the sermon: God's word to Eve is fulfilled in mankind's general doom; Eve's word to the serpent is fulfilled in the doubt concerning those who are alive at Christ's return; and the serpent's words are fulfilled in Christ's victory over the grave.

We shall see the death of Death it self in the death of Christ. As we could not be cloathed at first, in Paradise, till some Creatures were dead, (for we were cloathed in beasts skins) so we cannot be cloathed in Heaven, but in his garment who dyed for us.

This arresting idea appears again in a sermon preached on 1 Corinthians xv.26, in 1622—

Assoon as we were clothed by God, our very apparell was an Embleme of death. In the skins of dead beasts, he covered the skins of dying men.[49]

2 PS, II, sermon 15 preached at Lincoln's Inn just after his return from the Continent, January, 1620. The sermon as a whole, on John v.22, is on a different subject, but it contains one notable passage influenced by Genesis. We recall that he left Lincon's Inn in the spring of the previous year to accompany Viscount Doncaster on his embassy to the Continent, in an endeavour to prevent war between Catholics and Protestants over the succession to the throne of Bohemia. Donne was in a depressed and troubled mood. Parting from friends always strained him, and now, a

[49] VI. 292; discussions on the meaning of 'man'—see II. 78f, IX. 61f; X. 198; IV. 333; II. 197, 202f (cf. IV. 52).

widower, he felt intensely the parting from those whom he loved and who loved him.[50] A terrible storm was about to break on the Continent, and he wondered if he would return alive. As we have seen, his farewell sermon was inspired at a number of points by the opening of Genesis, and ended with a memorable contrast between the impending calamity of war among the kingdoms of men, and the Kingdom of Christ, which is a Kingdom of harmony and consent, and where for Christians there is

a *Venite benedicti*, in being called to the participation of an immortal Crown of glory: where there shall be no difference in affection, nor in mind, but we shall agree as fully and perfectly in our *Allelujah*, and *gloria in excelsis*, as God the Father, Son, and Holy Ghost agreed in the *faciamus hominem* at first; where we shall end, and yet begin but then; where we shall have continuall rest, and yet never grow lazie; where we shall be stronger to resist, and yet have no enemy; where we shall live and never die, where we shall meet and never part.

So the sermon ends, with the addition, in an earlier version, of the words, 'but here we must'. This version, the sermon as actually preached, brings out the meaning of *faciamus hominem* with the assertion, 'we shall praise the whole Trinity as unanimly as the Trinity concur'd in making us.'

He was spared to return home, his health improved. But the worst fears of war abroad were confirmed by what he had seen and heard; and when he preached again at Lincoln's Inn, in the course of the sermon, he declared:

who hath divided heaven into shires or parishes, or limited the territories and Jurisdictions there, that God should not have and exercise *Judicium discretionis*, the power of discerning all actions, in all places? When there was no more to be seen, or considered upon the whole earth but the garden of Paradise, for from the beginning *Deliciæ ejus esse cum filiis hominum*, Gods delight was to be with the sons of men, and man was only there, shal we not diminish God nor speak too vulgarly of him to say, that he hovered like a Falcon over Paradise, and that from that height of heaven, the piercing eye of God, saw so little a thing, as the forbidden fruit, and what became of that, and the reaching eare of God heard the hissing of the Serpent, and the whispering of the woman, and what was concluded upon that? Shall we think it little to have seen things done in Paradise when there was nothing

[50] See the poem written by him at this time, 'A Hymne to Christ, at the Authors last going into Germany', Grierson, I. 352f.

else to divert his eye, nothing else to distract his counsels, nothing else done upon the face of the earth? Take the earth now as it is replenished, and take it either as it is torn and crumbled into raggs, and shivers, not a kingdome, not a family, not a man agreeing with himselfe. . . .[51]

3. PS, II, sermon 17 on Genesis ii.18, which may be entitled: 'God brought the woman to the man.' One of Donne's first duties on returning from the Continent was to preach at the marriage of Doncaster's secretary, Sir Francis Nethersole, to Lucy, daughter of his lifelong friend Sir Henry Goodyear. The text prompted reflections on the Creation story. The command, 'Be fruitful and multiply' was given to the human race as well as to other living creatures (see Genesis i.22, 28), and it was accompanied with blessing; it was in this connection that the first reference to a blessing was made, the blessing being related to the process of generation, which involves repetition and renewal, and the perpetuation of what is good; in the case of man particularly God took special care that this generation should be directed and controlled, for the story immediately distinguishes mankind from the rest of creation—though both are related in verses 22 and 28, the fulfilment of the command in the case of man involved also the creation of woman, who was brought by God to man (see ii.22), and the command must be fulfilled within the relationship of marriage, when God brings a woman to a man: they do not simply seek each other.

God's concern is for the good of man, which must be considered in relation to mankind as a whole, not the individual in isolation. This 'good' concerns the public, not the individual—the text does not say *non bonum homini*, or *non bonum hunc hominem*, but *non bonum, Hominem*, referring to mankind (the text as he presents it has a comma after 'good', to stress that man's good is the good involving all, not individual self-interest); man's good is not simply the relief of solitariness, which could have been achieved by the creation of more men; marriage conveys the blessing of children, and ministers to man's needs, though, in the Creation, unspoilt by human infirmity and temptation, marriage is not referred to as a remedy against incontinence, for the problem had not arisen. What is good to God may be considered by the omission of reference to 'good' after the second and sixth days—the

[51] II. 249, 390, 316.

M

making of the firmament was to divide between waters and waters, and division, disunion, is not in itself good; the making of man could not be declared to be good, in itself, for man needed woman.

John Donne believed that the Creation story established the relationship of the wife to the husband; the primacy of Adam was indicated by the *faciamus*, the consultation of the Trinity, in his creation, whereas the text states, in the creation of woman, *faciam*, as though her creation were more arbitrary, not requiring the counsel and deliberation of the whole Godhead. This will seem to the modern reader mere trifling with words; yet the heart of the sermon is a positive statement of a woman's true place in society; she is not a duplication of man, the functions of man and woman are not interchangeable, and there is healthy human wisdom in his conclusion—

Since she was taken out of his side, let her not depart from his side, but shew her self so much as she was made for, *Adjutorium*, a Helper. . . . If she think her self more then a Helper, she is not so much.

The sermon is dramatic, he sees the woman standing at the man's side; she was not taken out of the foot, to be trodden on, or out of the head, to become an overseer; but out of his side, to be at his side, as a helper. It is not an insufficient view of the wife's place in Christian marriage that she should be at the man's side, and on his side, through life.

4. PS, IX, Two sermons, 1, 2, preached before Charles I, on Genesis i.26 in April 1629.

In April 1629 he preached a sermon on the words, 'And God said, Let us make man, in our image, after our likeness', and stated that a second sermon on this text would follow, but not on the same day. We have both sermons, which may be conveniently considered together, though it is significant to remember that he presented this theme as too large to be discussed adequately in one discourse: neither sermon is short, and the second is the longer of the two.

In these sermons he returns very deliberately, with the sense of wonder which was half of what Divinity meant to him, to the beginning of Holy Scripture, which held him fascinated, as though he never needed to travel farther. The act of Creation, he says, was incomparable; it involved the beginning of time, and the

[52] See II. 335ff, and p. 346; and also III. 241f, 246; VIII. 94.

world was made in fewer days than are required to make a map of it. One would like to know what volumes he had especially in mind when he said that the volumes written upon the Beginning are hardly less than infinite. As he reads the Scriptures, he remembers that the Holy Spirit is in the work of which he reads, and in the work that he reads; The Holy Ghost hovered upon the waters, and so God wrought; He hovered upon Moses, and so he wrote. The framework of the two sermons is the world, considered in its four compass-points—east and west (the first sermon), north and south (the second). The East is his emblem of rising, of beginning; he begins here, with God the Trinity speaking, and the confession of the Trinity is the beginning of the Christian Faith; the West is man, whose essential nature involves him in death, in the setting of the sun; the North signifies the image or likeness, and from this quarter come winds to drive away the storm-clouds of death; the South is God Himself, Whose image remains imprinted on the soul when the body dies.

The first section, the East, presents the beginning of Creation, which is also a representation of our spiritual beginning, for, as man was made by the Trinity, so he is remade by Baptism in the triune Name; the opening verse of Holy Scripture requires belief in the Trinity; when we are told that God spoke, to whom, in the beginning, could He speak but to Himself? The Trinity created man, and recreates him, for His preached Word joins with the ministry of His Spirit, even as in the beginning man was made through the Word and the Spirit.

'Tis true, that when God speakes this over againe in his Church, as he does every day, now, this minute, then God speakes it to Angels; to the Angels of the Church, to his Ministers; he says *Faciamus*, Let us, us both together, you and we, make a man; join mine Ordinance (your preaching) with my Spirit, (says God to us) and so make man. Preach the oppressor, and preach the wanton, and preach the calumniator into another nature. Make that ravening Wolfe a Man, that licentious Goate a man, that insinuating Serpent a man, by thy preaching.

We have here another example of his adaptation of *Faciamus hominem*, this time to the preacher's calling which, in its purpose and effect, reproduces the essential elements of the first Creation, when the three Persons of the Godhead, in concert, made man.

The second section, the West, is a statement on man's nature.

His misery is written into his biblical names; yet, even though man is lowly and of the earth, the day of his creation, which saw the creation of cattle, and creeping thing, and beasts of the earth, simply by command, saw also the holding of a consultation, and then a special creative act, not 'let there be' but 'let us make', for man is mentioned separately, though other creatures were made on this day. The distinction drawn is the one already discussed, between 'having' and 'being'[53]—the creation of that which was simply external to Himself could be accomplished by a Fiat; but the creation of man in His own image committed and involved the Godhead in a unique way, for the creation of man in His likeness involved Him in His essence as well as His will. Man, Adam, is not only earth, but red earth, carrying the blush of shame, contrasted with Christ's whiteness, and mankind is one in death; no limbeck, no scales, can determine which is the dust royal, which the plebeian, which the catholic, which the heretical dust.

The third section, the North, reminds us that this earth, man, has a nobler form than any other part or limb of the world, because he was made, not only by a special act, but after the likeness of his Creator. All things were created in conformity to an idea, and were declared to be good because they realized it; man was not declared to be good because his conformity to his pattern was to appear only in subsequent actions—other creatures obey the law of their nature instinctively, whereas man's nature endows him with the exercise of choice and the possibility of disobedience.

The last section, the South, considers the significance of the image. The images forbidden by God were inferior versions of that which they represented; but God, who spoke of His image, means that we should discern Himself, not a representation of Himself, in man. This Image is not in man's body, though its superiority denotes his possession of the image. Man's soul is made to fit this Image. Just as only the seal imprinted in the wax can fit the print afterwards, so only God can declare the origin of man to be Himself. Everywhere one may see the appropriate seal— the crown for the State, the mitre for the Church; only the right seal will fit the impression, nevertheless people make an infamous bargain, exchanging the true Image for one that will not fit. Man's nature derives from God, and is meaningless apart from Him.[54]

[53] See pp. 65ff *supra*.   [54] IX. 48, 57f.

The more unusual and interesting references to the Creation story have been noted; there are many more of a conventional kind. Even so, they occupy only a small place in the full range of the sermons, and there would be nothing surprising in a studious reader regarding them as no more than occasional scriptural illustrations. In the course of one hundred and sixty sermons, other interests of Donne, plainly represented, might excite his interest more. The character of a certain monotony would be given to them if it were supposed that this theme was omnipresent. This is by no means so. Its importance to Donne is corroborated by the sermons, but the evidence contained in them is not really significant unless related to his whole life, his poems, and his *Essayes in Divinity*; only when this evidence is collected together in an organic biographical relationship can its derivative nature be appreciated.

The characteristic features of the sermons do stand, nevertheless, in direct relation to the theme that launched him on his voyage. His religious position was orthodox; what made his utterances more than simply conventional was his infectious enthusiasm for the great doctrines of the Faith, notably the Trinity, and the Incarnation, which he associated with Genesis. It is not surprising that he should preach on the great occasions in the Church year; this was his duty; but he brought to the familiar subjects an astonishing fertility of mind, investing them with fresh authority and kindling a sense of their massive importance. The themes that he handled were made to matter. He obtruded upon the attention of his hearers the Christian doctrine of man, and this, like the doctrine of the Trinity, he linked with the Genesis story. Man was one of those fruits of paradise, ripe the first minute, a man the first minute, able to stand upright before God; but we have lost the sweet savour of our own spikenard; there was a time when we had a sweet savour of our own, but now man is fallen and corrupt; in sermon after sermon he presented man, through the sin of Adam and Eve, tainted and impure; but his presentation of man in his misery proceeds from a vision of God's true purpose for him. He gripped his hearers with his many-sided understanding of the solidarity of mankind in Adam; his descriptions of the unity of the race in the corruption of the body through death have never been equalled; his acute analysis of man's inner nature, his temptations, his subterfuges, his struggles and hopes, made his hearers feel themselves to be one with him and one another; especially did he repeat himself in severely condemning sins against society—counterfeiting; usury; the omission of one's own positive contribution to the public good and the perpetuation of the race and society; and, most conspicuously, the sin of corrupting others—

> Wilt thou forgive that sinne which I have wonne
> Others to sinne? and, made my sinne their doore?[55]

His revolt against nihilism constructed his view of man's future. Death was not the end, and the resurrection of the body was stressed by him perhaps more than any single article of the Creeds. The judgement upon the impenitent sinner would not exterminate him, he would not return to nothing, but would experience the anguish of separation, that last, most awful singularity; the believer's life here on earth would be, in important ways, determinative of his life beyond the grave. Even as the opening verse of Holy Scripture was linked with his doctrine of the Trinity, so the creation of man after the consultation of the Trinity was joined by him to his quite magnificent exposition of the essentially sociable nature of religion, expressed in the Church, the unity of which was essential to her nature, and he looked forward to the day when the differences that now tore her apart would be resolved. Meanwhile the Church, planted in these islands, made the Gospel accessible to all, a view he reinforced from Deuteronomy xxx.13: 'Neither is it beyond the sea, that thou shouldest say, Who shall go over the sea for us, and bring it unto us, that we may hear it, and do it?' His religious thought began with the acceptance of Creation, as a divine act, a divine initiative which should evoke wonder and gratitude, not criticism and speculation. He became reconciled to the Church established in England, and he became reconciled to the created order. Frequently in his preaching he discouraged what he regarded as improper investigation into the mysteries and secrets of God—the word 'curious', like the word 'singular', stood for a wrong attitude of mind. The Sacraments were accepted by him without question, and he discouraged speculation on the nature of the bread and wine after consecration, and any attempt to localize

---

[55] VI. 97, 207; VII. 108; Grierson, I. 369; on Donne and sins of omission see E. M. Simpson, *A Study of the Prose Works of John Donne*, pp. 78f.

and imprison within a moment of time what was essentially a mystery; and he cleverly suggested, characteristically reversing the expression 'real presence', that Christians might more fitly establish their own real presence, (rather than debate that of Christ,) and stress the transubstantiation of bread and wine into the soul of the believer: it is our transformation that should be our concern.[56]

The Christian doctrines which he principally stressed are closely related by him to the scriptural account of the origin of the world and man, and its influence upon him, amply illustrated in specific passages, may also be traced in the emphasis of his preaching. Not so much what a man says, reveals a preacher; rather what he says repeatedly, and emphasizes.

One of the ideas repeated by Donne was that the name of Jesus is Oriens, the East—He not only comes from the east, He is the East.[57] Only one sermon for All Saints' Day has come down to us; in it he preaches from Revelation vii.2f, beginning: 'And I saw another angel ascending from the east'. He has in mind the Vulgate of Zechariah vi.12 (A.V. has 'The Branch'), *Ecce vir oriens nomen ejus*, and the words of the New Testament Zechariah in St Luke i.78, *in quibus visitavit nos, oriens ex alto* ('whereby the dayspring from on high hath visited us'—A.V.). The name was his last thought in the epitaph which he prepared for his effigy, and which may still be seen above it in St Paul's: '. . . HIC LICET IN OCCIDUO CINERE ASPICIT EUM CUJUS NOMEN EST ORIENS' (. . . and here, though set in dust, he beholdeth Him whose name is the Rising).[58]

In a sermon he tells us that Athanasius, scarce three hundred years after Christ, found the Church following the custom, believed to be on apostolic authority, of turning to the East for prayer, to signify the desire of Christians to return to their lost country, paradise. Our last, abiding recollection of John Donne, preacher, as one contemplates him in the south choir aisle, is that his dying intention was to face the east, in hope of the coming again of Him whose name is the East. In ways which it has been our endeavour to indicate, there was his starting-place; there his message was launched. If the reading of his sermons kindles

---

[56] VII. 139f, 320f; see IX. 254.
[57] Another example of the 'identification' discussed on pp. 68f *supra*.
[58] As translated by Francis Wrangham, Gosse, II. 282.

even a small measure of affection for a struggling, often discordant Christian, and if the reading of the sermons, illuminated by his poems, reminds us that he was a poet to the end who read the opening verses of Holy Scripture, not as a scientist but as a poet, to our great enrichment, we will not be slow to turn eastward with him, as we hear him say again: 'Wee looke towards our ancient country, where the Gospel of our salvation was literally acted, and accomplished, and where Heaven, the end of the Gospel, was represented in Paradise.'[59]

[59] See letter to Sir Robert Ker, Gosse, II. 191; PS, V. 97; VI. 59; IX. 208f, X. 50f.

EIGHT

THE TRUMPET, AT WHOSE VOYCE THE PEOPLE CAME

('Of the Progresse of the Soule'—last line)

JOHN DONNE was a preacher; he valued preaching, at least for himself, above all other activities of the Christian Minister. There is no particular accent upon priesthood in his sermons, and the word 'minister' is used as often as 'priest'. The sacraments have their unquestioned place, and ceremonies are properly honoured and expounded. There is some reference to auricular confession, and to pastoral care. Sermons directly on the preacher's calling, and incidental references to preaching, abound, and his language reaches great heights as he considers the preacher's vocation. *Væ mihi si non* if not as frequently found, is as much a key-phrase as *Faciamus hominem* or *Subjicite & dominamini*. These words of the apostle Paul, 'Woe be unto me if I doe not preach the Gospell',[1] found in I Corinthians ix.16, were never far from his thoughts—

Who but my selfe can conceive the sweetnesse of that salutation, when the Spirit of God sayes to me in a morning, Go forth to day and preach, and preach consolation, preach peace, preach mercy, And spare my people, spare that people whom I have redeemed with my precious Blood, and be not angry with them for ever; Do not wound them, doe not grinde them, do not astonish them with the bitternesse, with the heavinesse, with the sharpnesse, with the consternation of my judgements. *David* proposes to himselfe, that he would *Sing of mercy, and of judgement*; but it is of mercy first; and not of judgement at all, otherwise then it will come into a song, as joy and consolation is compatible with it. . . . What a Coronation is our taking of Orders, by which God makes us a Royall Priesthood? And what an inthronization is the comming up into a Pulpit, where God invests his servants with his Ordinance, as with a Cloud, and then presses that Cloud with a *Væ si non*, woe be unto thee, if thou doe not preach, and then enables him to preach peace, mercy, consolation, to the whole Congregation.

[1] As in IV. 195; see Walton, p. 52.

Before he preached his sermon at the dedication of the new Chapel at Lincoln's Inn, he prayed:

> . . . let a full pot of thy *Manna*, a good measure of thy Word, and an effectuall preaching thereof, bee evermore preserved, and evermore bee distributed in this place.

More than once he claimed that the Reformation revived preaching in England, and he was proud to stand in the Reformed tradition. The preacher was a mark of the true Church, set in the Church, tracing his lineage back to the making of man '*in sermone*, in a consultation', and his function was not to proclaim a message external to himself, but to communicate the message through his personality, to be the living agency of the recreation of man. The preacher had a direct link, therefore, with Genesis, for he wrought by words even as God in the beginning spoke, and it came to pass. Donne gave himself with singleness of mind to the task of preaching, dedicating to it all his powers, finding fulfilment in this undertaking; and toward the end, when illness prevented him from preaching, he wrote to a friend: 'I have been always more sorry when I could not preach, than any could be that they could not hear me. It hath been my desire (and God may be pleased to grant it me) that I might die in the pulpit; if not that, yet that I might take my death in the pulpit, that is, die the sooner by occasion of my former labours.' This wish was essentially fulfilled, for the last sermon overstrained his waning strength and he returned home to die.[2]

We possess one hundred and sixty sermons. A substantial number were preached to the Court at Whitehall, extending throughout his ministry, and his last sermon was preached there. A comparable number were preached at Lincoln's Inn, but only in the earlier years—one recalls his inscription at the front of the first of his presentation volumes on leaving Lincoln's Inn, in which he states that for five years he was engaged, frequently and actively in preaching there.[3] Nine of the sermons were preached at

[2] Gosse, II. p. 268; Walton, p. 74; see Jessopp, p. 141; VII. 133f; IV. 363; some occurrences of '*Væ si non*'—II. 164, 309; IV. 192, 195, 374; VI. 93; IX. 285; X. 126; see II. 167f on the preacher as the Trumpet; see V. 255f, VIII. 164 on the Reformation revival of preaching; I. 289.

[3] 'Munere suo frequenter et strenue hoc loco concionandi per quinque annos functus.'

St Dunstan's following his appointment as Vicar. We have numerous sermons for special occasions, almost certainly preached in London or in connection with London society; six prepared for preaching in the open air (Paul's Cross, and the Spittle). Nearly all the remainder, just over a third in number, were preached at St Paul's Cathedral. His 'auditory', as he termed it, was, then, the Court; the Benchers and law students at Lincoln's Inn; a parish congregation at St Dunstan's; a cosmopolitan assembly at the Cathedral, and a congregation out-of-doors.

His contribution to the observance of the Christian Year was massive. As Dean he had to preach on Christmas Day, Easter Sunday and Whitsunday, and he first preached in the Cathedral as Dean on Christmas Day 1621. In addition we have sermons for Candlemas, Lent, Trinity Sunday, and in commemoration of St Paul's conversion—this was a self-appointed task, linked in his mind either with the Cathedral or his own ordination there at that time; or with both. To Donne himself the statutory obligations were a heavy responsibility. In a letter to Mrs Cokain, almost at the end of his life, he wrote: 'I was under a necessity of preaching twelve or fourteen solemn sermons every year, to great auditories at Paul's, and to the judges, and at Court . . . You know the ticklishness of London pulpits. . . .'[4]

The series of Christmas Day sermons at St Paul's was interrupted twice by illness, in 1623 and 1630, but we have sermons for each of the remaining years, eight in number. There are five Candlemas sermons; for most of his ministry he preached before the King at Whitehall on the first Friday in Lent, 'his old constant day' as Izaak Walton says[5] and there are ten Lent discourses in all; two uninterrupted series of nine Easter Day and nine Whitsunday sermons have survived; in addition we have an earlier Easter Day sermon, and also the longest that he preached, on Easter Monday, and one early Whitsun sermon. Two Ascension Day sermons, sermons for Trinity Sunday and Sundays following, one for All Saints' Day, Midsummer Day, New Year's Day, four on St Paul's conversion, sermons for a number of special occasions, five sermons on the five Psalms, lxii-lxvi, which as Prebendary of the Cathedral he had to read daily (there were thirty Prebendaries, each of whom read five different consecutive Psalms daily, the whole Psalter being thus recited daily), sermons at weddings, churchings, baptisms, funerals and a commemoration, comprise the remainder.

Sir Edmund Gosse says, 'He was essentially an extempore preacher',[6] a statement which would have surprised the preacher more than anyone, for he spoke frequently against 'extemporal' utterance, a word which keeps company with 'rude', 'barbarous'. It is a late time of meditation, he says, for a sermon, when the Psalm is singing.[7]

All his sermons were carefully prepared, the text chosen well in advance and the outline constructed; he probably used full notes in the pulpit, but was so familiar with them that he was not, seemingly, dependent upon them—the reading of a manuscript was strongly disapproved and he would have made no progress in his calling without freedom of utterance. Probably he prepared his sermon fully, delivered it within the normal limit of an hour, and afterwards wrote it out, allowing it to take whatever space it required. The sermons are unequal in length, but would be of much the same length when preached. Donne was against unprepared utterance, which then as now would be regarded by some as more 'spiritual'. It must be remembered, however, that his sermons contain many notable passages which are best described as ejaculatory, for, whether actually prepared beforehand or not, they use the form of direct address and create an atmosphere of spontaneity. This was a feature of his first exercises in his *Essayes in Divinity* which he carried over into his later preaching. It is doubtful if the word 'extempore' serves a useful purpose; in the sense of immediate, unprepared utterance, in preaching or praying, which he associated with 'separatists' and 'Nonconformitans', he was certainly not extemporaneous; neither was he dependent on his notes for the exact form of words, and he created an atmosphere of ease and freedom which was one secret of his power. If the word signifies free, self-directed preaching or praying, despite his dissociation from the word, he may legitimately be described as 'extempore'. Just as his poems, so free from sentimentalism were nevertheless the work of one who felt deeply the attachments of friendship, so his sermons, so carefully prepared,

[6] II. p. 313.   [7] I. 260f, II. 167, 171; see II. 50; IV. 99; V. 54; X. 174.

included strongly personal passages which distinguished them from a formal, objective preaching style.[8]

He preached for an hour, 'a Compasse, that all Ages have thought sufficient'. He began a Lent sermon at Whitehall on 1 Timothy iii.16 with the words, 'This is no Text for an Houre-glass' and ended a sermon on 1 Thessalonians v.16: 'It is time to end; but as long as the glasse hath a gaspe, as long as I have one, I would breathe in this ayre, in this perfume, in this breath of heaven, the contemplation of this Joy.'[9]

The sermon always had a text, and its selection was the first step in his preparation—preaching without one would have amazed, and alienated him. He distinguished a sermon from a lecture. The purpose of the former, he said, was exhortation, edification; of the latter, discussion of matters of doctrine and divinity. He once said, 'We are not upon a Lecture, but upon a Sermon'.[10] The important consideration was not the subject, as in a lecture, but the text itself, which controlled the sermon, being considered in detail, and from different points of view, and introduced repeatedly. A certain amount of repetition was inevitable, and an essential part of the method. Ingenuity in drawing fresh meanings from the text, in attaching great significance to minute details, was not considered misplaced. Certainly his reading of his text was close and meticulous; he would stress, for example, the significance of number—one doubts if he could have endured modern English, with its 'you' for the singular and the plural. Reading Job xix.26, 'And though, after my skin, wormes destroy this body, yet in my flesh shall I see God', he perceives that this flesh he now has is not his, it will return to the earth; but in Christ his flesh shall no more be none of his than Christ shall not be man, as well as God—this effective interpretation turns on the words 'this', objective to himself, and 'my', subjective and possessive.[11]

He believed, simply, that a text was given by God; that it contained hidden treasure; that a preacher, by preaching upon

[8] I. 250f; II. 70, 363; III. 244; VII. 361f are examples of prayers in sermons which create an 'extemporaneous' atmosphere.
[9] IV. 378; III. 206; X. 227; Walton, p. 75: 'measure out an hour'.
[10] See VIII. 95; II. 320, 12; IV. 2f.
[11] See III. 93, 113.

it, released new spiritual forces which acted upon speaker and hearers and communicated God Himself in His truth. The distinction which he seized in his poetry, and which runs throughout his writings, between 'having' and 'being', between talking about something objective to oneself, and communicating that which has gripped and become expounded in the writer, is deeply significant for his preaching. He was not a personal preacher in the allusions that he made; references to his own life and experience are not numerous; but he was a highly personal preacher in that he was involved in, and committed to, his message, to a degree that impressed his hearers deeply—

preaching the Word so, as shewed his own heart was posssest with those very thoughts and joys that he laboured to distill into others: A Preacher in earnest; weeping sometimes for his Auditory, sometimes with them: always preaching to himself, like an Angel from a cloud, but in none; carrying some, as *St Paul* was, to Heaven in holy raptures, and inticing others by a sacred Art and Courtship to amend their lives; here picturing a vice so as to make it ugly to those that practised it; and a vertue so, as to make it beloved even by those that lov'd it not; and all this with a most particular grace and an unexpressible addition of comeliness.[12]

The basis of this was not only personal religion; it was a conviction that the Holy Bible is God's living word, and that whenever it is handled, in any part, the living God quickens the reader, even to the extent of giving new insights into its meaning and reflections upon it which, without altering the sense, carry its meaning farther. Donne was submissive to the authority of Holy Scripture, but he was never fettered, imprisoned, by his text, as though it were an irksome necessity. It liberated him, and he liberated it.

He, in common with his age, made Christ central to the whole Bible. It is assumed by us that a chronological sense, a sense of history, is a modern insight; but it is fatally easy to think of the incarnation happening after the end of the Old Testament period, and of Jesus as connected with Old Testament times only in that its Scriptures spoke of His coming and mission. It is just as easy, then, to limit Him to the pages of the New Testament and disconnect Him from subsequent history. But to John

[12] Walton, p. 49, and see p. 52 on the sermon after his wife's death, and p. 75, on his last sermon; see also 'To Mr Tilman after he had taken orders', Grierson, I. 351f, lines 42f, and the whole poem for Donne's views on Holy Orders.

Donne, Jesus is in the first verse of Holy Scripture. He is the
agent of the creation of the world. He is as fully implicated in
history before His coming, as in His earthly life. Through the
Holy Spirit He is the living, risen Lord of the ages. There is
adequate New Testament justification for these views; whereas
the twentieth-century Christian would not deny them, he affirmed
them by the manner of his preaching. He expected to find Christ
in the Old Testament, and was uninhibited by the idea of chrono-
logy. He related Him naturally to his own contemporary scene.

The endeavour to determine what the original writer meant
was for him only part of the preacher's discipline. Integrity did
not require of him that he must not adapt, or amplify that original
meaning. The text must work on him, and, when he preached,
be seen to have worked upon him. A journey with Donne, when
he has a text in his hand, is essentially an adventure, and sometimes he penetrates where none has been before.

This view of the Scriptures gives the preacher much freedom,
and protects him against the charge of distortion. To the poetic
temperament, especially, this freedom is a great advantage, and
the insight into Holy Scripture which Donne shows is its justification. In Donne's day, as in medieval times, sermons were constructed in conformity with these views; a text would be
considered, first, 'literally' or historically, giving the meaning as
originally intended; then, 'morally', indicating the moral and
spiritual lessons to be derived by us from the text; and, thirdly,
'typically,' showing how the words prepared for, and predicted,
the coming of Jesus.

Reverence for the whole of Scripture equally gave a preacher
freedom to use the Old Testament with a confidence unknown in
our times. Seventy-nine Old Testament, and eighty-one New
Testament texts, are to be found in his sermons. The Book of
Psalms comes easily first of the Old Testament books, thirty-four
sermons being based on texts from seventeen different Psalms;
a long way after comes the book of Genesis with nine, Isaiah with
six, Job with five, the remaining books represented being Proverbs
(four) for which an epigrammatist had a natural appreciation;
Ezekiel (three) whom he regarded as the greatest of the four great
prophets—Jeremiah, Isaiah, Daniel and Ezekiel—because of his
extraordinary depth and mysteriousness;[13] Ecclesiastes (three),

[13] X. 141.

which not surprisingly appealed to him; Hosea, Exodus, Deuteronomy, Lamentations, Canticles, Micah (two each); Amos,
Judges, Esther (one each). When one turns to the New Testament,
one finds that sixteen texts were chosen from Matthew, sixteen
from John, three from Luke and two from Mark, so that thirty-
seven sermons were preached on texts from the Gospels, practically the same number as texts from the Psalms. There are eight
sermons from Acts, eight from 1 Corinthians, five from Revelation, four from Romans, three from 1 Timothy, three from 2
Corinthians, two from Colossians, two from 1 Thessalonians,
two from Galatians, one from Philippians, 1 Peter, 2 Peter,
Ephesians, 1 John, James, and Hebrews.

These facts harmonize with his statement that the Psalms
and the epistles of St Paul were his favourite reading in the
Scriptures,[14] but the sermons show that he had a ready, allusive
knowledge of the whole Bible, that he was able to illustrate the
Bible from the Bible, one place of Scripture taking light from
another—he would frequently pursue a word through the Scriptures and note its use, and ingeniously expound the various
occurrences of the word by reference of one to the others.

His freedom of exposition, his tendency to add to Scripture
and give its words a new twist, is noticeable. For example:

As Christ sayes, that as often as wee eate the Sacramentall Bread, we
should remember his Death, so as often, as we eate ordinary bread,
we may remember our death; for even hunger and thirst, are diseases;
they are *Mors quotidiana*, a daily death, and if they lasted long, would
kill us.[15]

No man ever saw God and lived—yet we shall not live until we
see God, and when we see Him we shall never die; Without faith
you cannot please—anybody; the light that lighteneth every
man going out of the world; to fall into the hands of the living God
is a fearful thing, but to fall out of the hands of God is a horror
unspeakable.[16]

He frequently took ordinary, familiar words, and pressed home
their meaning. The Virgin Mary was blessed, not only above all
other women, but among women, that is, by women. It is all
very well telling a person who is ill to take his rest, but rest cannot

[14] See II. 49.   [15] II. 203.
[16] III. 111; X. 70, 87; V. 266; further illustrations abound.

be taken; talk of a man's means, that is, his possessions? his means is the means he took to get them. Sin no more—more it will be, if you sin again, for sin grows. Coldly considered now, these examples are lacking in the dramatic power with which he invested these words, making the conventional significant.[17] Inevitably, the text glittered in his hands as he presented it, so that every facet could be seen, and sometimes a single word became memorable.

Not only did the text, analysed and repeated, remain in the memory; the sermon structure which he followed was designed to assist the hearer to follow the course of the sermon and to recall it afterwards. First, the text was 'placed', then 'divided', then 'expounded', and, finally, 'applied'. To place the text was to announce and introduce the text, with preliminary remarks, often quickening the interest—a number of the sermons begin arrestingly, and one suspects that he paid more attention to the beginning than to the ending, which is sometimes commonplace. Then the text was divided, that is, the divisions of the text and the stages of the exposition to be given were indicated; the exposition set forth the meaning which, finally, was applied, related, to the hearers. Thus every sermon—and in this he followed the best tradition of preaching—had a text controlling it, and a plan to be announced before being followed. In this way a bridge was built between the preacher, who had lived with his subject for many days, and his hearers, who could make no such preparation. Much of the physical difficulty of listening to a very long sermon was reduced by the assistance given at the beginning to follow the argument as it was assembled, and even to look forward, as one finds oneself doing when reading Donne, to the discussion still to come, promised and partly indicated at the start. Donne often speaks of a sermon as a tree, with different branches, or he thinks of a tree with roots, the tree itself, the fruit. On one occasion he speaks of it as a house with various rooms.[18]

Donne, as we know from the pun on his name, and from his poems, for example 'Elegie XI' on the angel (the angel, and the coin of that name) found the pun irresistible, and his sermons

[17] III. 249; II. 83; VII. 260; X. 80.
[18] See I. 286; IV. 291; IX. 298; X. 85; V. 70; IV. 146, 267; V, sermon 12.

N

abound in them—Son, Sun; Ordinance, Ordnance; if a word suggests another of similar sound he feels obliged to introduce it, sometimes quite unnecessarily—unction, function; traditions, additions; modify, mollify. Much of this is hardly clever, but it is the rough working by which occasionally he produces a brilliant phrase, as when he says that death comes equally to us all, and makes us all equal when it comes; or that Jesus was His name when He was carried to the altar to circumcision, when He carried His altar the cross; to us also will be given circumcision of heart, and a joyous 'consummatum est' on our last altar, our deathbed.[19]

He was specially fond of the device of using a term proper to a particular profession in another connection. This was done in the third stanza of 'Metempsychosis, The Progresse of the Soule':

> Nor, holy *Ianus*, in whose soveraigne boate
> The Church, and all the Monarchies did floate;
> That swimming Colledge, and free Hospitall
> Of all mankinde. . . .[20]

and in the powerful poem on 'The Storme', when the ship is described as a sick man:

> Then note they the ships sicknesses, the Mast
> Shak'd with this ague, and the Hold and Wast
> With a salt dropsie clog'd. . . .[21]

There are many references to legal matters, illustrating the Gospel —he can even speak of Chief Justice Moses; the device was effectively and suitably used in the closing passage of his 'Sermon of Valediction' at Lincoln's Inn; but other allusions frequently found are to the Government and Constitution; the Church; School and University; various Trades; in all these cases familiar terms and expressions are taken from their proper setting and applied to Christianity, as when he says, for example, '. . . here is my University and my Chair, here I must take my Degree, in my Heart, in my Conscience . . .'[22] Essentially this was a reversal of his youthful adaptation of sacred words or terms (see p. 29 *supra*), a practice continued to this day in the non-scriptural,

---

[19] See IV. 53; I. 312.   [20] Grierson, I. 296.
[21] Grierson, I. 177; cf. 'Elegie XIX', line 27, p. 120.   [22] I. 296.

non-ecclesiastical use of words like 'gospel', 'baptism', 'hierarchy', 'crusade'.

It is to be expected that certain ideas recur.

The fourth of his youthful Paradoxes is entitled: 'That good is more common than evil.' A conclusion, which may be included among his 'surprises', found often in the sermons, is that the practice of goodness is easier than its opposite—

. . . vicious men are put to more pains and to doe more things against their own mindes, then the Saints of God are in the ways of holinesse.

A man may go with more ease to Heaven than to Hell; the mystery of iniquity is greater than that of Godliness, for Heaven might be had with less pains than men bestow on hell.[23] This judgement, reinforced by his own experience, is given its firmest and most religious expression in the statement that we cannot be absolutely, entirely, essentially sinful as God is absolutely, entirely, essentially merciful.

A final example of a number of themes found repeatedly, is his insistence that the Godhead did not leave the dead body of Christ. He attached considerable importance to this, and stated it on many occasions. When Christ lay dead in the grave, the Godhead remained united to His body and soul, though they themselves were disunited; God was so united to man, as that He was with man when man was dead. The body is not to be despised, but respected; it will be restored to us again, for it is part of God's saving work to save the body as well as the soul. The body of a deceased Christian has been a temple of the Holy Ghost, and it must be treated with respect, as a sign of our Christian hope. As the divine nature did not depart from the body of Christ in the grave, so the love and power of God do not depart from a dead believer. He returned to this theme in his last sermon. It was a point of doctrine in which he saw concentrated the all-important truth of the redemption of our physical nature.[24]

Worthy of mention is his much practised art of developing an idea stage by stage, one word leading to another—reminding one

---

[23] II. 134, 215; see III. 211, 326; VI. 66, 330; VIII. 198; IX. 341.
[24] See III. 103, 204, 215; IV. 104, 332; V. 134; VI. 155; VII. 100; IX. 207, 348; X. 188, 236.

of the supreme example in 1 Kings xix.11f—not in the wind . . .
not in the earthquake . . . not in the fire . . . and after the fire a
still small voice. Sometimes he moves from the lesser to the
greater, sometimes from the greater to the lesser, but always there
is the sense of pursuit and in the end of penetration to unexplored
country beyond conventional frontiers of thought. He can
excitedly open up the theme of the various names for God, or
Man, in the Scriptures; he traces the development of human
sinfulness from fancies in the imagination, to thoughts, from
thoughts to deeds, and from deeds to habits; whispering sins
lead to speaking sins, and these to crying sins, and so to sins
buttressed by reason. He studies the various anthropomorphic
views of God in the Scriptures—He has eyes and ears, hands and
feet; is capable of joy, pity, laziness, drowsiness, corruptibleness,
prodigality, anger, inexorableness, scorn, even drunkenness—
he compiles a tremendous list of adjectives used to describe God
humanly, only to declare at the end, that the Scriptures never
say that God is proud—

God in the Scriptures is never made so like man, as to be made capable
of Pride; for this had not beene to have God like man, but like the
devill.[25]

Donne used in his preaching the remarkable insight into human
nature which makes his poetry psychologically outstanding. His
study of the love-relationship quickened his exploration of the
mind, and he opened up new territories for conquest—and study.
He can thrust a conventional phrase like 'with all my love' or
'at his side' into that newly discovered country. He does not
puzzle his hearers with new doctrine, new arguments, and
theories. He never has to struggle with an incapacity to follow,
on their part. He is not the prophet before his time, met with
prejudice and opposition. He takes thoughts that are simple,
even commonplace, and invests them with great meaning. His
central thought of Christ coming to the world is orthodox, and so
stated, conventional; but in his company the world was of greater
extent and interest than one knew before. This governing thought
made his exposition of 1 Timothy, i.15, '. . . Christ Jesus came
into the world to save sinners . . .', one of his finest sermons.

[25] II. 288-290; Leslie Stephen says: 'He is specially master of one device. He
reaches a climax, as you suppose, and that only leads to another more surprising,
and so to a third, which eclipses its predecessors.' (*Studies of a Biographer*, III. 75).

Perhaps there is more of novelty than one has allowed, in the thought that, through the Incarnation, the world He came to save is a greater world than we otherwise would have known it to be.[26] There are many notable passages in the sermons, following through an idea from stage to stage, passages which, with adaptation, may be made the basis of acts of devotion. One example is given, an excerpt from the close of the Easter Monday sermon, 1622, arranged to suggest a profitable use of this and similar material—

Look him in the face

> as he lay in the Manger, poor, and then murmur not at temporal wants; suddainly enrich'd by the Tributes of Kings, and doubt not but that God hath large and strange ways to supply thee.

Look him in the face,

> in the Temple, disputing there at twelve years; and then apply thy self to God, to the contemplation of him, to the meditation upon him, to a conversation with him betimes.

Look him in the face

> in his Fathers house; a Carpenter, and but a Carpenter. Take a Calling, and contain thy self in that Calling.

But bring him nearer, and
Look him in the face,

> as he look'd . . . when he whose face the Angels desire to look on, he who was fairer then the children of men . . . was so marr'd more then any man . . . *That they hid their faces from him, & despised him*; when he who bore up the heavens *bowed down his head*, and he who gives breath to all, *gave up the ghost*:

and then Look him in the face again,

> as he look'd . . . not lam'd upon the Cross, not putrifi'd in the Grave, not singed in Hell, rais'd, . . . Victoriously, triumphantly, to the destruction of the last Enemy, death;

Look him in the face

> in all these respects, of Humiliation, and of Exaltation too; and then, as a Picture looks upon him, that looks upon it, God upon whom thou keepest thine Eye, will keep his Eye upon thee.[27]

[26] See I, sermon 9, and esp. pp. 308f.   [27] IV. 130.

He once said that when Christ would 'pierce into' his Father, he prayed with the word 'Abba'.[28] To use his own phrase, he had power given him, as to few other men, to 'pierce into' reality, and part of his high art was not to bring his hearers too suddenly to the conclusion of his thought. The hearer is not immediately confronted with new truth to which his natural reaction is resistance; he meets it, after a journey, recognizing it as inevitable, indisputable, a fact to which he had capitulated somewhere on the way.

Drummond of Hawthornden said of Donne: 'I think, if he would, he might easily be the best Epigrammatist we have found in English.'[29] The gift of terse, clever expression was widely exercised in his sermons, and the following aphorisms are examples of a valuable element of his preaching—

To be changed so, as that we can never be changed more, is the greatest change of all.

. . . as the *eye* sees every thing but *it selfe*, so does *sinne*, too.

God, as God, is never represented to us, with Defensive Armes; He needs them not.

If our goods were not amongst Moveables, yet we our selves are; if they could stay with us, yet we cannot stay with them. . . .

The Church is the spouse of Christ: Noble husbands do not easily admit defamations of their wives.[30]

A feature of all his preaching is the quotation of Latin Fathers of the Church, and the introduction into his sermons of phrases and passages in Latin, which, unlike those in the *Essayes in Divinity* (not prepared for publication) are translated. Donne liked to allude to a subject in a phrase. His brief *Faciamus hominem* and even briefer *Faciamus* conjured up a great idea and a whole argument. Scattered through the sermons are Latin phrases which succinctly summarize for us much that he said at length —*Integritas Christi, Stabit Rex Christus, In domo Patris*, are examples of eloquent phrases. He was particularly fond of St John xiii.1,

---

[28] III. 267.   [29] H. W. Garrod, *John Donne: Poetry and Prose*, p. xlv.
[30] I. 232; II. 119; VII. 65, 271, 409. As Bishop Lightfoot says: 'Of such pithy sayings Donne's sermons are an inexhaustible storehouse.' (*Historical Essays*, p. 242).

with its closing words in the Vulgate, *in finem dilexit eos*, and stressed that, wonderful as it would be if He loved us *in fine*, at our end, it was much more wonderful that He should love us *in finem*, all the way to the end—not our end only, but His end; and, characteristically, amplified the words of Scripture, playing with the double meaning of 'end' as 'conclusion' and 'purpose', asserting that His end is, that He should love us still, for His love is endless.[31]

Donne's sermons are a noble, consistent tribute to Holy Scripture which he pondered and studied all his life. To him the Bible was part of that original utterance by which God created the world, and the Christian preacher, proclaiming, interpreting its message, was continuing that creative work. The canonical Scriptures satisfied him completely, and he discouraged speculation on matters outside their range. But interpretation was not a private matter. It must be as corporate as the world's creation, and he gave an important place to the Church as the interpreter. The preacher, the Church, the Scriptures, the created order, human society, were all held together in his experience by his imaginative, poetic interpretation of the opening chapters of the Bible. Within this fellowship of the Triune Being and of mankind he gave place to the individual, not as interpreter, but as recipient; there was, he would say, something for everyone in the Bible, it was manna for all tastes; and one must search the Scriptures, as one would search a wardrobe—not to make an inventory, but to find something to wear.

Through the Scriptures the story of Creation was embodied, realized for him. The world was created through a word, through the action of the Spirit on the word, through the divine fellowship. The Christian holds in his hands a book, a created word, interpreted by the Spirit through the fellowship of the Church. It had for him the characteristics of an emblem, communicating, in concentrated form, that of which it spoke.

Personal references are not found often in the sermons, and 'illustrations', to use the rather vague modern term, are not plentiful. But the various allusions found in the poems occur also

[31] See II. 182; III. 304; IV. 96; VI. 173; Devotions, 5, Prayer.

in the sermons: to scholastic and Protestant theology; law, casuistry, logic; anatomy, alchemy, medicine; astronomy; chemistry, science; geography, maps, navigation; and the same words, like 'balm', 'mithridate' require explanation—Grierson's commentary on the poems is enriched by many references to the sermons in which the same ideas are found. The student of the poems is all the time in the same world of thought and imagery as that of the sermons.

His sermons, no less than his prose letters and poems, abound in sentences constructed on 'as ... so'. His mind fed upon simple, familiar things and darted from one picture to another to express his meaning, and confirm it from the natural scene. He notes the porter in a great house, ever nearest the door, yet seldom beyond it;[32] the prisoner going to execution, suddenly reprieved, not stopping to enquire why, or how, but eagerly accepting the news without asking any questions; the man who often passes by a house but does not know it like the invited guest; the weary traveller who rejoices even to see the place of execution, because he knows that, though outside, it is near a city. With ease he could appropriately illustrate his meaning because he lived in this world with his eyes open and regarded familiar things as interpreters of mental concepts (conceits). Anything, everything, a book, a room, a rag, a taper, coins was useful to this end, and if it illumined thought it did not matter if it belonged to outmoded fashions or theories—the world of Ptolemy could be as serviceable as that of Copernicus to illustrate meaning. But while there were many good illustrations of ideas in familiar things, some were not just metaphors or even symbols, but emblems, concentrating significance and in their impact upon himself capable of agitating the emotions with an intense apprehension of meaning, awakening thought, not illustrating thought already awakened. Whereas he might look for some confirming illustration to give elegance to his thought, the emblem obtruded upon his thought, insisting upon attention. This is illustrated in his 'Hymne to Christ, at the Authors last going into Germany', the ship and the clouds and the sea, at this time of parting, coercing him into the now infrequent creation of a poem and demanding a Christian interpretation of the ship as the Ark, and the sea as Christ's Blood.

[32] Walton, p. 38.

Examples of the 'illustrations' found in the sermons are as follows:

(*1*) *the Picture:* the treasonable act of taking the picture of a Prince into any 'irreverend' place—but this is what we do to the image of God in our souls.[33]

(*2*) *the Bell:* Donne was much moved by the sound of bells, and references in the sermons are numerous. In one, altering the Vulgate version of 1 Corinthians iv.7, '*Quid autem habes quod non accepisti?*', he asks the question: '*Quid habes quod accepisti?*'; In the course of life it is good to remember that we have nothing which we have not received from God; but the passing bell says, as it tolls, What hast thou of all that thou hast received? Many passages in his sermons, and particularly his *Devotions*, show how the sound of the bell awakened an awareness of death, of man's true state, of man's interrelationship.[34]

(*3*) *the Circle:* The affinity of the sermons and the poems is seen in his use, for purposes of illustration, of the sun, light, a torch,[35] and, especially, the circle. References to this are frequent, and also to the connected idea of the globe of the world, and a map that brings east and west together on a globe; or to a pair of compasses, or simply to the fact that a circle has no angles or corners.

A study of John Donne which has sought to bring into equal prominence and full association the poetry and the sermons, and which has stressed the contribution of his learning in many fields to both, may not unsuitably end with examples of this in his verse and prose. There are references both in his poetry and sermons to mithridate, a universal antidote against poison made through compounding together various ingredients—it was said, over seventy in number; this preparation was named after Mithridates King of Pontus. Describing the fusion of all her qualities in one, John Donne extolled Elizabeth Drury, who had no quality excelling all the others—

> But as in Mithridate, or just perfumes,
> Where all good things being met, no one presumes

---

[33] I. 160.   [34] I. 161.
[35] See 'The Dreame'.
> . . . as torches which must ready bee,
> Men light and put out. . . .'
Grierson, I. 38; and PS, II. 131; III. 371.

> To governe, or to triumph on the rest,
> Only because all were, no part was best.[36]

The last line is an example of his powerful compression. Held within the picture of mithridate, or blended perfumes, is a conception which promoters of that cause which he served, Christian reunion, might contemplate with advantage. The example from the prose is of the preacher using his knowledge gained from the study of law, to describe the forlorn condition of a completely isolated individual, separated from society. In three of his sermons he depicts a man made intestable by law, who is not allowed to dispose of his own property by gift or legacy—he has no rights; not allowed to receive anything from the will of another and presumed to be disinherited; not permitted to testify, and so not to be believed; not to be assisted in any way by the testimony of another. In this way he described the misery of one who is cut off from his fellows, unable to give or to receive, to be believed or assisted. This was a vivid picture in his mind, of the misery of separation, an unnatural singularity, for God, though alone, is not solitary. The thought which satisfied him, and which excited him to write some of his finest prose, was the richness of the divine Being, a fellowship of Persons overflowing in its nature, seeking rest in man. The quintessence of misery, prolonged in hell itself, was the separation of a man, made in such an image, and after so deliberate a counsel and agreement, to be severed, dismembered, apart.[37]

[36] Grierson, I. 255.   [37] See I. 155f; IV. 275; V. 131f.

NINE

REANIMATED

('But I shall see it reanimated'—the last words of Izaak
Walton's Life of Dr John Donne)

SAMUEL TAYLOR COLERIDGE says, of a paragraph
in Donne's Christmas Day sermon, 1626: 'A beautiful
paragraph, well worth extracting, ay, and repreaching.'[1]
Can Donne be repreached? The republication of his sermons,
like that of all his other writings, is a literary necessity, compelled
by the revival of his fame. Grierson's edition of the Poems, 1912,
established the value of the sermons for a study of the poetry, but
their reappearance in an impressive edition invites the question
whether they can be repreached, or assist preaching, today.

It can hardly be an offence, remembering that Donne was the
most self-aware of writers, for a preacher to offer material for
some of his own sermons as a small contribution to the answer.
The five which now follow are a varied selection, from a much
larger number of suitable examples, indicating something of
Donne's influence; the title of each is a quotation from Donne's
sermons. The first reproduces an idea first found in the *Essayes
in Divinity*, and often in the sermons. The second considers an
aspect of Donne's view of man's nature, by means of one of his
most effective emblematic poems. The third presents Donne the
missionary, as he speaks of St Andrew, the one who finds, that he
may seek, and who holds the Christian Year in his hands. The
last two are based on striking expositions of Holy Scripture,
reinforced by passages from his poetry.

Thus the poems no less than the sermons are of value for the
contemporary presentation of the Gospel. Grierson's great work,
which illustrates the verse from the sermons, illustrates also, if
unintentionally, the value of the poetry for the sermons. The
preacher of the modern Church may turn, much to his profit,
to the concentrated insights of a master of words. C. S. Lewis,
a distinguished writer in the Christian cause, gives a flavour of

---

[1] *Notes on English Divines*, ed. Derwent Coleridge, I. 80, commenting on PS, VII.
281f, the paragraph beginning: 'In the first part then'.

Donne to *The Four Loves*, a consideration of Affection, Friendship,
Eros and Charity, introducing his book with the words from 'A
Litanie', 'that our affections kill us not, nor dye', which put the
matter as succinctly and memorably as words can do. That
Donne, aptly quoted, adds distinction, may be illustrated from
an exposition of Acts xxvi.26, 'this thing was not done in a corner',
suggested by the author in a sermon, tracing back this statement
to the fact that Christ's death was a public execution, an event of
history memorably compressed by Donne into the words, 'Pub-
lique at Golgotha'. This present work owes much to 'Metempsychosis, The Progresse of the Soule', which is not an obvious quarry
for preachers, with its concluding commendation of relativist
ethics—

> Ther's nothing simply good, nor ill alone,
> Of every quality comparison,
> The onely measure is, and judge, opinion,

yet, hidden in the poem, to contradict this, is

> A swan, so white that you may unto him
> Compare all whitenesse, but himselfe to none.

What better miniature of Christ could one desire? Tightly
compressed, involved; quickening thought, presenting an incontestable argument through a self-justifying familiar image, it has
the essential qualities of metaphysical wit. But, also incontestably,
it has an even greater claim to distinction—it says something.[2]

1. God loves his owne example, to doe as he hath done.
(From a sermon on Psalm xxxii.10f, PS, IX.409.)

Text: And they that did eat of the loaves were about five thousand
men . . . And they that had eaten were about four
thousand. . . . (St Mark vi.44, viii.9.)

The miraculous feeding of the five thousand is told with impressive consistency by all four Evangelists (Mark vi, Matthew xiv,
Luke ix, John vi). Mark (viii) and Matthew (xv) also narrate
another, similar miracle, the number on this occasion being four
thousand. Luke and John both omit this second story. There is
no confusion in the mind of Mark, our primary authority, he is
quite sure that both events took place, and the second is introduced

2 Grierson, I. 347, 335, 316, 304.

with the words: 'In those days, when there was again a great
multitude, and they had nothing to eat . . .' (viii.1, R.V.). A
little later he records our Lord's own reference to both occurrences
(verses 19f).

There is a spiritual significance in this repetition. His meditation on Holy Scripture had introduced John Donne to a thought
about God of which he became so fond that he brought it into his
sermons more than once. Suitably, the theme was that of God
repeating Himself. He was impressed with the story of Moses
and the tables of the Law, and refers to this early on in the *Essayes
in Divinity*—

For God, who first writ his Law in the *Tables of our hearts*; and when our
corruption had defaced them, writ it again in *Stone-tables*; and when
Moses zealous anger had broken them, writ them again in *other tables*, . . .

Later, he meditates upon the deliverance of God's people from
Egypt, and applies this story from the past to his own spiritual
history—

. . . thou, and all mankind are delivered from an Egypt. . . . And then,
camest thou, O Christ, thine own *Moses*, and deliveredst us. . . .

and his mind seizes hold of a truth which he would reiterate
in later sermons—

Lastly, descend, O my Soul, to the very Center, . . . and consider to
what a land of promise, and heavenly *Hierusalem* God will at last bring
thee, from the *Egypt* of this world, and the most Egyptiacal part, this
flesh. God is so abundantly true, that he ever performes his words
more then once. And therefore, as he hath fulfilled that promise,
Out of Egypt have I called my Son; So will he also perform it in every one
of his elect; and as when *Herod* dyed, his Angell appeared to *Joseph in
Egypt in a dream*, to call him thence; So when our persecutor, our flesh
shall dy, and the slumber of death shall overtake us in this our *Egypt*,
His Angels . . . shall call and invite us from this *Egypt* to that *Canaan*.[3]

God is so abundantly true, that He ever performs His words
more than once! This declaration gives distinction to these *Essayes*,
and value to the laboured, protracted discussions to which it
belongs, and which made it possible. The thought behind it is his
repeated insistence on the significance of Creation. This to him
is not a single event of time past, something that happened, but

3 *Essayes in Divinity*, pp. 9, 74-76.

as the first event which was the beginning of all that has followed. Creation, in its nature, is continuous. The Genesis story witnesses to the events of one day followed by the events of the next. One leads on to two, two to three. The distance between Nothing and One is infinitely greater than between any succeeding numbers. The act of Creation contains the promise of repetition. The first day was followed by the second. That which God does, He does again; all creation, and so all mankind, is included in this truth, and what has happened in the past records what, essentially, can be repeated. The Exodus is a past event which can be renewed in every age, even as the Spirit who moved once upon the face of the waters can always bring order out of chaos. And so for him the Scriptures could never be a book about the past. They were written for our learning.

God is so abundantly true, that He ever performs His words more than once! These words, at least, earn the right to be repeated. And they contain the essence of his message, for, in the ample pages of his sermons we find him repeating himself on the theme of the Mercy of God, God loving His own example, doing as He hath done. God remembers His former works, and we must cultivate the art of recalling our experience of His goodness towards us.[4]

The theme of God's mercy seen in Him repeating Himself occupied his close attention in the vast sermon of Easter Monday, 1622, the longest he ever preached. The text (2 Corinthians iv.6) prompted the thought. What was done in the Creation is done every day. God, who commanded the light to shine out of darkness, hath shined in our hearts, to give the light of the knowledge of the glory of God in the face of Jesus Christ. God compares Himself with His own past.

One generation is a precedent to another, and *God* is his own Example; whatsoever he hath done for us, he is ready to do again.

This is what happened when Moses came down from the mount and saw the molten calf set up by Aaron, and the people dancing and singing, and his anger waxed hot, and he cast the tables out of his hands, and broke them beneath the mount (Exodus xxxii.19); God turned to His own precedent, and wrote the Law again—'And the LORD said unto Moses, Hew thee two tables

---

[4] See II. 73f; VIII. 261f.

of stone like unto the first: and I will write upon these tables the words that were in the first tables, which thou brakest' (Exodus xxxiv.1, A.V.). Donne reminds his hearers of a recent experience in their national history, when Queen Mary had halted the Reformation; God turned to His own precedent and established the Reformation once more under her successor Elizabeth.

Donne was fond of this word 'precedent'—

God hath no law upon himselfe, but yet God himselfe proceeds by precedent: And whensoever we present to him with thanksgiving, what he hath done, he does the same, and more againe.

Rule by Precedent is, he declares, one of the secrets of State by which He governs. He gives, and gives more, to the one who has already received. And every good action is but His exercise by which to do better. 'The LORD hath heard my supplication; the LORD will receive my prayer' (Psalm vi.9)—the Lord hath, and therefore He will: that is the simple logic. Christ is the Samaritan who comes to the wounded man; not only did He see him, have compassion on him, go to him, bind up his wounds, pour in oil and wine, put him on his own beast, bring him to an inn and provide for him: He promised to come again. He will repeat His mercies. As long as He is God, He has more to give than we have received, and He is more than willing to give it.

How differently God argues! If a beggar comes to us, we say: 'I gave you something only yesterday.' But when we come to God, He gives to us today *because* He gave to us yesterday. By giving He learns to give, His practice makes Him perfect. Every blessing He bestows, instead of discharging an obligation, imposes a new one upon Him—

he delights to give where he hath given, as though his former gifts were but his places of memory, and marks set upon certain men, to whom he was to give more.

The ground of our confidence before God is not our love of Him; how little that argument will prevail upon Him; the ground of our confidence is His mercy toward us, for if He has given He will give again.

We have good reason to know that this theme was frequently in Donne's private meditations, for it was his duty as Prebendary of Chiswick to recite daily five Psalms lxii-lxvi;[5] he preached a

---

[5] See p. 173f, *supra*.

sermon on each of them, and in three of the five sermons, the
2nd, 4th and 5th, he refers to God's repeated mercies. God, he
declares, by having done much already, has bound Himself to
do more. 'Because thou hast been my help, therefore in the
shadow of thy wings will I rejoice' (Psalm lxiii.7). Every Decree
of God has written into it His will that the same should be done
again whenever there is need. The overthrow of Pharaoh and
of Sennacherib long ago contained the promise of the defeat
of the Armada and of the Gunpowder Plot, within living memory.
Prophecies become Histories in the day of their fulfilment. And
Histories are Prophecies of mercies still to come: yes, and of
warnings, for in Invasion and in Powder-treason, and in pestilence
God repeats His ancient cry, 'Heare the word of the Lord.'[6]

Thus, in his meditations upon Holy Scripture, and especially
his own five Psalms, his 'five loaves', as he called them[7], he found
a truth to which he gave expression in his *Essayes in Divinity*,
in many sermons, and in his *Devotions*, (5, Prayer). It is there, in
the Scriptures, for all to find—in Abraham and Sarah, Zacharias
and Elisabeth (Genesis xvii.15-19, Luke i.13-18); in the rewriting
of the roll after the first had been burnt by Jehoiakim, King of
Judah (Jeremiah xxxvi.27f); in the return of Christ to Cana,
where He made the water wine (John iv.46); in the voice out of
heaven, declaring of the Father's name: 'I have both glorified
it, and will glorify it again' (John xii.28). In Christian experience
the Lord's Day has been what it was to Thomas, the day of the
repeated blessing—on the first Easter evening, he was not with
the other disciples when Jesus came to them. 'And after eight
days again his disciples were within, and Thomas with them:
then came Jesus, the doors being shut, and stood in the midst,
and said, Peace be unto you.' (John xx.26).

Not many hours before he died John Wesley sang verses from
a hymn by his brother Charles—it was the last of his eighteen
Hymns for the Nativity of our Lord, and his farewell words, 'The
best of all is, God is with us', are much more significant when
interpreted by his meditation on the Nativity. He who was
made man is with His people to the end of the world. The hymn
that he sang expresses one of the central convictions of John
Donne, with an application that is intensely modern—

[6] IV. 97f, see p. 93; V. 272, 365; VI. 39, 50f, see IX. 335, VI. 174, VIII. 155f;
VI. 350f; VII. 62f, 313f, VIII. 112, 122; VI. 220—see I. 173.
[7] VII. 301.

All glory to God in the sky,
And peace upon earth be restored!
O Jesus, exalted on high,
Appear, our omnipotent Lord!
Who, meanly in Bethlehem born,
Didst stoop to redeem a lost race,
Once more to Thy creatures return,
And reign in Thy kingdom of grace.

O wouldst Thou again be made known!
Again in Thy Spirit descend,
And set up in each of Thine own
A kingdom that never shall end.
Thou only art able to bless,
And make the glad nations obey,
And bid the dire enmity cease,
And bow the whole world to Thy sway.[8]

God is so abundantly true, that He ever performs His words more than once. Whatsoever He hath done for us, He is ready to do again, for He loves His own example, to do as He hath done.

2. Man is a future creature.

(From a Sermon of Commemoration of the Lady Danvers, PS, VIII. 75).

Text: (Charity) . . . believeth all things . . . (A.V.)
    (Love is) . . . always eager to believe the best . . . (Moffatt)
    (1 Corinthians xiii.7).

On 1st July 1627 John Donne preached in Chelsea Parish Church a sermon of commemoration of Lady Danvers, formerly Mrs Magdalen Herbert, his friend for many years. The sonnet[9] addressed to her indicates her influence upon the religious poems, and we know that he stayed at the home of Sir John and Lady Danvers at Chelsea during the plague of 1625, writing out many of his sermons. She was the mother of Edward and George Herbert, and so a link between Donne, his works, and the 'school' which is sometimes named after him. Under the influence of the text (2 Peter iii.13) and the occasion, his thought turns to the future, to the new heavens and earth, the intimation of which in

[8] *The Poetical Works of John and Charles Wesley,* IV. 125f; *Methodist Hymn-book,* No. 902; *The BBC Hymn-book,* No. 29.
[9] Grierson, I. 317f.

o

man he declares to be an insatiable desire of more than this world can provide. Man's nature is to expect more, and part of the proof of the immortality of the soul is man's unsatisfied nature, ever reaching out to something beyond this life. 'Creatures of an inferiour nature are possest with the *present*; *Man* is a future *Creature.*' In a sermon on Proverbs viii.17, 'preached to Queen Anne' in 1617, soon after his ministry had begun, speaking of Christ's love for us, he declared:

He loves us as his ancient inheritance, as the first amongst his creatures in the creation of the world, which he created for us: He loves us more as his purchase, whom he hath bought with his blood; for even man takes most pleasure in things of his own getting; But he loves us most for our improvement, when by his ploughing up of our hearts, and the dew of his grace, and the seed of his word, we come to give a greater rent, in the fruites of sanctification than before.

In a sermon on Psalm xxxviii.9 he says that God is omniscient, not time-conditioned, knowing all things that were, are, and shall or may be, and that may not be; He knows things otherwise than they are, for He knows future things as present. In the sermon preached just before the burial of King James, considering a favourite theme Who are we? he says, unless we see ourselves in terms of the future, of the life to come, we are short-sighted. Do we see the man to be in the cradle? The present implies the future. Man's physical growth is the writing into his bodily nature of a spiritual reality. We are sinners, but we may grow in grace. The ladder is a fitting symbol of this, for men do not stand still upon it. Christ Himself increased in wisdom, and in stature, and in favour with God, and man, and a Christian must do the same, asking questions, informing his understanding, enlightening his faith. In the sermon preached at The Hague, in 1619, on Matthew iv.18-20, he considers the first disciples as men who were chosen to be made in the Master's hands into what He could see them, but they could not see themselves, to be—

Such men he took then, as might be no occasion to their hearers, to ascribe the work to their sufficiency; but yet such men too, as should be no examples to insufficient men to adventure upon that great service; but men, though ignorant before, yet docil, and glad to learne. In a rough stone, a cunning Lapidary will easily foresee, what his cutting, and his polishing, and his art will bring that stone to. A cunning Statuary discerns in a Marble-stone under his feet, where there will arise an Eye, and an Eare, and a Hand, and other lineaments to make it a perfect Statue. Much more did our Saviour Christ, who was himselfe the Author of that disposition in them, . . . foresee in these fishermen, an inclinablenesse to become usefull in that great service of his Church. Therefore hee tooke them from their owne ship, but he sent them from his Crosse; Hee tooke them weatherbeaten with North and South winds, and rough-cast with foame, and mud; but he sent them back soupled, and smoothed, and levigated, quickned, and inanimated with that Spirit, which he had breathed into them. . . . Hee tooke fisher-men, and he sent fishers of men.[10]

The love of God is universal. There are, within our experience, lovable people—though they have their off days which remind us of the uncertainty of human nature. To a limited extent we can imagine that God finds something to love in them. But we can find nothing lovable in some people, and imagination fails to help us when we contemplate God's love of them. We cannot base the love of God for 'every soul of man' on the lovableness of man, on some hidden excellence undisclosed to us, the something hidden that the mother sees in the child, or the lover, and only the lover, in the beloved. How can God love a monstrous tyrant, or 'the itchy Lecher'? and if He can, is His love admirable? George Bernard Shaw was against unlovable people trying to love one another. He denied that God is Love, and declared that the sentimental 'Love one another' and 'Our Father' of Jesus did not fit into a world of savages, whom to love would be unnatural vice.[11]

Christianity is aware of the objection which it makes personal, particular. The Christian's problem is not, 'How can God love so-and-so?' but, 'How can He possibly love me?' In my moments of self-awareness I know that there is nothing lovable in me. Inwardly I know, with Paul, that in me, that is, in my flesh, dwelleth no good thing (Romans vii.18); even if I quieten others' suspicions, I never silence my own. The New Testament and Christian Worship alike resound with the astonished cry of those who never cease to wonder that God should love them. When

---

[10] See PS, VIII. 75; I. 236, 241; II. 151; VI. 285f; see I. 315; II. 232-234, 276; II. 291 on the principle of growth as part of the meaning of life, corroborated by Genesis i. 28; VII. 108; VI. 308.

[11] Grierson, I. 323; Blanche Patch, *Thirty Years with G.B.S.*, pp. 169, 189.

the last secret of this mysterious universe has been wrested from
Nature by science, and the universe is mysterious no longer, the
Christian Gospel will hold mystery and wonder at its heart,
because—

> It is a thing most wonderful,
> Almost too wonderful to be,
> That God's own Son should come from heaven,
> And die to save a child like me.

'But God commendeth his love toward us, in that, while we were
yet sinners, Christ died for us. . . . the Son of God, who loved me,
and gave himself for me' (Romans v.8, Galatians ii.20).

> Jesu, what didst Thou find in me,
> That Thou hast dealt so lovingly? . . .

> And can it be that I should gain
> An interest in the Saviour's blood?
> Died He for me, who caused His pain?
> For me, who Him to death pursued?
> Amazing love! how can it be,
> That Thou, my God, shouldst die for me!
> 'Tis mystery all . . .[12]

Is there anything more to be said than to assert simply that God
loves us, and it is mysterious and wonderful? Are we to suppose
that, in our self-condemnation we are less than fair to ourselves
(and possibly to Him who created us) and that, even though we
cannot find it, neither can those who know us best, there is good
in the worst, some uncorrupted core of good, of worth, that is
dear to God? This assumption explains away the problem, but
does not explain the uneasiness remaining, that we do but flatter
and deceive ourselves. Or, not bankrupt of ingenuity, shall we
live by the slogan that God hates the sin yet loves the sinner?
This distinction, admittedly, human beings find difficult to apply
to these relationships. It is theoretical, untenable in experience,
for sin is not abstract, impersonal. Where there is sin there is a
sinner. Nevertheless, unsatisfactory as the distinction is, it points
the way to something more convincing.

When I say that God loves me, what do I mean? As there are
two sides to every question, so there are two or more aspects to

---

[12] See *Methodist Hymn-book*, Hymns 854, 438, 371.

human personality. When we cease to be governed by the awareness of immediate needs and experiences, when by mental reflection we link present with past and future, when the feelings of
the moment are set between remorse and hope, when, in brief,
that which makes us human beings and not animals rises to the
surface and dominates us, the simple statement, 'God loves me'
becomes complex. There is the historic self, oneself in retrospect;
there is the actual self, faced with immediate needs and duties
and circumstances; there is the ideal self, or the possible, potential
self, oneself seen in prospect, the self one would like to be, involving desires, ambitions, yet shadowed by uncertainty on how much
of life remains.

That which is potential, possible, is as much part of the true
self as the actual. The flower-seed is planted in the garden, and
one's concern at that moment is to provide right conditions for
growth, that the seed may flower. If a person gives me a hundred
pounds, he gives me, in addition to the actual money, its potential
earning power, the interest—a Latin word which means 'it
concerns, is important to', a suitable word, for the earning power
of money is not a by-product, it interests its possessor, and the
meaning would be given if one spoke, not of the 'interest', but the
'concern'. The gardener, the investor, the parent, all are concerned, have an interest in, the future.

When I say that God loves me, I do not mean that He likes
me, approves of me, delights in me, as I am. I mean that He
sees me, not only as I am and was, but also as He can make me.
This vision of the possible is a divine insight communicated to
those who themselves respond; and, as the New Testament so
strongly apprehends, the consequence of awakening to God's
love for us is that we begin to love others in the same way. It
is not a matter of intellectual gymnastics, like distinguishing
sin and sinners; it is a spiritual capacity, an endowment conferred
by God Himself Who is, as John Donne says, a future God.[13]

'Elegie V. His Picture' tells of Donne's departure on foreign
service—either the expedition against Cadiz in 1596 or the
expedition to the Azores, in the following year. He presents to
his beloved a portrait of himself; when he returns, weather-beaten,
bearing the marks of battle and exposure, and people say to her,
'what, did you once love *him*?', this picture will show what I was.

---

[13] PS, VIII. 75, immediately after the statement that man is a future creature.

But you will not be altered. My love for you will be unchanged.
And your love will have outgrown its first dependence on 'my
picture'; you will have discovered a more mature capacity to
love me, not as I was once, but as I shall be then.

His Picture.

Here take my Picture; though I bid farewell,
Thine, in my heart, where my soule dwels, shall dwell.
'Tis like me now, but I dead, 'twill be more
When wee are shadowes both, then 'twas before.
When weather-beaten I come backe; my hand,
Perhaps with rude oares torne, or Sun beams tann'd,
My face and brest of hairecloth, and my head
With cares rash sodaine stormes, being o'rspread,
My body 'a sack of bones, broken within,
And powders blew staines scatter'd on my skinne;
If rivall fooles taxe thee to 'have lov'd a man,
So foule, and course, as, Oh, I may seeme than,
This shall say what I was: and thou shalt say,
Doe his hurts reach mee? doth my worth decay?
Or doe they reach his judging minde, that hee
Should now love lesse, what hee did love to see?
That which in him was faire and delicate,
Was but the milke, which in loves childish state
Did nurse it: who now is growne strong enough
To feed on that, which to disused tasts seemes tough.[14]

Edward Dowden writes: 'His lady will have the greater joy in
knowing that she still owns her full beauty to bestow on one so
worn, and will feel that the loss of what was fair and delicate
in him is more than compensated by the manlier complexion of
his love.'[15]

Although this is one of a collection of secular poems, it illustrates
its author's alert and informed interest in religious matters, and
at the close, refers clearly to Holy Scripture—

And I, brethren, could not speak unto you as unto spiritual, but as
unto carnal, even as unto babes in Christ. I have fed you with milk,
and not with meat: for hitherto ye were not able to bear it, neither yet
now are ye able . . . For when for the time ye ought to be teachers, ye
have need that one teach you again which be the first principles of the
oracles of God; and are become such as have need of milk, and not of

---

[14] Grierson, I. 86f.   [15] E. Dowden, *New Studies in Literature*, p. 108.

strong meat. For every one that useth milk is unskilful in the word of righteousness: for he is a babe. But strong meat belongeth to them that are of full age, even those who by reason of use have their senses exercised to discern both good and evil. (1 Corinthians iii.1f, Hebrews v.12-14.)

In one of the most important and informing articles written on John Donne, Miss Helen Gardner in 'John Donne: a Note on Elegie V, "His Picture",'[16] shows that this poem not only refers to the New Testament, it alludes thereby to a tradition of devotional literature, of which Donne would be aware, which regarded love for Jesus in His Manhood as the beginning of Christian devotion, which became mature in love for Him as both God and man. The argument of the poem is that the woman, on his return, will have outgrown her dependence on his outward appearance, and become practised (as the passage in Hebrews stresses) in mature love. This distinction of love for the human Christ and love for the divine-human Christ, the first associated with milk and the second with meat, is found in Walter Hilton's *The Scale of Perfection*, one of the most popular devotional books in the fifteenth and sixteenth centuries; in St Bernard and St Augustine the same tradition of thought may be traced much earlier. Our Lord's words to Mary Magdalene, 'Touch me not' (John xx.17) were seen to discourage dependence on the visible and tangible and human, the point of the poem.

Christian Love believes all things, is always eager to believe the best, is optimistic about man, and bases judgements concerning him on his possibilities of good. As Percy Ainsworth, using the Genesis story, said, 'Love is the spirit brooding over all the possibility of good in life that is now without form and void'.[17] This Love makes no compromise with evil in the person loved, for, patient, it is prepared to wait, and to apply a rigorous, purging discipline to achieve its positive end. It is free from sentimentality, and untruth, from a pathetic, easy-going tolerance which trifles with reality in suggesting that what is black is only grey. It is a Love which is even prepared to hurt the beloved, and to question the credentials of a 'love' which will not rebuke and chasten—'For whom the Lord loveth he chasteneth, and scourgeth every son whom he receiveth' (Hebrews xii.6).

[16] *Modern Language Review*, 1944, pp. 333-337.
[17] P. Ainsworth, *St Paul's Hymn to Love*, p. 93.

The Christian Gospel is a proclamation of this Love in Jesus Christ.

> My song is love unknown;
> My Saviour's love to me;
> Love to the loveless shown,
> That they might lovely be—

these words of Samuel Crossman compress the truth into a few words. In the Gospels we see Him loving people in this quite miraculous way. It is the father, as Jesus sees him, who welcomes the prodigal son, and says: 'Bring forth the best robe, and put it on him; and put a ring on his hand, and shoes on his feet . . .' (Luke, xv.22), and always those who see with the eyes of Jesus see, not the prodigal, but the son, with the robe, the ring and the shoes. In His eyes the fishermen are apostles, fishers of men; the lepers, the dumb, the crippled, are healed, restored; he sees hidden possibilities in women, in little children, in publicans and sinners, in the woman of Samaria, in Zacchæus, in the Gentiles. Even those who cast Him out in crucifixion could be forgiven, because they did not see themselves as He saw them.

But the Gospel is not only a proclamation of His love. It is a communication of this love, in His Church, to the world, His world. The apostles, the sick whom He healed, the women who found a purpose for living in His service, the woman who left her waterpot, the tax-collector to whose house salvation came, these, the immediate objects of the Saviour's love, were quickened by it to love as they were loved, and the Christan Church began a vast, awakening work of renewal, of hope, with the world for its parish, to uplift the slave, the prostitute, the abandoned child, the primitive savage, the criminal. The missionary, the social reformer, the educator, the doctor, all who put protecting hands around human life, are communicating to mankind the Love that came to Bethlehem, to be subjected to the same conditions of growth and potentiality which should be the true 'interest' of the human race. Those who know the love of Christ, and learn, in however small degree, to love as He loved, are not weakened in their faith by scientific demonstrations that man's origins were different from what, by the Scriptures, he supposed. To know the value that Love can give to the least and to the worst is to trace forward the story of mankind, to see beginnings in the light of their

endings, and properly to give the deciding word to teleology and
not anthropology. Man is a future creature, and the Church,
though, like the race itself, begun in lowliness—even a greater
lowliness, of scourging, buffeting, spitting, nails and thorns—is
the company of those who communicate the Saviour's love, and
she knows that, whatever her imperfections and her blemishes
(and her lovers, not her detractors, know her unworthiness) her
destiny is noble and the purpose conceived for her the unchanging
purpose of Him who created her and for its sake bears with her
—to present to Himself a glorious Church, not having spot, or
wrinkle, or any such thing; but holy and without blemish. And
this, every Christian knows, 'is reserved for the Triumphant time
when she shall be in possession of that beauty, which Christ
foresaw in her, long before when he said, *Thou art all faire my love,
and there is no spot in thee*'.[18] The realization of this is yet to be, but
He foresaw, proleptically, the work accomplished. Meanwhile,
amid the struggle, we will sing of ourselves and all mankind,

> Finish then Thy new creation,
> Pure and spotless let us be;
> Let us see Thy great salvation,
> Perfectly restored in Thee.[19]

3. The fecundity of true Religion.

(From a sermon preached at The Hague, PS, II. 271.)

Text: One of the two which heard John speak, and followed him,
was Andrew, Simon Peter's brother. He first findeth his
own brother Simon, and saith unto him, We have found
the Messias, which is, being interpreted, the Christ. (St
John i.40f.)

Throughout his ministry John Donne referred frequently to St
Andrew. He would observe that, appropriately, his Day comes
first in the Christian Year. In his sermon for Whitsunday 1629,
on the second verse of Holy Scripture, 'And the Spirit of God
moved upon the face of the waters', he points out that this was
the first allusion to a Person of the Trinity, following upon the
reference in the first verse to the Godhead; and he illustrates his

---

[18] PS, V. 126; see The Song of Solomon, iv.7.
[19] See the hymn, 'Love divine, all loves excelling', by Charles Wesley (*Methodist
Hymn-book*, No. 431, *BBC Hymn-book*, Nos. 328, 329). The full version is reprinted
in Frank Baker, *Representative Verse of Charles Wesley* (London, 1962), No. 69.

meaning from the Church Year, in which St Andrew's Day is placed next to All Saints' Day. He made similar reference to Andrew ten years earlier, preaching at The Hague shortly before Christmas 1619, when accompanying Viscount Doncaster on his embassy of peace to the Continent, on the eve of the Thirty Years War—

And in *Andrews* thus early applying himselfe to Christ, we are also to note, . . . the fecundity of true Religion; for, as soone as he had found Christ, he sought his brother *Peter, Et duxit ad Iesum,* he made his brother as happy as himselfe, he led him to Jesus; (And that other Disciple, which came to Christ as soone as *Andrew* did, yet because he is not noted to have brought any others but himselfe, is not named in the Gospel). . . Therefore doth the Church celebrate the memory of *S. Andrew,* first of any Saint in the yeare; and after they have been altogether united in that one festivall of *All-Saints, S. Andrew* is the first that hath a particular day.

There is an earlier reference to Andrew in a sermon preached to Queen Anne in 1617, in a characteristic passage on the fellowship that is the authentic sign of the Christian Religion—

And let no man be afraid to seek or find him for fear of the loss of good company; Religion is no sullen thing, it is not a melancholly, there is not so sociable a thing as the love of Christ Jesus. It was the first word which he who first found Christ of all the Apostles, Saint *Andrew,* is noted to have said, *Invenimus Messiam,* we have found the Messias, and it is the first act that he is noted to have done, after he had found him, to seek his brother *Peter, & duxit ad Jesum,* so communicable a thing is the love of Jesus, when we have found him.

In his first sermon as Dean of St Paul's, the great Christmas Day sermon (1621) on John i.8, he refers at length to him, and in another sermon preached there on the same text, in the following year, he again underlines the significant omission of the name of Andrew's companion—

onely *Andrew* is named, who sought out his brother *Simon,* and drew *him* in, and so propagated the Church, and spread the Glory of God . . . It will be but Christs first question at the last day, *What hast thou done for me?* If we can answer *that,* he will aske, *What hast thou suffered for me?* And if we can answer *that,* he will aske at last, *Whom hast thou won to me, what soul hast thou added to my kingdome?*

St Andrew holds in his hands the two ends of the Christian

Year, and expounds its meaning. He is the disciple who notices
the lad with the five barley loaves and two small fishes. He is the
one to whom Philip comes, to speak of the Gentiles (St John
vi.9, xii.22). He understands that small, simple things can have
great significance and use, and human speech supreme importance. St John's Gospel, which is based upon its opening declaration, that, in the beginning, was the Word, takes us back, behind
the call of the apostles at the sea of Galilee, to the simple human
talk in which great movements have their commencement.
Historians, narrating the events of the past, point to an event at
which a movement began—a moment of conversion, a meeting on
a known date in a building made significant by it. Here, for
example, we may stand and say, the Edinburgh Missionary
Conference was held in 1910, the event which began the ecume-
nical movement of our century. But before it was—talk. John
takes us behind the event to the speech, to the encounter of
persons, that made it possible. And this tradition of St Andrew,
which we can trace throughout Donne's preaching, holds together
the Church, even as he holds together the Church Year. Some
things a man may know through his inward nature—human
reason, natural law, liberty, affection. A sense of awe and
mystery and worship is innate. The inward man can distinguish
beauty from ugliness, right from wrong. He may inwardly believe
in the immortality of the soul; but he cannot inwardly believe in
the Resurrection of Jesus, son of Mary. This he must be told. For
this beginning he is dependent absolutely on a word. John Donne,
meditating upon the Transfiguration and the fact that Moses and
Elijah talked with Christ, said, in one of his sermons preached at
Lincoln's Inn:

As there is a *Communion* of Saints, so there is a *Communication* of Saints.
Think not heaven a Charter-house, where men, who onely of all
creatures, are enabled by God to *speak*, must not speak to one another.
The Lord of heaven is *Verbum*, The word, and his servants there talk
of us here, and pray to him for us.

On Wednesday, 13th November 1622, he preached what
Augustus Jessopp called 'the first *missionary sermon* ever preached
in England since Britain had become a Christian land'[20] before

[20] Jessopp, p. 148; for a criticism of this statement, and an assessment of the
sermon, see Stanley Johnson, 'John Donne and the Virginia Company', *ELH* XIV.
(1947) 127-138 and especially p. 128f.

the Honourable Company of the Virginian Plantation, founded
some years earlier. The sermon was published, and, addressing
the Company in a dedicatory epistle, he says: 'I had some place
amongst you, before: but now I am an Adventurer; if not to
VIRGINIA, yet for VIRGINIA.' The young colony was faced with
great problems and discouragements, but Donne urged his hearers
to persevere, realizing the importance of what was being
attempted. He was fully persuaded of the universality of the
Gospel, and of the responsibility of the Church to evangelize the
peoples of the New World. Recalling the last words of St Matthew
he presented the apostolic succession in missionary terms—those
whom Christ addressed would not themselves live to the end of the
world, but their successors would link them to the end of which
they were the beginning. We who so often think of this succession
from our age back to theirs need to remember that it is as much
for the future as the past. These Adventurers, to whom he
preached, would be succeeded by others, their work would
develop, grow. His sermon, on Acts i.8 is, principally, a vigorous
plea that the propagation of the Gospel among the natives and
colonists of Virginia should be accepted as their primary task.
Characteristically he drives home the significance of the word
'Acts' in the title of the book, and thinks of them as actors on a
stage, the world, on which they present the drama of the Gospel;
declaring:

O, if you could once bring a *Catechisme* to bee as good ware amongst
them as a bugle, as a knife, as a hatchet: O, if you would be as ready
to hearken at the returne of a *Ship*, how many *Indians* were converted
to *Christ Iesus*, as what Trees, or druggs, or Dyes that Ship had brought,
then you were in your right way, and not till then . . . let your principall
ende, bee the propagation of the *glorious Gospell*. . . .

The Gospel is universal, to be proclaimed in the countryside as well
as in the city, for

Christ was not whip'd to save Beggars, and crown'd with Thornes to
save Kings: he dyed, he suffered all, for all.[21]

Seek, and ye shall find. Find, and ye shall seek.

[21] See PS, IX. 92f; II. 271f; I. 246; III. 350f; IV. 234; III. 122; IV. 264, 280, 269,
271, 277; also III. 239, 307 for further references to Andrew, and I. 286, 307f, V. 51
for some further references to evangelism.

4. Stabit Rex Christus.

(In the margin of the last paragraph of a sermon preached to the King at Whitehall, PS, VIII. 252).

Text: The woman saith unto him, Sir, give me this water, that I thirst not, neither come hither to draw. Jesus saith unto her, Go, call thy husband, and come hither. (St John iv.15f.)

To consider the conversation between Jesus and the woman of Samaria is a profitable spiritual exercise. It also tests and stretches the intelligence. A study of a conversation is different from that of a book. One expects prose to be orderly in arrangement. One listens to a speaker more easily if one can see the relationship of what is being said to the subject as a whole. The digression sometimes irritates and confuses, and one says: 'What has all this to do with the subject?' A well-arranged address, the material logically ordered, is rewarded by intelligent, responsive listening. But when it comes to conversation, human talk, the matter is different. Only imaginary conversations, literary dialogues, will be orderly, arranged, free from interruption, and complete in expression. Real conversations are spontaneous, unprepared; they lack form and order, the thought moves forwards and backwards, digressions must be tolerated, for what seems irrelevant to the hearer has a bearing on the subject for the speaker. One remark leads on to another. The speaker, the writer, communicates himself fully, but a reported conversation reveals part only of the encounter of persons. It says nothing of the silences, and whether they were awkward or enjoyable; of the stress on the words spoken and the expression on the face at the time; of the meaning in the voice; of the understanding, or the doubt, when the eyes of one meet the eyes of the other; the words reported as spoken are the least part of the encounter. All this makes the study of a conversation so interesting; each student can be his own interpreter; the scholar will help to determine the meaning of the words, but each of us can be expert in their interpretation, in so far as we know human nature. We must bring to our study now the exercise of imagination, and read into the recorded words the gestures, the looks, the silences, the subdued voices and the rising flush on the face, as two people talk beside a well.

This conversation has an inexhaustible fascination. It is real

talk, not ordered dialogue. The story begins with Jesus coming
to Jacob's well, in Samaria, outside Sychar. He is tired, after a
long journey, and rests, alone, on the well head. A woman comes
to draw water, and He asks her for a drink.

> Was not his pity towards thee wondrous high,
> That would have need to be pittied by thee?[22]

The request by a Jew for a service from a Samaritan, and by a
man of a woman, neither knowing the other, was sufficiently
unusual to begin a conversation, in which He discloses that He
has more to give her than she has to give Him. He is as puzzling as
His words, and she can comprehend neither. There is a literal
meaning which one can follow, and if all fails one can take Him
literally, though one has the strange feeling that He does not mean
what the words literally, obviously mean. She is in the presence
of Mystery. He refers to living water—the well water is spring
water, 'living'—which He is able and ready to give her, water
in endless supply which will last for ever. The situation quickly
changes. He asked her for water, but now she finds herself asking
Him! 'The woman saith unto him, Sir, give me this water, that
I thirst not, neither come hither to draw.' 'Jesus saith unto her,
Go, call thy husband, and come hither.' Between these two statements there is not only a full stop in print, there is a full stop in the
conversation. We have to discover the connection of thought,
the argument not fully revealed in the words. We need to know
what they are thinking to understand the relationship between
her words to Him, 'give me this water', and His words to her,
'Go, call thy husband'. No human talk moves on like this without
pauses. And there was not only a pause. Their eyes met. Donne's
early love poems are often encounters of persons, and they are
living, colloquial arguments, conversations, and he expresses well
the power of the eyes to confirm affection, and to interpenetrate
to hidden depths. The lovers' silence in 'The Extasie' is simply
expressed—

> All day, the same our postures were,
> And wee said nothing, all the day,

and the power of the eyes of the one meeting those of the other—

[22] Grierson, I. 319.

Our eye-beames twisted, and did thred
Our eyes, upon one double string. . . .[23]

The encounter of Jesus and this woman was not the tranquil, unembarrassed, confirming union of 'The Extasie', but it requires the same elements of silence and the penetrating gaze to understand it. The text should be read with a pause between 'draw' and 'Jesus'.

Why did Jesus abruptly change the conversation? We follow her meaning, her dull, literal interpretation of His words; we see the immediate advantage to her as plainly as she sees it. But why does He so speak? what is the connection of thought? After His words to her she says, 'I have no husband', and Jesus says, 'Thou hast well said, I have no husband: for thou hast had five husbands; and he whom thou now hast is not thy husband: in that saidst thou truly'. Thus Jesus gives her convincing evidence of His extraordinary powers—He knows about her personal life although they have never met before. It is not surprising that she says: 'Sir, I perceive that thou art a prophet.' It is not in character, however, that Jesus should advertise Himself in this way, and though this was the effect, it was not the purpose, of His words. It may be suggested that, for her to receive this living water from Him, she must own, and end, her immoral life; so He comes to the point suddenly, ruthlessly, like an accuser in a cross-examination, showing that all has been but preparation for this moment of devastating exposure. This is even more unlike Jesus. His relationships with women were courteous, respectful, and every woman in His presence felt herself invested with a new self-respect and worth. In another story which John tells, of the woman taken in adultery, her heartless accusers are contrasted with Jesus, who embarrasses the men, not the woman—'He that is without sin among you, let him first cast a stone at her'—to whom He says: 'Neither do I condemn thee: go, and sin no more' (viii.7, 11). Was it not good news to her that she, in this man's eyes, was capable of not sinning?

The thought of this simple Samaritan woman, so superficial and

[23] Grierson, I. 51f; see 'The good-morrow', lines 15f, (p. 7), 'Witchcraft by a picture', pp. 45f, 'A Hymne to Christ, at the Authors last going into Germany', 1st stanza, p. 352. F. P. Wilson, *Elizabethan and Jacobean*, p. 57, quotes Coleridge, 'To read Donne, you must measure *time*, and discover the time of each word by the sense of passion', and stresses that the pauses, no less than 'the emphases and the disturbances of the syntax', communicate his meaning; see T. M. Raysor, *Coleridge's Miscellaneous Criticism*, p. 133.

talkative, is that she can be saved this journey to the well. But she has forgotten that she would not be saved the journey if the gift is for her alone. She has commitments. She must still draw water for the man with whom she lives. The root of all her trouble is her self-concern, and the domination of her thought by the instinctive self-interest which governs her feelings and actions. Though she associates all too freely with others, she lives, morally and spiritually, alone, apart: 'give me . . . that I. . . .'

Salvation of the individual involves more than the individual, for we live in a community, and His gifts are only for those who are willing to share them. The man is not brought into the situation to embarrass the woman, but to present the truth that His gifts cannot be exclusive, and His concern for her must include him. As Matthew Henry comments: '*Call thy husband*, that he may learn with thee; that then you may be *heirs together of the grace of life.*' This interpretation may be found in many commentators, and notably in William Temple's *Readings in St John's Gospel*, and in a sermon preached by John Donne to King Charles I at Whitehall in 1628 on Isaiah xxxii.8.

Therefore said Christ to *Iames*, and *John*, *Non est meum dare vobis*, It is not mine to give, to set you on my right, and on my left hand; *Non vobis, quia singuli separatim ab aliis rogatis*, not to you, because you consider but your selves, and petition for your selves, to the prejudice, and exclusion of others. Therefore Christ bad the Samaritan woman call her husband too, when shee desired the water of life, *Ne sola gratiam acciperet*, saith *S. Chrysostome*, That he might so doe good to her, as that others might have good by it too.[24]

The sermon is on the subject of liberality, set forth supremely in King Jesus, and the text is applied to Him. The chapter to which the text belongs begins, 'Behold, a king shall reign in righteousness, and princes shall rule in judgment', and the sermon is an eloquent exposition of a Christian community, ruler and people, moved by the spirit of liberality, giving to the community and receiving blessing in return, and all prospering together; by this exercise of liberality the King shall stand in safety and in triumph, the Magistrate shall stand established, and the People shall stand secure. The Liberality of God is seen in His ministry to mankind through the Holy Spirit the Comforter, and Donne himself, as a Christian Minister, giving liberally, bestows this

[24] PS, VIII. 244.

comfort through the preaching of the Gospel, and, receiving blessing in return, stands, and prospers.

Jesus Christ is established, and stands, through His liberality. It is, says Donne, the best character of the best things, that they can be communicated.

. . . . it is the best character of the best things, that they are communicable, diffusive. Light was Gods first childe; Light opened the wombe of the Chaos; borne heire to the world, and so does possesse the world; and there is not so diffusive a thing, nothing so communicative, and self-giving as light is. And then, Gold is not onely valued above all things, but is it selfe the value of all things; The value of everything is, Thus much gold it is worth; And no metall is so extensive as gold; no metall enlarges it selfe to such an expansion, such an attenuation as gold does, nor spreads so much, with so little substance. Sight is the noblest, and the powerfullest of our Senses; All the rest, (Hearing onely excepted) are determined in a very narrow distance; And for Hearing, Thunder is the farthest thing that we can heare, and Thunder is but in the ayre; but we see the host of Heaven, the starres in the firmament. All the good things that we can consider, Light, Sight, Gold, all are accompanied with a liberality of themselves, and are so far good, as they are dispensed and communicated to others; for their goodnesse is in their use.[25]

This living water proffered by Jesus, is, like light, and gold, and sight, to be communicated. At the side of the last paragraph of the sermon he has written the words, *Stabit Rex Christus;* He is the liberal Person who deviseth liberal things, and who by His liberality shall stand. It destroys the nature, the office, the merit of Christ, to restrict His redemption. That which He offers to one, He offers to all. 'Give me this water. . . . Go, call thy husband. . . .'

5. I am sinfull inough to infect thee.
(From a sermon on Psalm xxxii.5; PS, IX. 310.)

Text: When Simon Peter saw it, he fell down at Jesus' knees, saying, Depart from me; for I am a sinful man, O Lord. (St Luke v.8.)

In the opening verses of the fifth chapter, St Luke narrates the miraculous catch of a great multitude of fishes. Jesus makes a

[25] PS, VIII. 240.

P

pulpit of Simon Peter's boat; and when He has finished teaching, He commands him to launch out into the deep and let down their nets. With Christ in the boat, they succeed where before they had failed, the catch of fish so great that the weight breaks the net, and they call to the other boat for help, but both boats begin to sink under the burden. It is also too much for Simon. Fear of being overwhelmed forces from him the strange ejaculation: 'Depart from me; for I am a sinful man, O Lord.'

The authenticity of these words is established by their unsuitability to the occasion. They are a confession, not under torture, but freely given; no one, so far as we know, had spoken of sin, and he was engaged with others in his normal occupation, yet in the midst of this demonstration of the Master's powers he speaks, not of Christ as wonderful but of himself as sinful, and sees Him separated from himself by an unbridgeable chasm. In a flash he knows himself as a sinner. He does not belong to this Man's world. Nancy, who can say to Rose Maylie, 'If there was more like you, there would be fewer like me', nevertheless knows where she belongs, and must go back to her companions—'Back! Why do you wish to return to companions you paint in such terrible colours?' '. . . I must go back. . . .' is her reply.

If the eye wanders over this fifth chapter of Luke, it comes upon the story, a few verses farther on, of a man full of leprosy, whom Jesus healed. So John Donne once wandered freely through these verses, and suddenly the fancy crossed his mind, as he moved from the first to the next episode, that Simon Peter's cry was the cry of a leper. One of the familiar, terrible sights of life in Palestine was the leper standing afar off, away from the people. Did not Leviticus say: 'And the leper in whom the plague is, his clothes shall be rent, and his head bare, and he shall put a covering upon his upper lip, and shall cry, Unclean, unclean. All the days wherein the plague shall be in him he shall be defiled; he is unclean: he shall dwell alone; without the camp shall his habitation be' (xiii.45f). And to this burden of isolation and banishment was added the sense of guilt and punishment of sin. Separation was the one idea written into all their actions: they were men apart. And Donne interpreted the words of Simon in the light of their pathetic cry. Simon Peter, who under the stress of emotion and religious awe could not control his choice of words, found himself saying what the leper said: 'Unclean, unclean.' In a moment of self-disclosure, unable to speak words that were his own, he took up their cry.

I consider often that passionate humiliation of S. *Peter, Exi à me Domine, He fell at Iesus knees, saying, Depart from me, for I am a sinfull man, O Lord*; And I am often ready to say so, and more; Depart from me, O Lord, for I am sinfull inough to infect thee; As I may persecute thee in thy Children, so I may infect thee in thine Ordinances; Depart, in withdrawing thy word from me, for I am corrupt inough to make even thy saving Gospel, the savor of death unto death; Depart, in withholding thy Sacrament, for I am leprous inough to taint thy flesh, and to make the balme of thy blood, poyson to my soule; Depart, in withdrawing the protection of thine Angels from me, for I am vicious inough to imprint corruption and rebellion into their nature. And if I be too foule for God himselfe to come neare me, for his Ordinances to worke upon me, I am no companion for my selfe, I must not be alone with my selfe; for I am as apt to take, as to give infection; I am a reciprocall plague; passively and actively contagious; I breath corruption, and breath it upon my selfe; and I am the Babylon that I must goe out of, or I perish.[26]

Religious thought is familiar with the revulsion of the holy from the unholy. 'Depart from me, ye evildoers: for I will keep the commandments of my God.' 'Surely thou wilt slay the wicked, O God: depart from me therefore, ye bloody men.' 'Thou art of purer eyes than to behold evil, and canst not look on iniquity....' (Psalms cxix.115, cxxxix.19, Habakkuk i.13). Our Lord says, '... depart from me, all ye workers of iniquity.... Depart from me, ye cursed ...' (Luke xiii.27, Matthew xxv.41). These words express a revulsion of the holy from the unholy which is one aspect of the encounter of good and evil.

It is equally important to remember that evil shrinks from good. 'And they heard the voice of the LORD God walking in the garden in the cool of the day: and Adam and his wife hid themselves from the presence of the LORD God amongst the trees of the garden. And the LORD God called unto Adam, and said unto him, Where art thou?' (Genesis iii.8f). Before they were banished, they banished themselves. 'In the year that King Uzziah died I saw also the Lord sitting upon a throne, high and lifted up.... Then said I, Woe is me! for I am undone; because I am a man of unclean lips, and I dwell in the midst of a people of unclean lips:

[26] PS, IX. 310f.

for mine eyes have seen the King, the Lord of hosts' (Isaiah vi.1-5).
In the remainder of the paragraph quoted Donne recalls the biblical confession, *Non dignus*—Jacob's 'I am not worthy of the least
of all the mercies, and of all the truth, which thou hast shewed
unto thy servant'; the centurion's 'I am not worthy that thou
shouldest come under my roof' which he states was the form of
words in which communicants received the Sacrament in the
Primitive Church; the prodigal's 'I . . . am no more worthy to be
called thy son'; and John the Baptist's 'I am not worthy to stoop
down . . .' (Genesis xxxii.10, Matthew viii.8, Luke xv.21, Mark
i.7). Charles Wesley, in his Communion hymn, makes notable
use of this theme, relating it to the 'passionate humiliation' of
Peter—

> Saviour, and can it be
> That Thou shouldst dwell with me?
> From Thy high and lofty throne
> Throne of everlasting bliss,
> Will Thy Majesty stoop down
> To so mean a house as this?
>
> I am not worthy, Lord,
> So foul, so self-abhorred,
> Thee, my God, to entertain
> In this poor polluted heart:
> I a frail and sinful man; ·
> All my nature cries: Depart!
>
> Yet come, Thou heavenly Guest,
> And purify my breast;
> Come, Thou great and glorious King,
> While before Thy Cross I bow;
> With Thyself salvation bring,
> Cleanse the house by entering now.[27]

Tom, the chimney-sweep, came down the chimney and into
the bedroom of a little girl, fast asleep in bed. 'The room was all
dressed in white—white window-curtains, white bed-curtains,
white furniture, and white walls, with just a few lines of pink
here and there. . . . The next thing he saw . . . was a washing-
stand, with ewers and basins, and soap and brushes, and towels,
and a large bath full of clean water—what a heap of things all for

[27] *Methodist Hymn-book*, No. 760.

washing! "She must be a very dirty lady," thought Tom, "by my master's rule, to want as much scrubbing as all that. But she must be very cunning to put the dirt out of the way so well afterwards, for I don't see a speck about the room, not even on the very towels." And then, looking toward the bed, he saw that dirty lady, and held his breath with astonishment. Under the snow-white coverlet, upon the snow-white pillow lay the most beautiful little girl that Tom had ever seen. Her cheeks were almost as white as the pillow, and her head was like threads of gold spread all about over the bed. . . . No, She cannot be dirty. She never could have been dirty, thought Tom to himself. And then he thought, "And are all people like that when they are washed?" And he looked at his own wrist, and tried to rub the soot off, and wondered whether it ever would come off. . . . And looking round he suddenly saw, standing close to him, a little, ugly, black, ragged figure, with bleared eyes and grinning white teeth. He turned on it angrily. What did such a little black ape want in that sweet young lady's room? And behold, it was himself, reflected in a great mirror, the like of which Tom had never seen before. And Tom, for the first time in his life, found out that he was dirty; and burst into tears with shame and anger; and turned to sneak up the chimney again and hide. . . .'[28]

Only the pure in heart can bear the vision of God. Evil has its hour of bold, brash insensitivity, but its home is the shadows.

Simon Peter was much more than an impulsive talker, who knew not what he said; or the person who breaks an awkward silence and begins a discussion, for no higher purpose than to 'set the ball rolling'. Rather it may be said of him that he ends talk. He says what others want to, but cannot, say. He grips truth, and there is no more to be said. 'Thou art the Christ.' 'Can any man forbid water, that these should not be baptized, which have received the Holy Ghost as well as we?' (Mark viii.29, Acts x.47). Here, at the beginning of his association with Jesus, in a moment of awakening, from the depths of his being rises the confession about man's nature which is the truth we need to learn. Here is his primacy, for incontrovertibly, he speaks the truth. He sweeps away the easy, confident approach of man to God. He is a leper, who has no right to associate with Jesus, who will defile and corrupt all he touches, even God Himself.

[28] Charles Kingsley, *The Water Babies*, ch. 1.

All that is left to man is the leper's last act of decency, his warning
and estranging cry, 'Unclean!' 'Depart from me; for I am a sinful
man, O Lord.'

A little under two years before his ordination, John Donne was
riding westward on Good Friday, 1613, and as he rode he reflected
upon his westward journey, turning his back upon the Cross,
riding away from the Saviour. 'Goodfriday, 1613, Riding Westward' was the fruit of his meditation.

> Let mans Soule be a Spheare, and then, in this,
> The intelligence that moves, devotion is,
> And as the other Spheares, by being growne
> Subject to forraigne motions, lose their owne,
> And being by others hurried every day,
> Scarce in a yeare their naturall forme obey:
> Pleasure or businesse, so, our Soules admit
> For their first mover, and are whirld by it.
> Hence is 't, that I am carryed towards the West
> 10   This day, when my Soules forme bends toward the East.
> There I should see a Sunne, by rising set,
> And by that setting endlesse day beget;
> But that Christ on this Crosse, did rise and fall,
> Sinne had eternally benighted all.
> Yet dare I'almost be glad, I do not see
> That spectacle of too much weight for mee.
> Who sees Gods face, that is selfe life, must dye;
> What a death were it then to see God dye?
> 20   It made his owne Lieutenant Nature shrinke,
> It made his footstoole crack, and the Sunne winke.
> Could I behold those hands which span the Poles,
> And turn all spheares at once, peirc'd with those holes?
> Could I behold that endlesse height which is
> Zenith to us, and our Antipodes,
> Humbled below us? or that blood which is
> The seat of all our Soules, if not of his,
> Made durt of dust, or that flesh which was worne
> By God, for his apparrell, rag'd, and torne?
> If on these things I durst not looke, durst I
> 30   Upon his miserable mother cast mine eye,
> Who was Gods partner here, and furnish'd thus
> Halfe of that Sacrifice, which ransom'd us?

Though these things, as I ride, be from mine eye,
They'are present yet unto my memory,
For that looks towards them; and thou look'st towards mee,
O Saviour, as thou hang'st upon the tree;
I turne my backe to thee, but to receive
Corrections, till thy mercies bid thee leave.
O thinke mee worth thine anger, punish mee,
40   Burne off my rusts, and my deformity.
Restore thine Image, so much, by thy grace,
That thou may'st know mee, and I'll turne my face.[29]

line 13: But: Unless, except.
    27: Made: 'Make' is a probable alternative reading.
    38: leave: stop.

It is Good Friday, the day of all days in the year to turn to the east and contemplate the Saviour of the world; but he is riding westward (probably from Sir Henry Goodyear's home in Warwickshire to stay with the Herberts in Wales). The conflict between this westward journey and the spirit of devotion within him turning his thoughts eastward involves him in tension and discord (like St Peter, fleeing from Rome along the Appian Way, to escape from the persecutions of Nero, challenged by Christ, whom he sees journeying toward the city). This conflict is like that of the spheres, which, if left free to follow their nature ('naturall forme'—6) would travel from west to east; but the *Primum Mobile* (the 'first mover'—8) and other influences, like the ninth sphere ('forraigne motions'—4) resist this successfully and cause them to travel from east to west, as Donne himself is doing. Every sphere has its Intelligence or Angel in control (like Raphael in charge of the sun), and Devotion is the controlling influence in his soul, considered as a sphere. Devotion ought to have its way and turn him eastward, but, protest as it may, with 'pleasure or businesse' (7) in command, he must travel westward, away from Christ.

This is not a descriptive poem about a journey, despite the title; it states, considers, resolves, the problem which the journey creates. The clash of the two journeys awakens in him the spirit of contradiction; as he travels westward he meditates upon the Crucified, and so travels eastward in his mind. This he can do without real conflict because the memory is seated at the back of

---

[29] Grierson, I. 336f; II. 238f; see Bibliography, p. 234, *infra.*

the brain (35; 'in the hindermost part of the brain'—PS, II.235), and can look, naturally and without effort, upon Him.

A substantial part of the poem is given to the contemplation of Christ; the conflict of the two journeys excites the spirit of paradox; and as he makes these tremendous statements—e.g. 'a Sunne, by rising set' (11)—the horror of the Crucifixion so grips him that his mood changes, and he is almost glad not to make the eastward journey (15f). This shift of position, due to his repulsion from the Cross by its inherent nature (and so, religiously acceptable), begins his reconciliation to his westward journey, and emboldens him to question the conventional devotion of contemplating Christ. The basic antithesis of the poem has conditioned him to apprehend truth by contrast. The paradoxes which he has uttered so surely now turn back upon their creator to involve him directly. The moment of revelation comes, when the spirit of contradiction within him shatters the devotional attitude of looking at Christ. How glibly we can talk of surveying the wondrous Cross! self-confidently supposing that all its purpose is achieved by so doing. But the truth, which had never occurred to him before, is that He looks upon us: 'For that looks towards them/and thou look'st towards mee' (35)—the contrast between our devotion towards Him, and Christ looking towards us, is the dramatic moment of truth when the conflict is resolved.

Devotion has been in control all the time, turning him away from the east; but the eyes of Christ have been upon him, and now he understands that his back is turned that he may receive correcting chastisement, by which Christ will restore him to His likeness; so that, when he turns, He will recognize him.

Much that is characteristic of Donne is to be found in this poem—

(a) his intense self-awareness, causing him to argue with himself, and wrestle with his state, leading on to an increasing awareness of Another, implied by reason of his problem in the beginning, who at the end is the One to whom he speaks; thus from self-scrutiny he moves, by argument and conversation, to devotion;

(b) the use of the learned 'conceit' of the sphere and its Intelligence, with its 'correspondence' between microcosm and macrocosm, fusing emotion and thought; at first it seems a far-fetched analogy, but he works it out accurately, fully, and in the end justifies it as an exact, appropriate illustration of his meaning, capable of bearing the weight of the whole poem;

(*c*) the use of contrast, paradox, and argument—the poem, by changing and developing the discussion, resolves the conflict —it embodies, is, the experience, not a description of it;

(*d*) the adaptation and reversal of the familiar and conventional —just as the title 'The Extasie' introduces a different experience from ecstasy as normally understood, the emphasis being upon the return to and not emancipation from the body, so the title 'Riding Westward' introduces a journey which has significance in relation to the east. In the same way the conventional Good Friday devotion is reinterpreted to emphasize our Lord looking upon us; and, yet another example of adaptation, 'turning one's back' is no longer an act of separation or repudiation—the poem could be called, 'Turning one's back on Christ'—but becomes an act of penitence. Often it is the opposite of something familiar which provides him with fresh insight;

(*e*) finally, we have here, impressively, his reconciliation to the created order, to life as it must be lived; the journey which, at the beginning, is opposed to true devotion, is continued, and accepted at the end as directed by its Intelligence, Devotion. It is a journey westward.

Simon Peter cries, 'Depart from me'. But He does not go. That the leper can infect Him does not weigh with Him, because He can remove the leprosy. Neither God's revulsion from man, nor man's revulsion from God, is, ultimately, in His purpose. We fall, to rise. We sleep, to wake. We turn away, to look. We cry 'Depart', to be with Him for ever.

The republication of Donne's sermons raises the question whether they contain useful material for the preacher today; the foregoing five sermons are an attempt at an answer. Another question awaits an answer. Will John Donne, who through his Poetry has exercised enormous influence upon contemporary art in its rebellion against conventional forms, and who through his *Devotions* has gained a hearing for himself which a preacher might envy, assist, through his sermons, this generation to return to Christ and His Church? This is not likely if the sermons are studied apart from his life and his poetry; but when he is taken altogether he is as powerful an advocate as can be named for the presentation of the claims of the Christian religion. His mission to this century is unfinished. The realism of his early poetry leads on to the realism of his reconciliation to the created order, to life, to Jesus Christ, and to His Church, based firmly on the realism of man's essentially religious nature. If he could lead back to Christ all whom he has influenced in our age, if he could persuade those who have had him as companion for part of the way that it leads on to Him, his revival would be completed, its true aim achieved.

The answer to the question raised lies in the future, but the possibility of its being affirmative has a realistic basis. His powerful influence on Robert Browning, Gerard Manley Hopkins, Alice Meynell, Francis Thompson, W. B. Yeats, Rupert Brooke, T. S. Eliot, Herbert Read, Day Lewis, Dylan Thomas, to mention only a selection of poets, is established. Mario Praz begins his essay 'The Critical Importance of the Revived Interest in Seventeenth-Century Metaphysical Poetry'[30] by noting the general bewilderment of people in face of *avant-garde* literature, art and music, and proceeds to explore the influence of Donne, which, at the end of the essay, he describes as having a catalytic function. Certainly anyone who seeks to come to grips with our modern scene, to understand what is happening to it, can do no better than begin with a study of Donne and the effect of his genius upon our age.

But how completely is he known? It is possible to be influenced by him without being affected by him altogether, to turn eagerly to his secular poems and leave unread the *Essayes in Divinity* or the sermons. All too easily his life and work can be considered as a series of distinct, unrelated episodes. And how accurately and adequately is he known? Izaak Walton forced him into an Augustinian mould and contrasted the youthful sinner and the saintly convert. He has been regarded as a mystic; as a lonely ascetic; as a secret Catholic and medievalist, whose favourite sermon themes were sin, death and the grave; as a High Churchman; or, simply, an enigma. One must say of him, what he so often said of the Scriptures, that here is meat for all tastes. The

[30] See *English Studies Today: Papers read at the International Conference of University Professors of English held in Magdalen College, Oxford, August 1950*, pp. 158-166.

present writer would urge the importance to Donne of the practice
of meditation; his *Holy Sonnets, Essayes in Divinity, Devotions,*
Prebend sermons and reflection on the story of Creation, are
evidence of a habitually contemplative nature. This deeply
personal religion made him, what the stanzas from 'Metempsychosis, The Progresse of the Soule', demonstrate him to be, a
prophet, with intensely proleptic powers, at the heart of whose
verse was an insight into religious realism as the creature's return
to his Creator. Is there here, embedded in his poetry, a prediction
of our journey 'towards home'?

Whatever the vestiges of medievalism to be found in him, he is
intensely modern in his realistic attitude to sex, and in his inclusion
of the ugly and discordant elements of experience in his poetry.
We share his disappointment that increased knowledge ministers
so little to our salvation; we feel that he understands us when he
speaks of the mathematician who claimed that he could have
removed the whole world with his engine, if there had been any
place elsewhere for it—now there is;[31] or when he speaks of
plenty as a disease, or of a cloud cast upon the whole world.[32]
The man who can say,

> For man can adde weight to heavens heaviest curse. . . .
> Thus man, that might be'his pleasure, is his rod,
> And is his devill, that might be his God[33]

articulates our own frustration. We follow him as he seeks a lost
unity for individual and community; from us also, coherence has
gone.

Donne discovered for himself that life had meaning at the
moment of conjunction—this is most memorably expressed in
the three poems, 'A nocturnall upon S. Lucies day, Being the
shortest day' (the year and the day), 'The Annuntiation and
Passion' (Gabriel's message of joy and the Crucifixion), 'Goodfriday, 1613. Riding Westward' (east and west). Donne experienced intensely the truth embedded in every human happening,
which is always at the conjunction of space and time. Those who
have studied Donne's poetry to our great profit have stressed
the fusion in him of thought and feeling, of the claims of body and
soul, of the individual and society; as one reads one becomes
aware of him holding together two different elements of

---

[31] PS, I. 179, 193; V. 365.   [32] II. 63; III. 167.   [33] Grierson, I. 194.

experience, one in each hand, the trivial and the tremendous, the familiar and the cosmic. Inevitably the moment of conjunction demanded concentrated expression, packed, compressed speech; as one stands at the cross-roads, aware of two divergent ways intersecting at this one point, one must speak in paradox, in which two truths have joint mastery. The tremendous paradoxes of Donne have meaning for a generation which turns from simple statements because its own life is a paradox of success and bitter failure.

Writers on Donne and the metaphysical poets speak often of the embodiment of thought[34] as a distinguishing characteristic especially appreciated in our own day. This is not only a controlling feature of Donne's verse; it is in his verse because it is in his life. He writes about Nothing because of his experience of it. He predicts his return, but himself is destined to return to Oxford, and to Lincoln's Inn. Truth is embodied in his poetry and in his life. For him the Christian religion as he shared in it was a presentation, in compressed, human terms, within the limitations of time and space, of reality. The Word was made flesh in Jesus Christ, and the Word is manifested among men still in the Church which is His Body, in the Scriptures, in Worship, in the Sacraments, in the ordained Ministry and the calling of the Preacher, in the daily life of Christians; the distinction, which permeates his writings, of 'being' from 'having', expressed his understanding that in the Incarnation truth is realized, Jesus is the Way, the Truth and the Life, and the Christian's quest is to know God, the Being from whom our being is derived. The controversies of the modern Church involve the same issues which mattered so much to him, and in the search for Christian unity, and a fuller understanding of the nature of the Ministry, the Scriptures and the Sacraments, in the discussion of the true nature of Christian Worship, Christians must consider if anything that has to do with the Incarnate Lord can be simply a means to an end, variable and changeable to meet the convenience of a particular age. If the embodiment of truth is the principle of the Incarnation, if form and meaning are as closely related as body and soul, the way in which we worship is not to be determined by aesthetic

[34] See, e.g., Hugh Fausset, *John Donne, A Study in Discord*, pp. 175, 224; Rosemary Freeman, *English Emblem Books*, p. 147; George Macdonald, *England's Antiphon*, pp. 114f; E. M. Simpson, *A Study of the Prose Works of John Donne*, p. 111; George Williamson, *The Donne Tradition*, pp. 22f.

preferences of worshippers but by the truth to be embodied; the administration of the Church is not to be decided by what is thought by the majority to work best, but is to be constructed to set forth the Gospel; the meaning of ordination is to be sought in relation to the truth that it embodies; the Scriptures embody the Word; sacraments are not arbitrary symbols but embodiments of meaning; the high privilege of individual and corporate Christian living is to present the Church as the Gospel being preached. Without agreement on these outworkings of the Incarnation no permanent reconciliation of Christians in one outward, visible community is possible; with such agreement, no limits need be set to what can be accomplished to resolve our problems. A major reason for expecting that Donne will help us find our way back to Christ and to His Church is that in him these consequences of Christ's coming are persuasively presented; and, if one feels with his ardour, irresistibly communicated.

For there is, as Browning detected, something magisterial about Donne.[35] Coleridge spoke of his 'absolute right of dominion over all thoughts, that dukes are bid to clean his shoes, and are yet honored by it!'[36] In this century the Monarch of Wit has greatly extended his fame, and many have come under his imperious rule. He has taught us much. But he would have us chiefly know that it was the taking of orders that was his coronation; and that the pulpit was his throne.

[35] *The Elegies upon the Author* included in Grierson contain many references to him as Monarch—I. 379 (lines 49f), 380 (lines 95f), 380 (line 2), 382 (lines 76, 81-end), p. 386 (lines 11f.).

[36] *Coleridge's Miscellaneous Criticism*, ed. T. M. Raysor, p. 135.

BIBLIOGRAPHY

THE following list is a selection only from the large number of books and articles on John Donne. For further information, see

Sir Geoffrey L. Keynes: *Bibliography of Dr John Donne, Dean of St Paul's*, 3rd edition (1958)

Theodore Spencer, and Mark van Doren: *Studies in Metaphysical Poetry: Two Essays and a Bibliography* (1939). Contains: (1) 'Recent Scholarship in Metaphysical Poetry'; (2) 'Seventeenth-century Poets and Twentieth-century Critics'; (3) Bibliography, 1912-1938

William White: *John Donne since 1900: A Bibliography of Periodical Articles* (1942);

and bibliographies in books listed below, marked '(B)'.

The Year's Work in English Studies, published annually, should be consulted for new writing.

Abbreviations in this list:

* Reprinted in *John Donne: A Collection of Critical Essays*, edited by Helen Gardner (1962).

† Reprinted in *Seventeenth-Century English Poetry*, Modern Essays in Criticism, edited by William R. Keast (1962).

†† *A Garland for John Donne 1631-1931*, edited by Theodore Spencer (1931).

PQ	*Philological Quarterly*
RES	*Review of English Studies*
MLQ	*Modern Language Quarterly*
MLR	*Modern Language Review*
TLS	*The Times Literary Supplement*
NQ	*Notes and Queries*
ELH	*A Journal of English Literary History*
SP	*Studies in Philology*
KR	*The Kenyon Review*
SR	*The Sewanee Review*
MP	*Modern Philology*

TSL   *Tennessee Studies in Literature*
JEGP   *Journal of English and Germanic Philology*
ESEA   *Essays and Studies by Members of the English Association*
PMLA   *Publications of the Modern Language Association of America*

Books referred to in this book by an abbreviation:

Abbreviation

Jessopp   Augustus Jessopp: *John Donne, Sometime Dean of St
              Paul's* (1897) (in the series *Leaders of Religion*).

Gosse   Edmund Gosse: *The Life and Letters of John Donne,
              Dean of St Paul's* (two volumes, 1899; reprinted
              1959).
              Places the letters in a chronological order; interprets
              the poems autobiographically; many statements
              must be questioned in the light of later study, but
              remains indispensable.

Grierson   *The Poems of John Donne*, edited by Herbert J. C.
              Grierson—
              Volume I—the Text of the Poems with Appendixes.
              Volume II—Introduction and Commentary. (1912).
              Walter de la Mare described the commentary as 'an
              olla podrida of curious and far-fetched knowledge
              and scholarship, and a kind of natural history of
              Elizabethan ideas' (*The Edinburgh Review*, CCVII
              (1913) p. 375.
              *pp. xxxiv-xlix under the title 'Donne's Love-
              Poetry'.
              The Poems of John Donne edited by Herbert J. C.
              Grierson, Oxford Standard Authors (1933), is,
              essentially, Volume I, with a new Introduction.

Gardner   *John Donne: The Divine Poems*, edited with Introduc-
              tion and Commentary by Helen Gardner (1952).
              *pp. xxi-xxxvii under the title 'The Religious Poetry
              of John Donne'.

PS   *The Sermons of John Donne*, edited by George R.
              Potter and Evelyn M. Simpson, in Ten Volumes
              (1953-1962). Volume I begins with Introductions
              on (1) the bibliography of the sermons, (2) the
              manuscripts, (3) the text, and (4) the literary

value of Donne's sermons (* pp. 83f, 88-103 under
the title, 'The Literary Value of Donne's Sermons'
by Evelyn M. Simpson). The volumes contain the
160 extant sermons, as far as possible in chronological order, with introductions and textual notes
on each, and, in volume IV, an account of contemporary London life. There are numerous
illustrations, and Part II of the last volume is
principally a consideration of Donne's sources (1)
the Scriptures and the versions which he used, (2)
the early Fathers (especially St Augustine), commentators and controversialists.

Walton   Izaak Walton: *Life of Dr John Donne* (1675), the final
text as printed in The World's Classics (1927).
The original Life, the tribute of a parishioner, was
published in 1640, prefixed to the *LXXX Sermons*
of Donne, with the title 'The Life and Death of
Dr. Donne', and the death was thus deliberately
emphasized. This version, given in H. W. Garrod,
John Donne: Poetry and Prose, pp. xvii-xliv, was
amplified in 1658 and issued separately, and
further enlarged in 1670 and 1675 (see Garrod,
p. 107, note on p. xvii). The original version is
more accurate than the expanded versions in some
respects.

Devotions   John Donne, *Devotions vpon Emergent Occasions and
Seuerall Steps in my Sicknes* (1624). This was edited,
with an introduction, by John Sparrow in 1923,
and is included in *Ann Arbor Paperbacks* (1959),
together with Donne's last sermon *Death's Duel*
and Donne's Life, taken from Izaak Walton's *Life*.

Essayes   John Donne, *Essayes in Divinity*, edited by Evelyn M.
in Divinity;   Simpson (1952). Published as *Essays in Divinity;*
or Essayes   with Introduction; and Notes which incorporate
notes from Augustus Jessopp's edition of 1855.

Subjects discussed:

The Life of John Donne (chapter I)
Walton, Jessopp, Gosse.

Q

R. C. Bald: *Donne and the Drurys* (1959).

H. C. Beeching: '*Izaak Walton's Life of Donne—An Apology*', *The Cornhill Magazine*, n.s. VIII (1900), pp. 249-268. (A defence of Walton against criticisms by Gosse and Leslie Stephen.)

A. R. Benham: 'The Myth of John Donne the Rake', *PQ*, XXIII (1941), pp. 465-473.

H. I'A. Fausset: *John Donne: A Study in Discord* (1924). In four parts: (1) The Pagan, (2) The Penitent, (3) The Pensioner, (4) The Preacher; follows Gosse closely and interprets the poems autobiographically; see pp. 126f for a discussion of 'Metempsychosis, The Progresse of the Soule'.

K. W. Gransden: *John Donne* (1954). (B) A guide to his life and writings.

E. Hardy: *John Donne: A spirit in conflict* (1942).

F. Kermode: *John Donne* (1957). (B) No. 86, *Writers and their Work*, published for the British Council and the National Book League.

L. Stephen: *Studies of a Biographer* (Second Series), III. 36-82 (1902).

A. Symons: 'John Donne', *The Fortnightly Review*, n.s. LXVI. (1899), 734-745; also in his *Figures of Several Centuries* (1916), pp. 80-108.

J. Bryson: 'Lost Portrait of Donne', *The Times*, 13th October 1959.

H. W. Garrod: 'Donne and Mrs Herbert', *RES*, XXI.(1945), 161-173.

L. C. Knights: 'On the Social Background of Metaphysical Poetry', *Scrutiny*, XIII.(1945), 37-52. May be read in connection with chapter III on Donne's friendships.

M. F. Moloney: 'John Donne and the Jesuits', *MLQ*, VIII.(1947), 426-429.

E. M. Simpson: 'Donne's Spanish Authors', *MLR*, XLIII.(1948), 182-185.

J. Sparrow: 'The Date of Donne's Travels', ††.

P. Thomson: 'John Donne and the Countess of Bedford' *MLR*, XLIV.(1949), 329-340.

F. P. Wilson: 'Notes on the Early Life of John Donne', *RES*, III. (1927), 272-279.

I. A. Shapiro: 'John Donne and Lincoln's Inn 1591-4', *TLS*, 16th and 23rd October 1930, pp. 833, 861.

I. A. Shapiro: 'John Donne and Parliament', *TLS*, 10th March 1932, p. 172.

H. W. Garrod: 'The Date of Donne's Birth', *TLS*, 30th December 1944, p. 636.

W. Milgate: 'The Date of Donne's Birth', *NQ*, CXCI 16th November 1946—criticism of H. W. Garrod's theory, pp. 206-208.

J. Sparrow: 'Two Epitaphs by John Donne', *TLS*, 26th March 1949, p. 208.

W. Milgate: 'Dr Donne's Art Gallery', *NQ*, CXCIV (23rd July 1949), pp. 318f.

W. Milgate: 'The Early References to John Donne', *NQ*, CXCV (27th May, 10th June, 8th July, 2nd September 1950), pp. 229-231, 246f, 290-292, 381-383.

I. A. Shapiro: 'Donne's Birthdate', *NQ*, CXCVII (19th July 1952), pp. 310-313.

B. W. Whitlock: 'Donne at St Dunstan's', *TLS*, 16th and 23rd September 1955, pp. 548, 564.

B. W. Whitlock: 'The Heredity and Childhood of John Donne', *NQ*, CCIV (July-August 1959) pp. 257-262, 348-353.

B. W. Whitlock: 'The Family of John Donne 1588-1591', *NQ*, CCV (October 1960) pp. 380-386.

Poems:

For general consultation

R. G. Cox: 'A Survey of Literature from Donne to Marvell', and 'The Poems of John Donne', *From Donne to Marvell*, edited by Boris Ford, (*The Pelican Guide to English Literature*, volume 3), 1956.

H. Gardner (selected and edited by): *The Metaphysical Poets* (1957). With an Introduction (reprinted in †), a representative selection of Donne's verse, and biographical notes. (B).

Gransden (*q.v., supra*); Grierson.

J. B. Leishman: *The Monarch of Wit* (5th edition, 1962). 'An Analytical and Comparative Study of the Poetry of John Donne'.

† * chapter one, 'Donne and Seventeenth-Century Poetry'.

T. Redpath (edited by): *The Songs and Sonets of John Donne*, with Introduction and Explanatory Notes (1956). (B).

J. Reeves (edited with an Introduction, Notes and Commentary): *Selected Poems of John Donne* (1952). The notes offer a paraphrase of or extended comment on the poems selected.

'A nocturnall upon S. Lucies day, Being the shortest day' (pp. 14-20).

E. H. Duncan: 'Donne's Alchemical Figures', *ELH*, IX.(1942), 280-284. Studies, pp. 257-285, Donne's use of alchemical theories and practices, such as the elixir, the nature and properties of gold, the processes of distillation and transmutation, to express serious thoughts, e.g. the embodiment of virtue; the influence of a person on others (strikingly seen in 'Resurrection, imperfect' lines 9-16) (Grierson, I. 333f), with reference to the death and resurrection of Christ who was all gold in death, but, rising, had become refined into a tincture, or elixir, with power to make others like Himself, i.e. to transmute baser metals into gold, His own nature. 'Made like Him, like Him we rise' [Charles Wesley].

F. Kermode: *John Donne*, pp. 21-24.

J. B. Leishman: *The Metaphysical Poets:* Donne, Herbert, Vaughan, Traherne (1934), p. 57f. A general introduction, pp. 6-98, to Donne, relating the poetry to his life and ministry in the Church, with many quotations from Walton and Gosse, the poems and sermons; stresses the disappointment of learned men, 'polymaths', that the great increase in knowledge in their times had not taken them much farther.

D. Louthan: *The Poetry of John Donne: A Study in Explication* (1951), pp. 140-148.

W. A. Murray: 'Donne and Paracelsus: An Essay in Interpretation', *RES*, XXV.(1949), 115-123. Refers also to 'Loves Alchymie' (Grierson, I. 39f.)

E. M. Simpson: *A Study of the Prose Works of John Donne* (2nd edition, 1948), p. 116.

R. Sleight: In *Interpretations*, edited by John Wain (1955), pp. 31-58.

E. M. W. Tillyard: *The Elizabethan World Picture* (1943), p. 75.

—— *The Metaphysicals and Milton* (1956), pp. 20-22. Paraphrases Holy Sonnet XVII, 'The Blossome', and discusses 'A nocturnall . . .', 'A Valediction: of weeping', Holy Sonnet

VII, 'Lovers infinitenesse', and 'The Extasie', especially emphasizing the realization of self-knowledge as the goal and achievement of the ecstasy; the combination in man of the three souls, vegetative, sensitive, and rational; and man's correspondence with the macrocosm; argues that the poet Donne regards the journey as more important than the arrival.

L. Unger: *Donne's Poetry and Modern Criticism* (1941), pp. 46-50, 72.

E. L. Wiggins: 'Logic in the Poetry of John Donne', *SP*, XLII. (1945), pp. 45, 51; see pp. 41-60 for the whole essay.

G. Williamson: *The Proper Wit of Poetry* (1961), pp. 36f. Contains a consideration of Donne's poems, especially the *Songs and Sonets*, pp. 31-42.

'Metempsychosis, The Progresse of the Soule' (pp. 33-41)

Gosse, I. 131-141.

W. A. Murray: 'What was the soul of the apple?', *RES*, X.(1959), 141-155.

'Lovers infinitenesse' (pp. 57-60)

R. W. Ingram: In *Elizabethan Poetry, Stratford-upon-Avon Studies, 2* (1960), pp. 145-147.

F. Kermode: *John Donne*, pp. 11, 19.

M. M. Mahood: *Poetry and Humanism* (1950), pp. 95f. A discussion of Donne and other seventeenth-century devotional poets; see chapter IV, 'Donne: The Progress of the Soul', pp. 87-130; chapter V, 'Donne: The Baroque Preacher', pp. 131-168.

M. F. Moloney: *John Donne: His Flight from Mediaevalism* (1944), p. 145.

R. Sencourt: *Outflying Philosophy* (1924), p. 55. A Literary Study of the Religious Element in the poems and letters of John Donne, and in the works of Sir T. Browne and of Henry Vaughan the Silurist.

A. Stein: *John Donne's Lyrics: The Eloquence of Action* (1962). Appendix I. The Stanza of 'Lovers Infinitenesse', pp. 213-216.

E. M. W. Tillyard: *The Metaphysicals and Milton*, pp. 30-32.

G. Williamson: *The Proper Wit of Poetry*, pp. 39, 41.

'The Blossome' (pp. 79-81)

Gosse, I. 75.

C. Hunt: *Donne's Poetry* (1954), pp. 44-50, 219-224. Essays in Literary Analysis. A consideration of 'The Indifferent', 'Elegie XIX', 'Loves Alchymie', 'The Blossome', 'The good-morrow', 'The Canonization', 'Hymne to God my God, in my sicknesse', with some conclusions.

J. B. Leishman: *The Metaphysical Poets:* Donne, Herbert, Vaughan, Traherne, pp. 23f.

E. M. W. Tillyard: *The Metaphysicals and Milton*, pp. 13-19.

'An Anatomie of the World' and 'Of the Progresse of the Soule' (pp. 85-95)

Gosse, I. 273-278.

†† pp. 190f.

D. C. Allen: 'The Double Journey of John Donne', *A Tribute to George Coffin Taylor:* Studies and Essays, *chiefly Elizabethan*, by his Students and Friends, edited by Arnold Williams (1952), pp. 83-99. Considers 'Metempsychosis, The Progresse of the Soule', *Of the Progresse of the Soule*, and their relationship.

M. Bewley: 'Religious Cynicism in Donne's Poetry', *KR*, XIV (1952), 619-646. Interprets 'The Anniversaries' as a cryptic reference to the Roman Church and the Anglican Settlement under Elizabeth, and the final expression of religious cynicism found earlier in the *Songs and Sonets*.

F. Manley (edited by): John Donne: *The Anniversaries:* with Introduction and Commentary (1963).

L. L. Martz: 'John Donne in Meditation: The Anniversaries', *ELH* XIV.(1947), 247-273, reproduced in *The Poetry of Meditation:* A Study in English Religious Literature of the Seventeenth Century (1954, 2nd [revised] edition, 1962). Refers to many other writings of Donne. † * (B).

'The Primrose' (p. 109)

W. J. Courthope: *A History of English Poetry*, (1903), III, p. 161, notes 1, 2.

R. A. Durr: 'Donne's "The Primrose" ', *JEGP*, LIX. (1960), 218-222.

R. Sencourt: *Outflying Philosophy*, p. 50.

E. M. Simpson (edited by): *Essayes in Divinity*, p. 111.

'The Extasie' (pp. 109-111)

F. A. Doggett: 'Donne's Platonism', *SR*, XLII.(1934), 284-289; See pp. 274-292 for the whole essay, which strongly resists both a Platonic interpretation and that given by Legouis.

W. Empson: *Some Versions of Pastoral* (1935), pp. 133-135.

H. Gardner: 'The Argument about "The Ecstasy",' *Elizabethan and Jacobean Studies Presented to Frank Percy Wilson* (1959), Essay 17, pp. 279-306. Argues that Leone Ebreo's *Dialoghi d'Amore* was the source of the poem; studies Legouis and his critics; also 'Elegie X. The Dreame'; emphasizes Donne's meditation on the doctrine of creation and his disparagement of the idea of ecstasy.

M. Y. Hughes: 'The Lineage of "The Extasie" ', *MLR*, XXVII. (1932),1-5. Suggests possible French and Italian sources for the poem.

P. Legouis: *Donne the Craftsman*, An Essay upon the Structure of the Songs and Sonnets (1928). * pp. 47-61, 71-79 under the title 'The Dramatic Element in Donne's Poetry'.

G. R. Potter: 'Donne's *Extasie*, contra Legouis', *PQ*, XV. (1936), 247-253.

R. Sencourt: *Outflying Philosophy*, p. 44.

A. J. Smith: 'The Metaphysic of Love', *RES*, IX.(1958), 362-375. Shows that the questions considered in 'The Extasie' were frequently debated by Italians in Florence and Padua, and discusses the poem on pp. 370-375.

E. M. W. Tillyard: *The Elizabethan World Picture*, pp. 71-73; *The Metaphysicals and Milton*, Appendix B, pp. 79-84, 'A Note on Donne's "Extasie" ', reprinted from *RES*, XIX.(1943), 67-70.

A. Warren: 'Donne's "Extasie" ', *SP*, LV.(1958), 472-480.

G. Williamson: 'The Convention of "The Extasie" ', *Seventeenth-Century Contexts* (1960), pp. 63-77. † Studies the poem in relation to other poets, e.g. Lord Herbert.

'Elegie V. His Picture' (pp. 199-201)

H. Gardner: 'John Donne: a Note on Elegie V, 'His Picture'',
   MLR, XXXIX.(1944), 333-337.

'Goodfriday, 1613. Riding Westward' (pp. 216-219)

Gosse, I. 267, II. 25f.

Gardner, pp. xxx, xxxiiif, 89-100.

L. L. Martz: *The Poetry of Meditation*, pp. 54-56.

G. Williamson: *The Proper Wit of Poetry*, pp. 39f.

A. B. Chambers: 'Good Friday, 1613. Riding Westward. The
   Poem and the Tradition', *ELH*, XXVIII.(1961), 31-53.

K. Raine: 'John Donne and the Baroque Doubt', *Horizon*, XI.
   (1945), 371-395. Studies the conflict of Donne's age; this
   poem illustrates the power of poetry to hold together truths
   of different orders.

Du Bartas and the Hexaemeral Literature (pp. 115ff)

A. B. Grosart (edited by): *Complete Works of Joshuah Sylvester*
   (Chertsey Worthies' Library, 1880).

U. T. Holmes: *The Works of Du Bartas* (1935).

J. Chiari (edited by): *The Harrap Anthology of French Poetry* (1958).
   Pp. 165-168: gives selections from '*Premiere Semaine*'; pp.
   40-42 of the Introduction: links Du Bartas and metaphysical
   poetry, summarizes the contribution of Du Bartas to this,
   and indicates his belief that Donne read Du Bartas and found
   in him a congenial blend of erudition, imagination, and
   striking imagery.

G. Brereton: *An Introduction to the French Poets* (1956). Gives
   extracts from Du Bartas on pp. 37-39.

E. M. W. Tillyard: *The English Epic and Its Background* (1954).
   'Part III: The Renaissance, Chapter XII: The Great
   Translations, 6: Sylvester's Du Bartas', pp. 351-360. Gives
   excerpts from Du Bartas and their translation by Sylvester.

H. Ashton: *Du Bartas en Angleterre* (1908). On Du Bartas, his life,
   popularity and its decline; Sylvester's translation; the
   influence of Du Bartas on Milton and William Browne;
   Dunster's theory, he declares, '*est poussée trop loin*' (p. 340).

J. Craigie (edited by): *The Poems of James VI of Scotland* (The
   Scottish Text Society, 1955).

A. E. Creore: 'Du Bartas: A Reinterpretation', *MLQ*, I.(1940),

503-526. On his style, which makes language fit thought, not thought language.

W. Lauder: 'An Essay on Milton's Use and Imitation of the Moderns in His *Paradise Lost*' (1750). The first presentation of the theory that Du Bartas influenced Milton.

C. Dunster: *Considerations on Milton's Early Reading, and the Prima Stamina of his* Paradise Lost; together with extracts from a poet of the 16th century (1800). Examines parallels between the two poets.

D. H. Willson: *King James VI and I* (1956), pp. 59-67, 80.

G. C. Taylor: *Milton's Use of Du Bartas* (1934).

J. H. Hanford: *A Milton Handbook* (1926), pp. 174, 252f. 'The Youth of Milton', *Studies in Shakespeare, Milton and Donne* (University of Michigan Publications, Language and Literature, Volume I, 1925).

D. Daiches: *Milton* (1957), pp. 14, 145.

J. H. B. Masterman: *The Age of Milton* (1897), pp. xvf, 3.

D. Bush: *English Literature in the Earlier Seventeenth Century, 1600-1660* (Oxford History of English Literature, Volume V, 1945), pp. 73-75, 384.

L. B. Campbell: *Divine Poetry and Drama in Sixteenth-Century England* (1959). Chapter 9, 'Du Bartas and King James and the English Muse'; chapter 10, 'Du Bartas and English Poets'.

W. J. Courthope: *A History of English Poetry* (1903). Volume III, chapter 5, 'English Translators under Elizabeth and James I'. See also chapters 6, 8 on Donne.

V. Harris: *All Coherence Gone* (1949). Contains many references to Donne and Du Bartas, and considers the ideas of mutability and decay; and Creation according to Du Bartas.

S. Lee: *The French Renaissance in England*: an account of the literary relations of England and France in the sixteenth century (1910).

C. S. Lewis: *English Literature in the Sixteenth Century* (The Oxford History of English Literature Volume III, 1954), pp. 541-544. Stresses the importance of Du Bartas in relation to Metaphysical poetry, and links him with Donne, to whom reference is made especially on pp. 546-551.

L. Magnus: *English Literature in Its Foreign Relations 1300-1800* (1927).

J. Reeves: *A Short History of English Poetry* (1961), pp. 76f. Also discusses Donne (in chapter 6); and the legitimate avoidance of 'smoothness' in poetry (p. 41f).

F. E. Robbins: *The Hexaemeral Literature*, A Study of the Greek and Latin Commentaries on Genesis (1912).

R. A. Sayce: *The French Biblical Epic in the Seventeenth Century* (1955), pp. 41-46.

A. H. Upham: *The French Influence in English Literature* from the accession of Elizabeth to the Restoration (1908).

A. Williams: 'Commentaries on Genesis as a Basis for Hexaemeral Material in the Literature of the late Renaissance'. *SP*, XXXIV.(1937), 191-208.

—— 'Milton and the Renaissance Commentaries on Genesis', *MP*, XXXVII.(1939/40), 263-378.

—— *The Common Expositor*, An Account of the Commentaries on Genesis 1527-1633 (1948). Discusses the great popularity of commentaries and books on the Creation story and references to this subject, as part of Renaissance culture.

G. Williamson: 'Mutability, Decay, and Seventeenth-Century Melancholy', *ELH*, II.(1935), 121-150.

F. P. Wilson: *Elizabethan and Jacobean* (1945), pp. 69f, 77. Also discusses Donne and Bishop Andrewes as preachers, and Donne the poet, pp. 44f, 54-60.

Donne the preacher

S. Addleshaw: 'A Famous Dean: Dr John Donne of St Paul's', *The Church Quarterly Review* (1932), pp. 38-54.

D. C. Allen: 'Dean Donne Sets His Text', *ELH*, X.(1943), 208-229. A study of Donne's use of versions of Holy Scripture, of his knowledge of Hebrew, Greek, and Latin; concluding that he was a poet, not a disciplined scholar, using the version that appealed to him, or that was available on a particular occasion.

A. Clutton-Brock: *Essays on Books* (1920), pp. 78-91.

C. M. Coffin: 'Donne's Divinity', *KR*, XVI.(1954), 292-298. Reviews PS I, VI; the sermons contain the unifying theme of the story of Being, made from nothing (p. 296).

D. Coleridge (edited by): *Notes on English Divines*, by Samuel Taylor Coleridge (1853), pp. 65-120.

T. S. Eliot: 'Lancelot Andrewes', *Selected Essays* (1951), pp. 341-

353. Contrasts Donne and Andrewes to the advantage of the latter.

T. Gill: (selected and introduced by): *The Sermons of John Donne* (1958). A selection of nine sermons, almost in full, each preceded by an introductory note, with an introduction on Donne the preacher.

J. Hayward: 'A Note on Donne the Preacher', ††. On the preparation of the sermons and their manuscript versions.

R. L. Hickey: 'Donne's Art of Preaching', *TSL*, I.(1956), 65-74. Stresses Donne's understanding that a preacher should be *en rapport* with his audience, for whom he must make proper use of secular as well as sacred learning.

—— 'Donne's Art of Memory', *TSL*, III.(1958),29-36. Discusses the deliberate endeavour of Donne, when preaching, to stir the memory of his hearers, an emphasis consequent upon him beginning to preach late in life.

F. E. Hutchinson: 'The English Pulpit from Fisher to Donne', *Cambridge History of English Literature*, IV.(1909), 239-241.

—— 'Donne the Preacher', *Theology*, March 1931, pp. 155-163.

S. Johnson: 'John Donne and the Virginia Company', *ELH*, XIV.(1947), 127-138.

J. B. Lightfoot: 'Donne, the Poet-Preacher', *Historical Essays* (1877; published in this form 1895), pp. 221-245.

H. H. Milman: *Annals of S. Paul's Cathedral* (1868), pp. 322-330.

W. F. Mitchell: *English Pulpit Oratory from Andrewes to Tillotson: A Study of Its Literary Aspects* (1932). The main discussion is in chapter 5, 'General Considerations: The Anglo-Catholic Preachers, including Donne', pp. 179-194; this study, originating in the revived interest in the prose works of Donne, seeks to determine his relation to contemporary pulpit orators; stresses the metaphysical character of his preaching, seen, for example, in the 'conceits', the background of remote learning, and the probing analysis of personality; studies the structure of the sermons.

W. R. Mueller: *John Donne: Preacher* (1962). Five chapters on (1) the life and death of Dr Donne; (2) Dr Donne views his calling—the Priest, the Temple, the Written Word, the Spoken Word; (3) 'Golden Chrysostome . . . Alive Again . . .' —structure, rhetoric, imagery, tone; (4) interpreter of God's ways to men—*via media*, sin and redemption, grace and free will, death and resurrection; (5) ' . . . But for all Time!'

G. R. Potter: 'John Donne: Poet to Priest', *Five Gayley Lectures, 1947-1954* (1954), 105-126. On his early years as a preacher, 1615-1621.

A. Quiller-Couch: 'Some Seventeenth-Century Poets', *Studies in Literature,* (1st series 1918), pp. 96-117. The praise is given to the sermons, which contain the most magnificent pulpit prose in our language.

D. B. Quinn: 'Donne's Christian Eloquence', *ELH,* XXVII. (1960), 276-297. Studies the sermons on Psalms xxxviii (pp. 287-295) and vi (pp. 295f), and stresses that Donne, following St Augustine, regarded the Scriptures sacramentally as embodying divine truth, and not simply historical documents requiring philological study; and that, in consequence, he regarded preaching also sacramentally as an endeavour to communicate, embody, re-enact the truth contained in the Bible.

—— 'John Donne's Principles of Biblical Exegesis', *JEGP,* LXI. (1962), 313-329. Reiterates the 'embodiment' principle; the Bible is an event of history as well as a history of an event, an organic manifestation of God's encounter with men, as well as an account of it, which is re-enacted in Christian preaching (see pp. 324f); studies the *Essayes in Divinity* as well as the sermons.

L. P. Smith: *Donne's Sermons: Selected Passages with an Essay,* (1919). Contains 155 excerpts, with notes.

J. Sparrow: 'John Donne and Contemporary Preachers: Their preparation of sermons for delivery and for publication', *ESEA,* XVI.(1931), 144-178.

H. H. Umbach: 'The Rhetoric of Donne's Sermons', *PMLA,* XXI.(1937), 354-358. Examines Donne's treatment of his text.

—— 'The Merit of Metaphysical Style in Donne's Easter Sermons', *ELH,* XII.(1945), 108-129.

A. Warren: 'The Very Reverend Dr Donne', *KR,* XVI.(1954), 268-277.

J. Webber: *Contrary Music:* The Prose Style of John Donne (1963). This analysis of Donne's prose, begun as a study of the *Devotions,* here included, studies briefly the *Juvenilia, Biathanatos,* and *Essayes in Divinity,* and at full length the sermons, based on the Potter-Simpson edition.

F. P. Wilson: *Seventeenth Century Prose*, 1960.

Dietrich Bonhoeffer: *Creation and Fall:* A Theological Interpretation of Genesis 1-3 (1937). These lectures, delivered in the University of Berlin in 1932/3, may be studied as a modern contribution to hexaemeral literature. The Resurrection is presented as creation out of nothing (p. 16); the fusion of the imperative and the indicative is impressively declared (p. 20); a penetrating study of Genesis i.26 distinguishes the work of creation, which He loves, from man, in whom He sees Himself (p. 33f) as one beholds oneself in a mirror. Thus God Himself distinguishes 'having' from 'being', the created order which is the object of His love, and man, in whom He is. This book by a martyr of the modern Church illustrates the essentially timeless character of these insights, which are to be found also in Donne.

W. Barrett: *Irrational Man:* A Study in Existential Philosophy (1958), and
Helmut Thielicke: *Nihilism:* Its Origin and Nature—with a Christian Answer (delivered as lectures, 1945), (1951). Recommended for reading especially in connection with Donne's first sermon, Sold for Nothing, to show the essentially modern nature of Donne's spiritual pilgrimage from nothing to something, Creation; or, if one wills, the unoriginal nature of modern irreligion. Barrett illustrates the nihilism of our age by reference to William Faulkner's *The Sound and the Fury* [signifying nothing] and Ernest Hemingway's *A Clean, Well-lighted Place*, with its profane parody of Catholic devotion, 'Hail nothing, full of nothing, nothing is with thee'. Many other references to various art forms—the writings of James Joyce and Samuel Beckett; Cubism; modern sculpture—expound contemporary art as influenced by the realistic rebellious colloquialism of the treatment of the subject and its expression which we have found in the poet Donne. The rejection of nihilism finds modern presentation in the lectures of Thielicke, who proclaimed to great audiences of young men in the University of Tübingen, more hungry in mind and spirit even than in the body, just after total defeat in 1945, that God is Love, summoning us to say 'yes' to life.

Donne and our age:

R. M. Adams: 'Donne and Eliot: Metaphysicals', *KR*, XVI. (1954), 278-291.

R. C. Bald: *Donne's Influence in English Literature* (1932).

J. E. Duncan: 'The Intellectual Kinship of John Donne and Robert Browning', *SP* L. (1953), 81-100; 'The Revival of Metaphysical Poetry, 1872-1912', *PMLA*, LXVIII.(1953), 658-671. Both incorporated in *The Revival of Metaphysical Poetry*: The History of a Style, 1800 to the Present (1959). Contains, in addition, a chapter on early conceptions of metaphysical poetry; discusses the influence of metaphysical poetry on American writers, Yeats, and contemporary poets.

T. S. Eliot: 'Donne in our Time', ††.

G. R. Hamilton: 'Wit and Beauty: A Study of Metaphysical Poetry', *The London Mercury*, XIV.(1926), 606-620. With references to Francis Thompson.

F. R. Leavis: 'The Influence of Donne on Modern Poetry', *Bookman*, LXXIX.(March 1931), 346f.

W. de la Mare: 'An Elizabethan Poet and Modern Poetry', *The Edinburgh Review*, CCXVII.(1913), 372-386.

R. L. Mégroz: *Francis Thompson: The Poet of Earth in Heaven* (1927). (See chapter 8.)

D. Morris: *The Poetry of Gerard Manley Hopkins and T. S. Eliot in the Light of the Donne Tradition*: A Comparative Study, 1953.

M. Praz: 'The Critical Importance of the Revived Interest in 17th-Century Metaphysical Poetry', *English Studies Today*. Papers read at the International Conference of University Professors of English held in Magdalen College, Oxford, August 1950, (1951), pp. 158-166.

A. Stein: 'Donne and the 1920's: A Problem in Historical Consciousness', *ELH*, XXVII.(1960), 16-29.

—— *John Donne's Lyrics: The Eloquence of Action.* Postscript, 'On Donne's Modern Career' (1962), pp. 198-210.

K Tillotson: 'Donne's Poetry in the Nineteenth Century', *Elizabethan and Jacobean Studies Presented to Frank Percy Wilson* (1959), pp. 307-326.

G. Williamson: 'Donne and the Poetry of Today', ††.

M. Willy: 'The Poetry of Donne: Its Interest and Influence Today', *ESEA*, VII.(1954), 78-104. Presents the poetry

of Donne and of modern writers (particularly Yeats and
Dylan Thomas) as comparable reactions from Elizabethan
and Victorian times respectively, caused by scientific progress which disturbed people out of their security; which
became new material for poets, but which was discredited
by them because of its essential inadequacy—at heart the
metaphysical poetry of both ages is a rebellion against new
knowledge which is not a greater knowledge.

Some specific subjects:

D. C. Allen: 'John Donne's Knowledge of Renaissance
Medicine', *JEGP*, XLII.(1943), 322-342. Studies Donne's
interest in and knowledge of the human body and its sick-
nesses (especially his own, which stimulated him creatively),
and the many allusions embedded in his writings to medical
matters which set him in the context of the conflict between
traditional views based on Galen and the modern views of
Paracelsus. Donne studied medicine ('the grounds and use
of *Physicke*'—Grierson, I.377) seriously, but, as with
astronomy, he took what appealed to him from the old
and the new to communicate his thought.

C. Brooks: *The Well Wrought Urn*, Studies in the Structure of
Poetry (1947). * Part of the first chapter, under the title
'The Language of Paradox: "The Canonization." '

R. A. Bryan: 'John Donne's Use of the Anathema', *JEGP*, LXI.
(1962), 305-312. The anathema is found in a non-ecclesiastical context in three poems; the medieval formula for
excommunication was used in these poems as the vehicle
of his thought.

C. M. Coffin: *John Donne and the New Philosophy* (1937).

J. B. Douds: 'Donne's Technique of Dissonance', *PMLA*, LII.
(1937) ,1051-1061. Expounds his dissonance of style which
embodies inwardly experienced discord.

W. Empson: *Seven Types of Ambiguity* (1930). * 'A Valediction:
Of Weeping' (part of chapter 4).

R. Freeman: *English Emblem Books* (1948). Studies emblem books
from their introduction into England from the Continent
in Elizabeth's reign to the end of the tradition in John
Bunyan; places Donne in the tradition of emblematic writing.

H. J. C. Grierson: *Criticism and Creation*, Essays and Addresses

(1949). 'The Metaphysics of Donne and Milton', pp. 35-45; 'John Donne and the "Via Media" ', pp. 49-68. In addition to a study of Donne's views on the Church, and the Sacraments, and of the *via media* of Donne's later life, raises religious questions of perennial interest.

J. Lederer: 'John Donne and the Emblematic Practice', *RES*, XXII.(1946), 182-200. Studies the emblem—the 'picture' with a 'motto'—and the externalizing of an inward state of mind, in Donne, especially the poems, with detailed reference to examples like the heart, clock, lodestone, phœnix.

J. Mazzeo: 'Notes on John Donne's Alchemical Imagery', *Isis*, XLVIII.(1957), pp. 103-123.

D. L. Peterson: 'John Donne's *Holy Sonnets* and the Anglican Doctrine of Contrition', *SP* LVI.(1959), 504-518.

G. Phelps: 'The Prose of Donne and Browne', *From Donne to Marvell*, edited by Boris Ford (The Pelican Guide to English Literature, Volume 3, 1956). (B—Part IV, by Margaret Tubb.)

G. R. Potter: 'John Donne's Discovery of Himself', *Essays in Criticism, 2nd Series*, pp. 3-23, University of California Publications in English, Volume IV (1934). Expounds the view that, dominated by a desire to know, Donne sought the truth about himself, this quest for 'self-solution' being the constant theme of his writings.

M. Praz: 'Donne's Relation to the Poetry of His Time', *, ††.

M. P. Ramsay: 'Donne's Relation to Philosophy', ††.

T. M. Raysor (edited by): *Coleridge's Miscellaneous Criticism* (1936), pp. 131-145.

D. R. Roberts: 'The Death Wish of John Donne', *PMLA*, LXII. (1947), 958-976. Argues that Donne, believing in a contrary destructive principle within life, had a persistent wish to die, which found recurring expression throughout his life.

M. A. Rugoff: *Donne's Imagery*, A Study of Creative Sources (1939).

E. M. Simpson: *A Study of the Prose Works of John Donne* (2nd edition, 1948). After an outline of his life, considers Donne as man of letters, and theologian; reviews the medieval and renaissance elements of his thought, and studies all the prose works.

T. Spencer: 'Donne and His Age', ††.

A. Stein: 'Donne and the Satiric Spirit', *ELH*, XI.(1944), 266-282.

Studies the scientific nature of Donne's realism; his melancholy and its causes—namely, the new astronomy; his sex
obsession; his thirst for and disappointment with human
knowledge.

E. M. W. Tillyard: *The Elizabethan World Picture* (1943). Considers the idea of the Correspondences (e.g. the four elements
of nature corresponding to the four humours of man), a
basic belief in the interrelationship of all things held by his
contemporaries and expressed by Donne when he spoke of
'the correspondence and relation of all parts of Nature to
one Author, the concinnity and dependance of every piece
and joynt of this frame of the world' (PS I p.289f).

H. H. Umbach: *The Prayers of John Donne* (1951). Includes an
essay on Donne's idea of prayer; the prayers are in six
groups, from (1) *The Divine Poems*, (2) *Essayes in Divinity*, (3)
Devotions, (4) Letters, (5) sermons, and (6) miscellaneous,
including his will.

Some relevant books and articles of general interest:

A. Alvarez: The School of Donne (1961). Notices the obscurity
and difficulty of the poetry, and his consequent relationship
with his readers; his friendships; his use of traditional and
contemporary ways of thought.

J. Bennett: 'The Love Poetry of John Donne—A Reply to Mr.
C. S. Lewis', in the same volume as the essay by C. S. Lewis
(q.v. infra), pp. 85-104; †.

Rupert Brooke: 'John Donne', *The Prose of Rupert Brooke*, edited
by Christopher Hassall, pp. 85-98; written 1913 on the
publication of 'Grierson', (published in this form 1956).

D. Bush: *English Literature in the Earlier Seventeenth Century, 1600-
1660* (1945). Oxford History of English Literature, Volume
V [B].

J. E. V. Crofts: 'John Donne', *ESEA*, XXII.(1937), 128-143.*
An exposure, with many effective phrases, of Donne haunted
by his self-awareness, only half-serious in his wit as a thinker.

T. S. Eliot: 'The Metaphysical Poets' (1921), in *Selected Essays*
(1951), pp. 281-291; †. A basic document of the metaphysical
revival, stressing (a) the embodiment of meaning which it
achieved and which has its modern counterpart in difficult

R

poetry; (b) its immediacy of communication; (c) its power of unifying disparate experiences.

H. Gardner: *The Business of Criticism* (1959). Studies 'Aire and Angels' (pp.62-75); 'The Poetry of St Mark', and the original last verse xvi.8 (ἐφοβοῦντο γάρ), the discussion of which should be considered in connection with pp. 66ff *supra*; and refers in 'The Historical Sense' to Donne's interpretation of Holy Scripture.

H. J. C. Grierson (edited by): *Metaphysical Lyrics and Poems of the Seventeenth Century: Donne to Butler* (1921). The notable introduction is included in his *The Background of English Literature and Other Essays*, 1925, and in †.

D. W. Harding: 'Coherence of Theme in Donne's Poetry', *KR*, XIII.(1951), 427-444. Shows that Donne imaginatively, proleptically, anticipates the future, seeking to prolong it when it is pleasurable and to draw all possible significance from it, knowing that it will pass away, leaving disappointment.

M. Y. Hughes: 'Kidnapping Donne', *Essays in Criticism*, 2nd *Series*, pp. 61-89, University of California Publications in English, Volume IV (1934). Asserts that we kidnap Donne from the past, making him a modern scientific intellectual, and a sceptical philosopher; urges that Donne was not a mystic, and that he was inclined toward the Ptolemaic rather than the Copernican astronomy, being disappointed with new knowledge; Donne was a medievalist at heart, but essentially a poet, making all knowledge serve his purpose of self-expression; pp. 83-86: discusses 'The Extasie' and illustrates its affinity with the sixteenth-century writing of Antoine Héroët, *La Parfaicte Amie*.

F. Kermode: 'Dissociation of Sensibility', *KR*, XIX.(1957), 169-174. Discusses the views of T. S. Eliot and Eliot's later revision of them.

F. R. Leavis: 'The Line of Wit', *Revaluation*, Tradition and Development in English Poetry, pp. 10-36, 1936. †.

C. S. Lewis: 'Donne and Love Poetry in the Seventeenth Century', *Seventeenth Century Studies Presented to Sir Herbert Grierson*, pp. 64-84, 1938 († * (in part)). A critical appraisal, which emphasizes the importance of the tradition of love poetry against which Donne, it is supposed, rebelled; and which denies to Donne any real profundity, or understanding of love itself.

J. A. Mazzeo: 'A Critique of Some Modern Theories of Metaphysical Poetry', *MP*, l.(1952), 88-96. †.

M. F. Moloney: *John Donne: His Flight from Mediaevalism* (Illinois Studies in Language and Literature, XXIX, nos. 2-3), 1944. (B). Notable for quotations from T. E. Hulme, Ruskin, H. Adams, R. A. Cram, G. K. Chesterton, Patmore, Berdyaev, and others; asserts that Donne was untroubled by the disintegration of the medieval world and the loss of unity; that, though there are traces of Catholicism in his works, though he spoke the language and used the terms of scholasticism, he recognized that the synthesis of the universal Church unifying theology, politics, economics, and the arts had gone; that he used all knowledge indiscriminately to serve his art; and that he was not a mystic.

M. H. Nicolson: *The Breaking of the Circle*: Studies in the effect of the 'new science' upon seventeenth-century Poetry. Revised edition, 1960.

H. Read: 'The Nature of Metaphysical Poetry', *Collected Essays in Literary Criticism*, pp. 69-88; 1938.

G. Saintsbury: *Prefaces and Essays*, pp. 273-291, written 1896, published in this form 1933. *.

R. Skelton: 'The Poetry of John Donne', chapter X in *Elizabethan Poetry, Stratford-upon-Avon Studies*, 2, pp. 203-220; 1960. Discusses Donne's realistic normality in his attitude to sex; also, emblems and their function.

J. Smith: 'On Metaphysical Poetry', *Scrutiny*, ii (1933-1934), pp. 222-239, or *Determinations: Critical Essays* (with an Introduction by F. R. Leavis), pp. 10-45, 1934. Metaphysical problems are the problems of opposites in relation to each other—individual and community, body and soul, and are so expressed in Donne.

W. B. Smith: 'What is Metaphysical Poetry?', *SR*, XLII.(1934), 261-272.

A. Stein: 'Donne's Obscurity and the Elizabethan Tradition', *ELH*, XIII.(1946), 98-118. Shows the poet discouraging shallow, impatient readers who want everything ample, self-explanatory; imperiously demanding concentrated attention from those who will persevere and become 'understanders';

nevertheless, establishing a fruitful relationship with them, as he stimulates their thought.

R. Tuve: *Elizabethan and Metaphysical Imagery*: Renaissance Poetic and Twentieth-century Critics, 1947.

F. J. Warnke: *European Metaphysical Poetry*, 1961. With a substantial Introduction, pp. 1-86.

H. W. Wells: *Poetic Imagery illustrated from Elizabethan Literature*, 1924.

H. C. White: *The Metaphysical Poets: A Study in Religious Experience*, 1956. Especially the first five chapters, (1) 'The Intellectual Climate', (2) 'The Religious Climate', (3) 'Metaphysical Poetry', (4) 'The Conversions of John Donne', (5) 'The Divine Poetry of John Donne'.

B. Willey: *The Seventeenth-Century Background:* Studies in the Thought of the Age in relation to Poetry and Religion, 1934.

REFERENCES TO GRIERSON'S ONE-VOLUME EDITION OF THE POEMS

Page	Note	Grierson reference (1912)	One-volume edition (1933)
4	4	341	312
8	17	55	49
	20	241	217
9	23	185	164
14	37	254	230
15	38	328	299
		19	18
19	—	368	336
20	41	322	293
	42	44f	39–41
22	52	125	111
		182	161
23	55	288	262
	57	66	59
	58	16	15
24	62	323	294
		328	299
27	1	279	254
29	7	28	26
32	15, 17	26	24
34	20	221	199
		334	305
	21	334–336	305f
	22	352f	321
		336f	306–308
		198	175
		24f	22f
		44f	39–41
35	24	298	272
		319	290
		368	337
	25	294	268
37	30	295	269
	31	298	272
		302	276
		308	280
39	35	296f	270f
	36	295	269
	37	181	160
		328	299
	38	329	300
	39	53	48
		303	276
40	44	41	37
41	45	368	337
43	49	330	301

Page	Note	Grierson reference (1912)	One-volume edition (1933)
43	49	353	322
		394	364
44	1	353	321f
45	6	30	28
47	17	212	187
	18	189	166f
48	19	191	168
49	20	224f	202f
	21	18f	17f
		49–51	44f
		102f	92
51	1	318	289
	2	320	291
	4	51	45
52	5	293	267
	6	182	162
53	11	369	337f
	12	7	frontispiece
54	13	378f	347
	14	211	187
	15	96	85f
55	16	7	7
	17	69	61
		9	9
		48	43
	19	8f	8f
		11f	10f
		16	15f
		25–28	23–26
		28f	26f
		43	39
		51–53	46–48
		61f	54f
		65f	58f
		67f	59f
		10	9f
		44f	39–41
56	20	13	13
		39	35
		63	57
	21	13	12
58	23	17f	16f
60	26	37f	33f
	27	7	7
61	29	11f	10f
		46	42
		47	42
		295	269
	31	7	7
	33	310f	282f
62	35	210	186
63	39	326	297
	40	53	48
	41	330	301
66	49	318	289
	50	7	7
		30	28
67	54	14f	14f

Page	Note	Grierson reference (1912)	One-volume edition (1933)
67	55	157	139
68	56	112f	100
	57	24f	22f
	58	11	11
		20	19
		37	34
		47	42
		63	56
		70	62
		178	158
		186	165
		368	336
69		231	208
		264	239
		158	140
		201–203	177–179
		202	178
		216	191
		219	194
		221–223	199–201
72	70	347	317
73	72	178	158
	73	175	155
	74	22	21
74	75	353	322
77	1	331	302
	2	324	295
78	4	328	299
81	7	59f	53f
82	10	197	173
83	15	28	26
84	19	393	363
		53	47
	20	343f	313f
85	21	245–248	221–224
87	22	229–245	208–221
	23	249–266	227–242
103	43	241	217
104	44	127	113
108	4	369	337
		328	299
109	6	22	21
		95	84f
		37f	33f
		49–51	44f
		86f	77f
		336f	306–308
	7	61f	54f
111	12	51–53	46–48
112	13	24f	22f
113	14	11	11
	15	246	221
		49	44
114	17	293	267
116	26	267–270	243–246
	28	91	81
124	39	24	22
		26	24

Page	Note	Grierson reference (1912)	One-volume edition (1933)
124	39	266	241
		328	299
		175	155
		177	157
		241f	217f
		252	227
132	1	212f	188
133	2	387	357
	3	157	139
134	8	17f	16f
		13f	13
		34f	31f
135	10	44f	39-41
		22	21
		38f	34f
		347f	317f
		178-180	157-159
		195	172
138	21	49	44
144	31	85	76
146	35	177	157
150	41	197	173
157	44	50	45
		52	47
		51	46
		64	57f
159	47	258f	234
162	50	352f	321f
168	55	369	337
176	12	351f	319-321
180	20	296	270
	21	177	156
		120	107
187	35	38	34
188	36	255	230f
190	2	347	317
		335	305
		316	287
		304	277
195	9	317f	288f
197	11	323	294
200	14	86f	77f
208	22	319	290
209	23	51f	46
		7	7
		45f	41
		352	321
217	29	336f	306-308
221	33	194	171
223	35	379	347
		380	349
		382	351
		386	355
230	—	333f	304f
		39f	35f
241	—	377	345

INDEX

(see also Summary of Contents, pp. xi-xiii)